IMAGES
of America

SOUTHEAST ROCHESTER

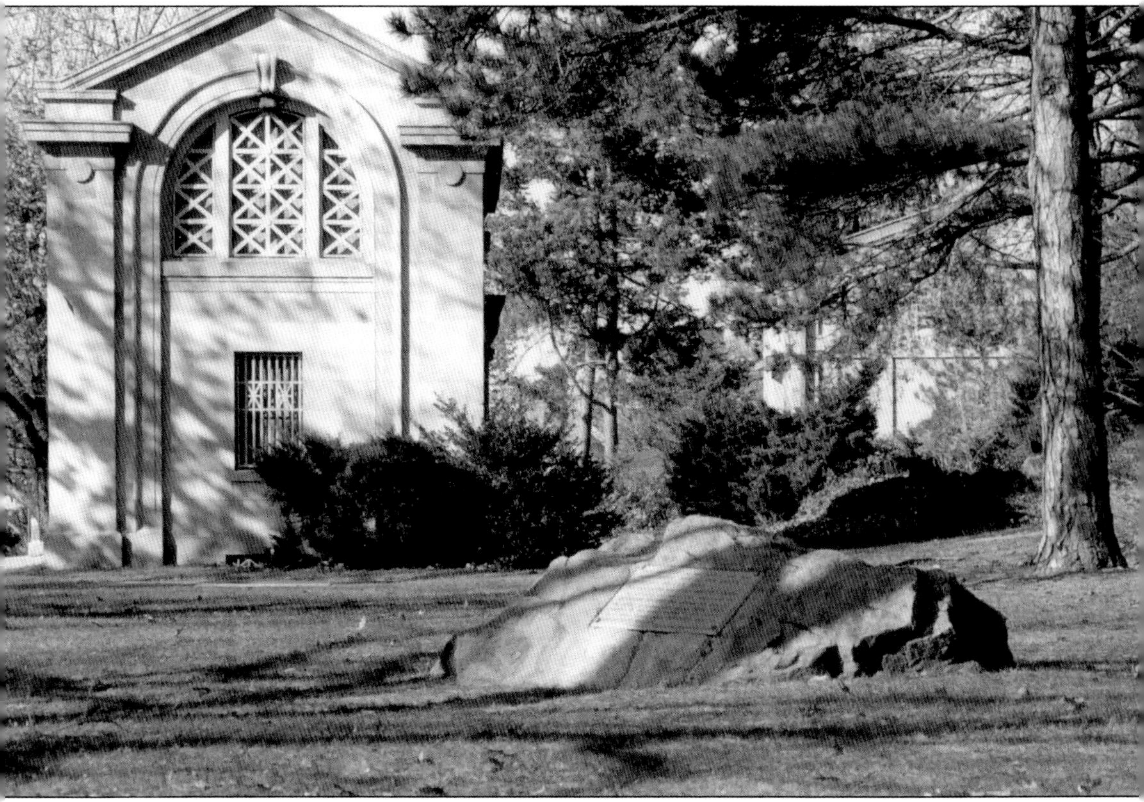

PAST THIS SPOT. This plaque was placed on a boulder at the base of Cobbs Hill for the Rochester Centennial in 1912. It reads, "Past this spot ran the Portage Trail from Irondequoit Bay to Red Creek in Genesee Valley Park. Its eastern end was at the Indian Landing. The portage followed the direction of Highland Avenue and skirted the base of Mt. Hope. It formed part of the Ohio Trail. Famous in the early history of this country as a short route from Canada into the Mississippi Valley." (Courtesy Robert P. Meadows.)

On the cover: please see page 34. (Courtesy City of Rochester Photo Lab.)

IMAGES
of America

SOUTHEAST ROCHESTER

Rose O'Keefe

ARCADIA
PUBLISHING

ISBN 978-0-7385-4509-7

Published by Arcadia Publishing
Charleston, South Carolina

Printed in the United States of America

Library of Congress Catalog Card Number: 2006921060

For all general information, please contact Arcadia Publishing:
Telephone 843-853-2070
Fax 843-853-0044
E-mail sales@arcadiapublishing.com
For customer service and orders:
Toll-Free 1-888-313-2665

Visit us on the Internet at www.arcadiapublishing.com

This book is dedicated to all those who helped make it happen, with special thanks to Bob Meadows, my husband and photographer, for his patience and support, and to South Wedge native Josh Canfield, whose generosity continues to brighten my day.

Contents

ACKNOWLEDGMENTS

Images in this book are used with the permission of the following organizations and groups: Al Sigl Center; Cinema Theater; City of Rochester Archives; City of Rochester Photo Lab; Ellwanger and Barry Neighborhood Association; Monroe Community Hospital; Rochester Psychiatric Center; St. John's Home; Landmark Society of Western New York Inc.; Rochester Photo Images, Central Library of Rochester and Monroe County; Roman Catholic Diocese of Rochester; St. Thomas Episcopal Church archives; South Wedge Planning Committee; and University of Rochester Rare Books and Special Collections.

In identifying and describing the images, information from the above and also the following was used: American Baptist Historical Society; Ask-a-Librarian, Central Library of Rochester and Monroe County; Congregation Beth Sholom; Dan McBride, Rochester Fire Department; the online Rochester History Series, Central Library of Rochester and Monroe County; and Rochester Institute of Technology Photography Department. Special thanks go to Dave Mohney, City Photo Lab; Marylee Wilk, Central Library; Ruth Rosenberg-Naparsteck, City Archives; Sr. Connie Derby and Bob Vogt, Catholic Diocese archives; Jim Malley, Mercury Posters; Steve Bartlett, Monroe Community Hospital; Rowe Photo staff, and Arcadia Publishing's staff specialists.

Individual contributors include: David "Josh" Canfield, Agnes Coon, Robert Good and Susan Schickler, Tom Leavitt, Robert P. Meadows, Tom Page, Bernice Reinhardt, Bob Schnacky, Donovan A. Shilling, Cheryl Stevens and Mary Williams, Marva Corbin and JoAnn Thomas, Charlie and Emily Westfall, and Martha and Billy Yatteau. Special thanks also go to Jeanne DeKeyserling and Mike Thompson.

INTRODUCTION

The ancient glacial mounds of the Pinnacle Range define southeast Rochester. The Pinnacle Range, which is the remainder of ice age deposits called kame moraines, includes Mount Hope Cemetery, Highland Park, Pinnacle Hill, and Cobbs Hill.

Before the American Revolution, the Senecas followed animals tracks and portage trails from Lake Ontario, Irondequoit Bay, and the Genesee River to the Ohio River and on to the Mississippi. In the 1790s, early settlers hacked paths between Seneca Lake and the Genesee River. The area of Rochester's southeast quadrant began as crude wagon roads to grist and sawmills downtown across the river. There were so few bridges across the river, few pioneers moved to the southeast side before construction of the original Erie Canal in 1819.

Natural landmarks determined the early route of the original Erie Canal whose construction caused the city and southeast to expand. Because of the Erie Canal, Rochester was the number one boat builder in the nation from 1820 to 1895, with boat yards east and west of downtown.

Much of the southeast side was in primitive Brighton before 1834. Mount Hope Cemetery, which was formed in 1838 to move burial plots a safe distance from downtown, is the first municipal Victorian cemetery in the nation. The Ellwanger and Barry Nurseries, that started with seven acres along Mount Hope Avenue in the 1840s, had 650 acres by the Civil War. The nurseries were so famous, Rochester's nickname of Flour City changed to Flower City.

Conductors on the Underground Railroad network crisscrossed the southeast taking fleeing slaves to the river, north to Lake Ontario and freedom in Canada. The Frederick Douglass family lived in Rochester from 1847 to 1872, with 18 of those years on South Avenue, then on a remote edge of the city.

The industrial expansion from the 1880s to the beginning of the 20th century led to a surge in construction throughout the city. So many of the changes brought by the railroads and the early subway bed that were the precursor to Interstate 490 have faded with time. Hope Hospital, the Monroe County Penitentiary, the old almshouse, and a surprising number of churches have come and gone. The University of Rochester, Strong Memorial Hospital, Iola Sanitarium, Colgate-Rochester Divinity School, and Cobbs Hill Reservoir are 20th century additions to the southeast area.

Maps, roads, bridges and public building projects measure the area's changes and expansion. The Images of America series blends family snapshots, old postcards, and one-of-a-kind photographs from public records to provide vivid glimpses into earlier days.

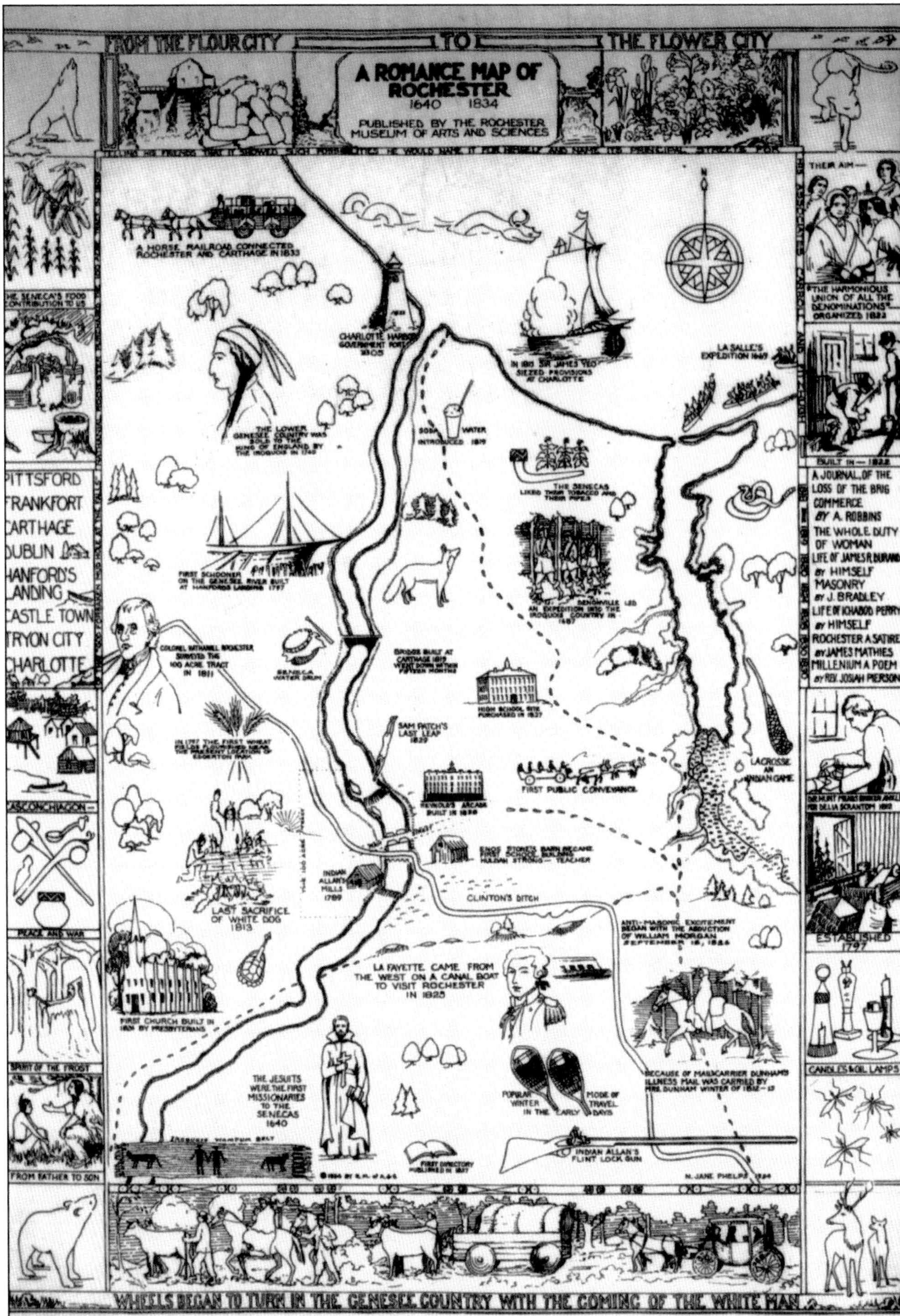

ROCHESTER, 1640–1834. Rochester was full of civic pride when it was incorporated as a city in 1834. This 1934 centennial map highlights the transition from Seneca times to Flower City. (Courtesy City of Rochester Photo Lab.)

One

ALONG THE GENESEE RIVER

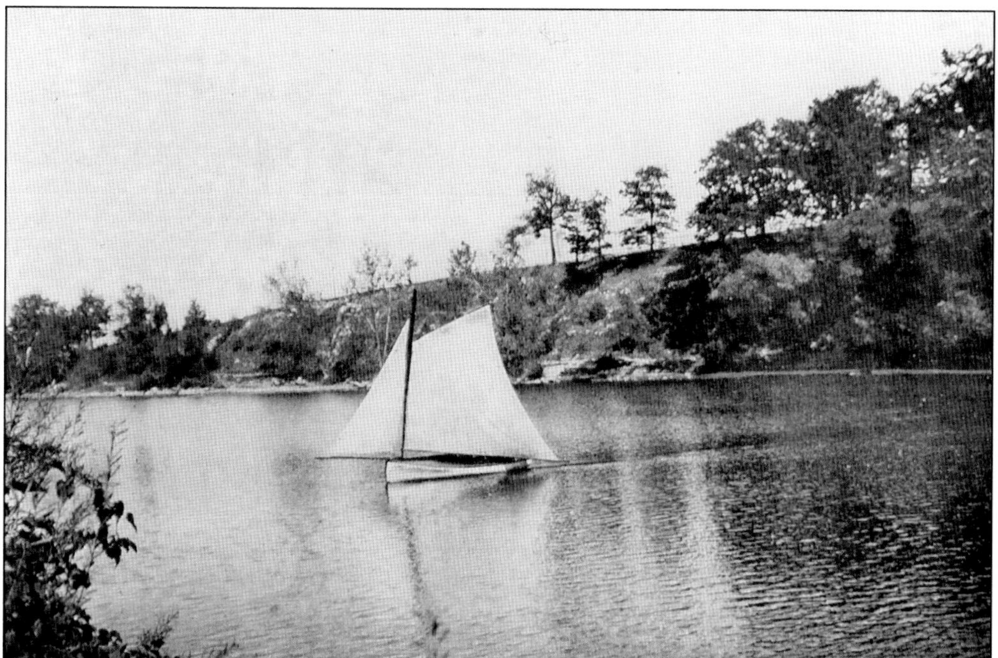

OAK HILL, 1898. This was the site of an Algonkin village about AD 1200. After the American Revolution, ancient animal and hunting trails were widened into rough wagon roads along the river. There is a marker on the east side of the river, between the Elmwood Avenue Bridge and the Interfaith Chapel that reads, "Indian town. In primitive wilderness here was a large Algonkin village whose bark cabins and tilled fields covered nine acres. University of Rochester, June, 2002." (Courtesy City of Rochester Photo Lab.)

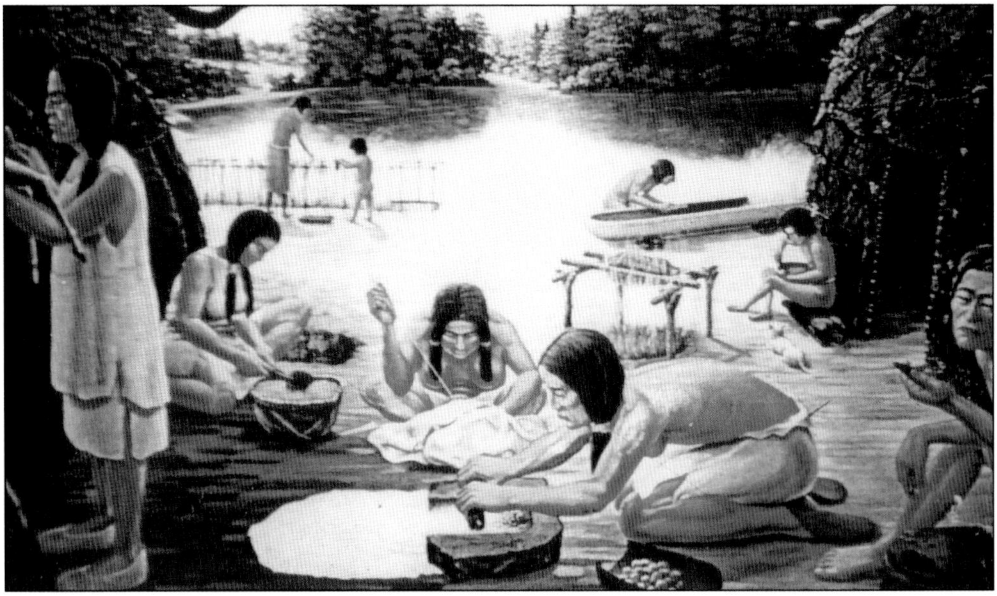

SENECA WOMEN AT WORK. The Senecas had traditional hunting and fishing grounds between Seneca Lake and the Genesee River, seasonal fishing camps, and sacred burial and ceremonial sites throughout the Genesee Valley. They used the area by the University of Rochester as a fishing camp and avoided the swampy downtown area. This rendering shows the work native Genesee Valley women did, from grinding, weaving, sewing, drying foods, to hollowing out a canoe. (Courtesy City of Rochester Photo Lab.)

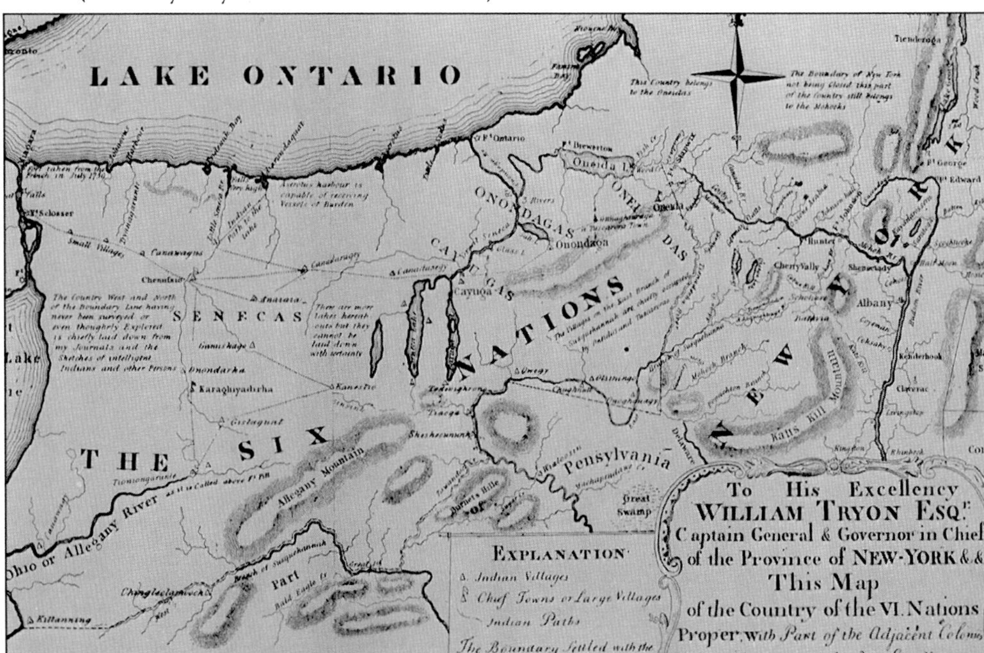

THE SIX NATIONS. This map shows the territory of the Six Nations created when William Tryon (1729–1788) was governor-in-chief of the province of New York from 1771 to the beginning of the American Revolution. (Courtesy City of Rochester Photo Lab.)

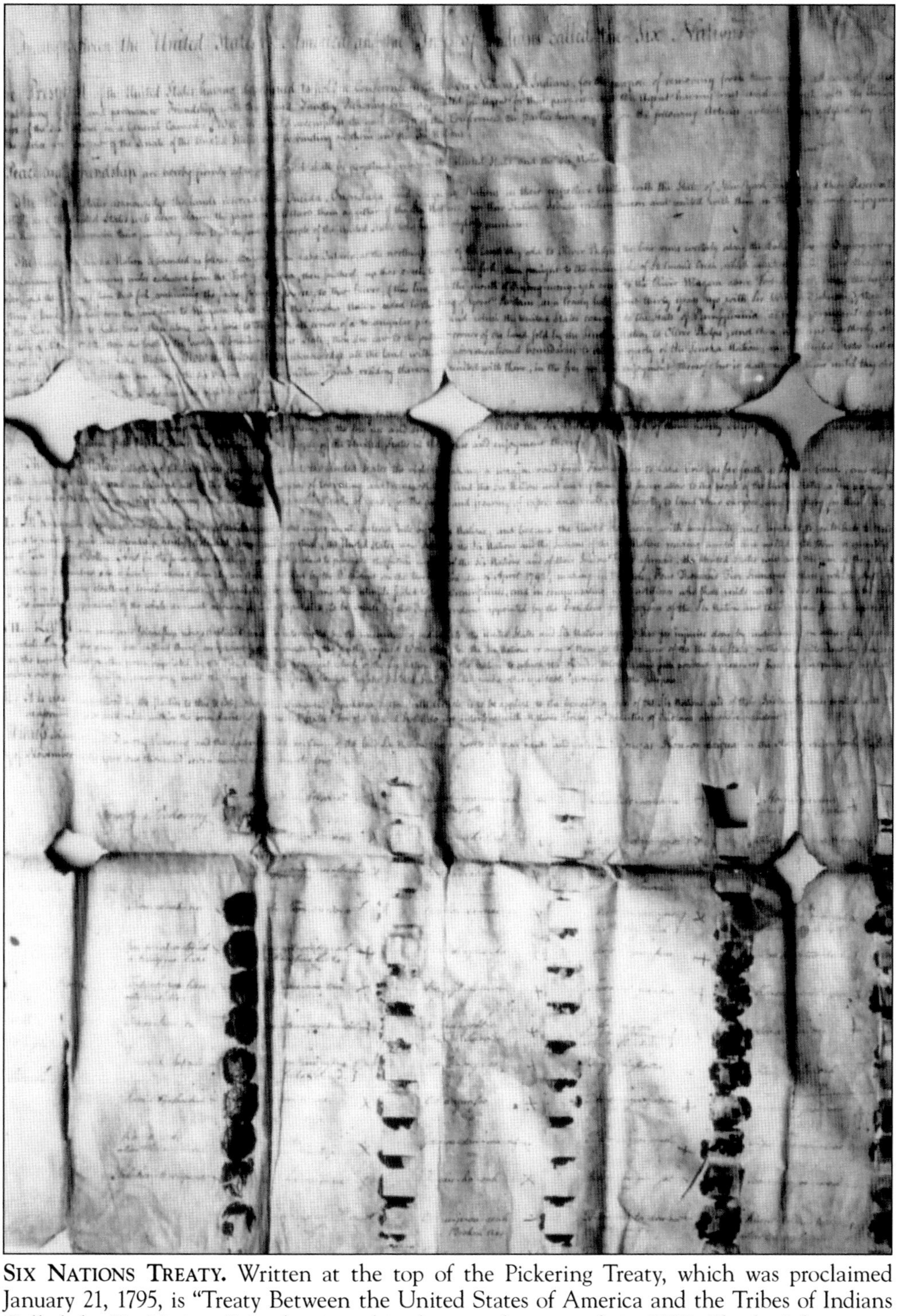

SIX NATIONS TREATY. Written at the top of the Pickering Treaty, which was proclaimed January 21, 1795, is "Treaty Between the United States of America and the Tribes of Indians Called the Six Nations." At the time this photograph was made in 1920, Charles Johnson, or How-In-Ya-Nus, a Seneca Indian residing on the Tonawanda Reservation, owned the original copy of the treaty. (Courtesy City of Rochester Photo Lab.)

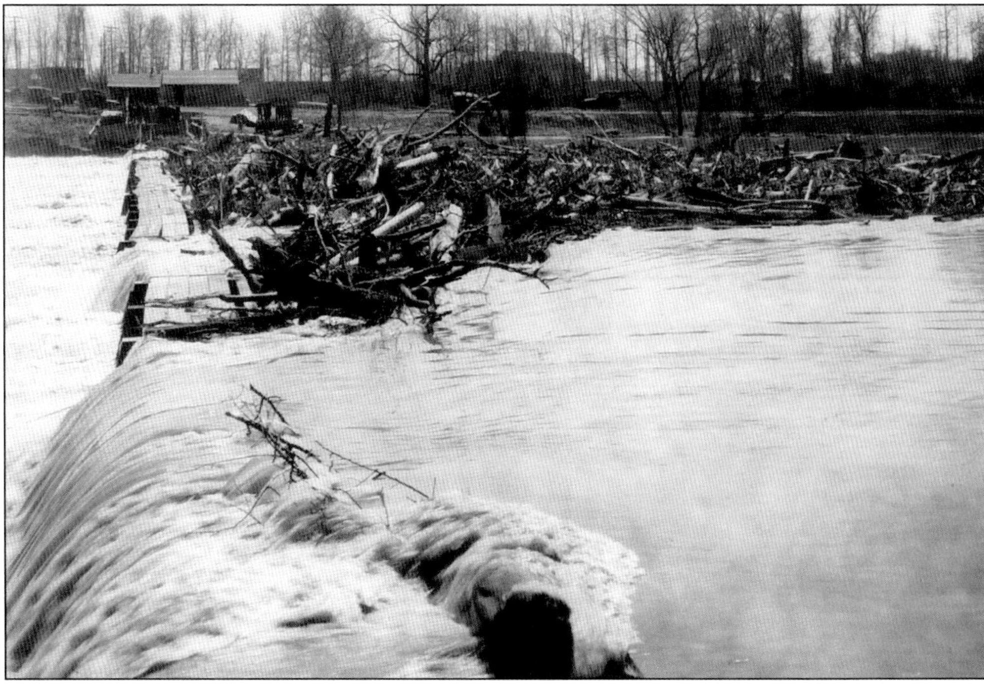

LOGJAM. A movable dam was built near the Elmwood Avenue Bridge to slow the flow of the Genesee River and keep the Barge Canal functioning during a construction project begun in 1915 to deepen the river and control future flooding. This logjam happened after flooding in 1919. (Courtesy City of Rochester Photo Lab.)

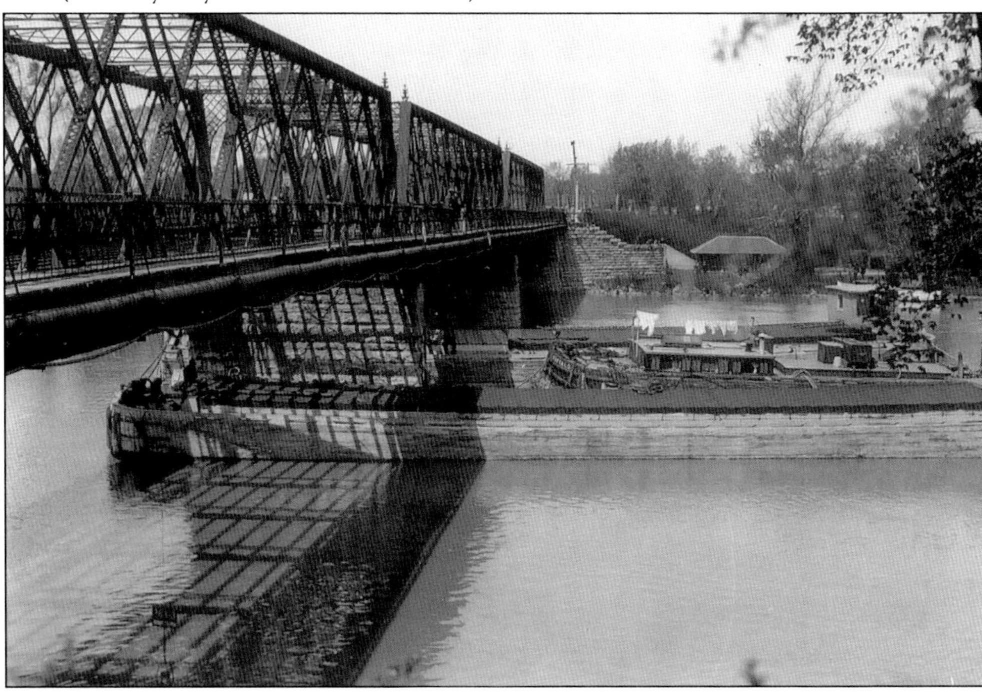

BRIDGE WORK. Repairs are underway on the old Elmwood Avenue Bridge in May 1933. (Courtesy City of Rochester Archives.)

MOORE STATUE. Edward Mott Moore (1814–1902) taught surgery in several medical colleges before becoming surgeon-in-chief of St. Mary's Hospital and starting the Infant Summer Hospital in 1887. He was also the first president of the Rochester Park Commission. This statue is in Genesee Valley Park, south of the University of Rochester campus. (Courtesy Robert P. Meadows.)

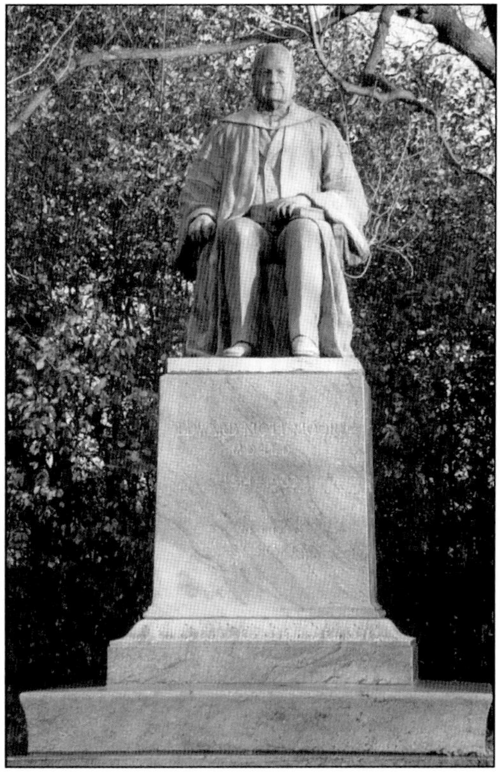

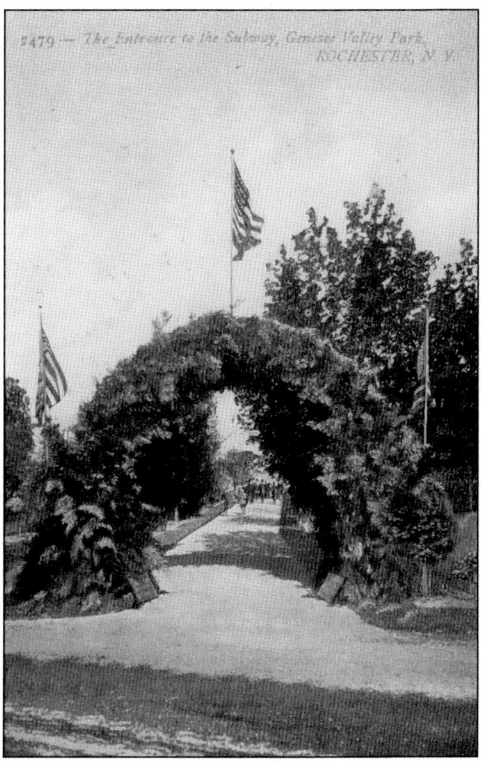

SUBWAY ENTRANCE. This fancy arch was located on the east side of the Genesee River, south of the University of Rochester campus. This colorful postcard is from the 1920s. (Courtesy City of Rochester Photo Lab.)

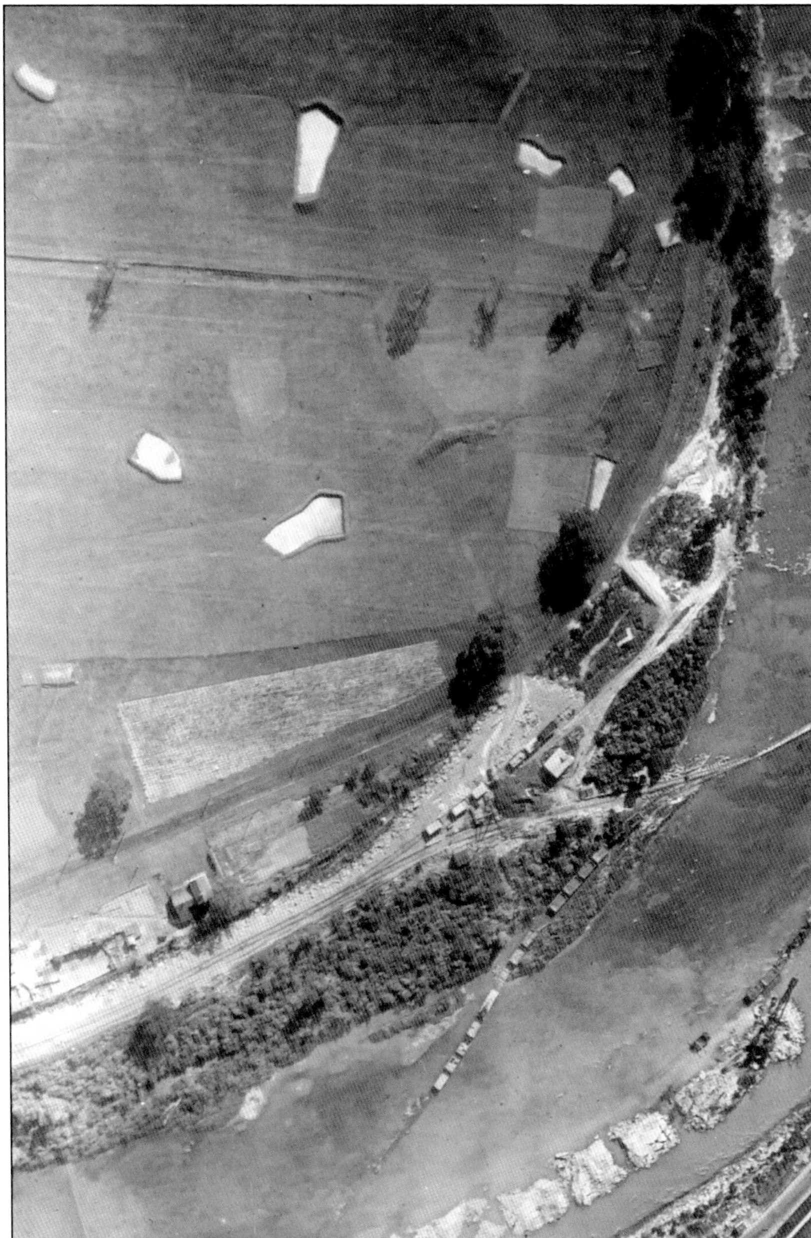

Bird's-Eye View of Oak Hill. In the early 1800s, Daniel Harris of Massachusetts built a house, choosing a treeless spot along the river with fine spring water and fertile land. It was near the University of Rochester's Women's Residence. Two farms covered most of the area: the Lewis-Aldington farm in the southern part and the Wolcott property near the football field. West of Strong Auditorium, Chapin and Loder built a small factory in 1847 for glue manufacturing. It was listed in the 1878 city directory on "Wolcott Street near the rapids." A Boughton and Chase's Shingle Factory advertisement in the 1859 city directory placed it on "Wolcott Street, (east side of the river) 25 rods south of Clarissa Street Bridge." The Oak Hill area was a part of Brighton until the city of Rochester annexed it in 1874. Oak Hill Country Club leased most of the area of the Aldington and Wolcott farmlands from 1901 until 1926. This aerial view is from 1918. (Courtesy City of Rochester Archives.)

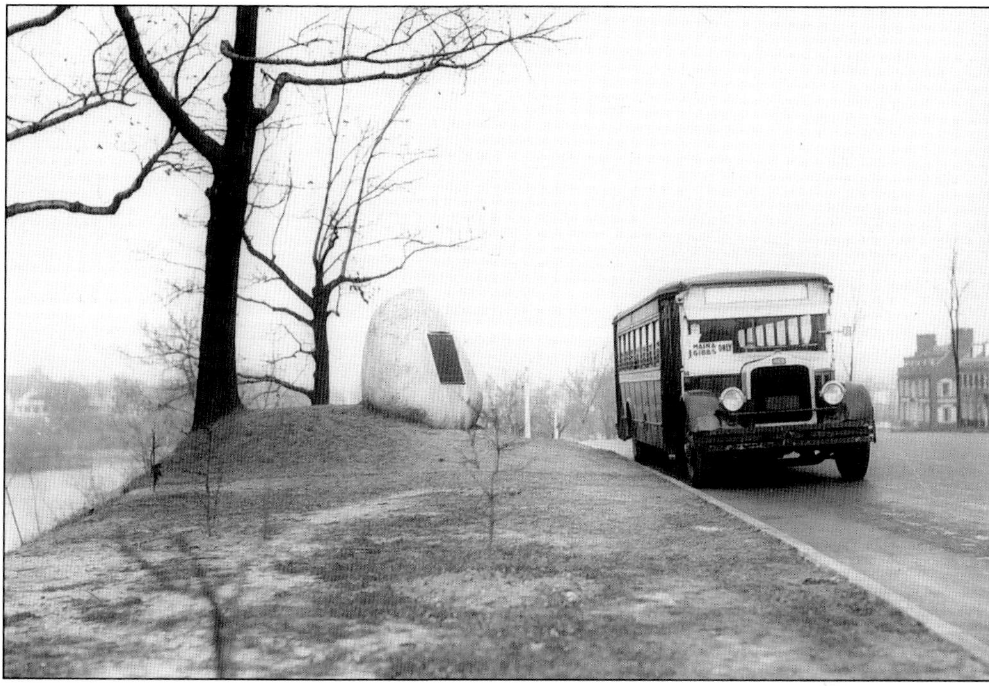

Bus Stop. These two utilitarian views of a bus stop on River Boulevard, dated December 3, 1932, are from the city files. The top photograph also shows the boulder and memorial plaque to Thomas Swinburne, the University of Rochester student who wrote the alma mater. (Courtesy City of Rochester Archives.)

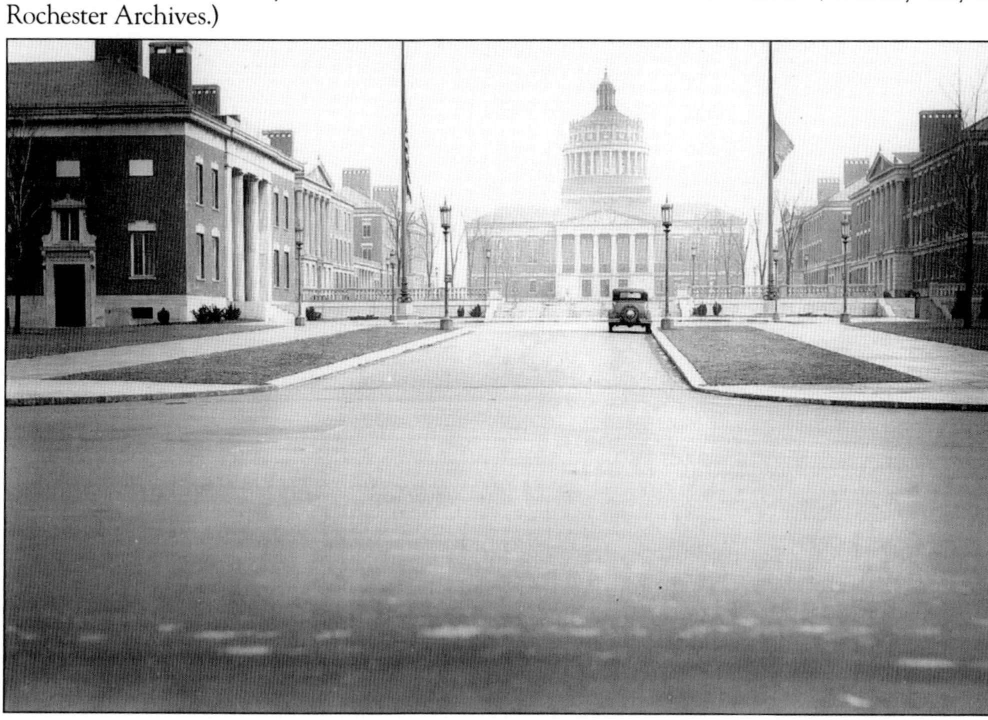

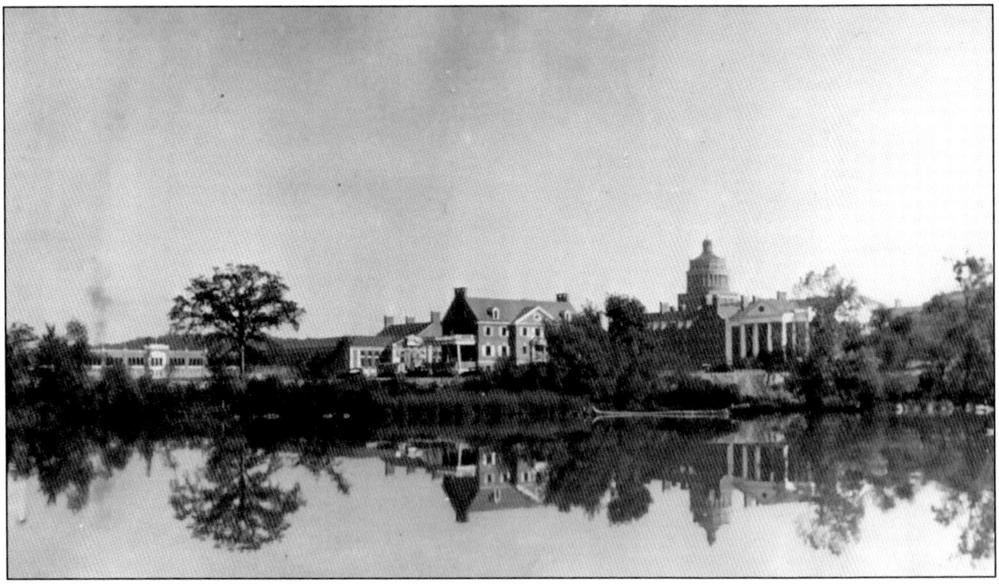

Smooth as Glass. The Genesee River mirrors the trees and buildings of the River Campus with Rush Rhees Library near the center. The photograph, *Genesee River and University of Rochester*, by Albert Stone (1866–1934) was printed in the *Democrat and Chronicle* on November 26, 1930. It is from the Albert Stone Negative Collection of the Rochester Museum and Science Center. (Courtesy City of Rochester Photo Lab.)

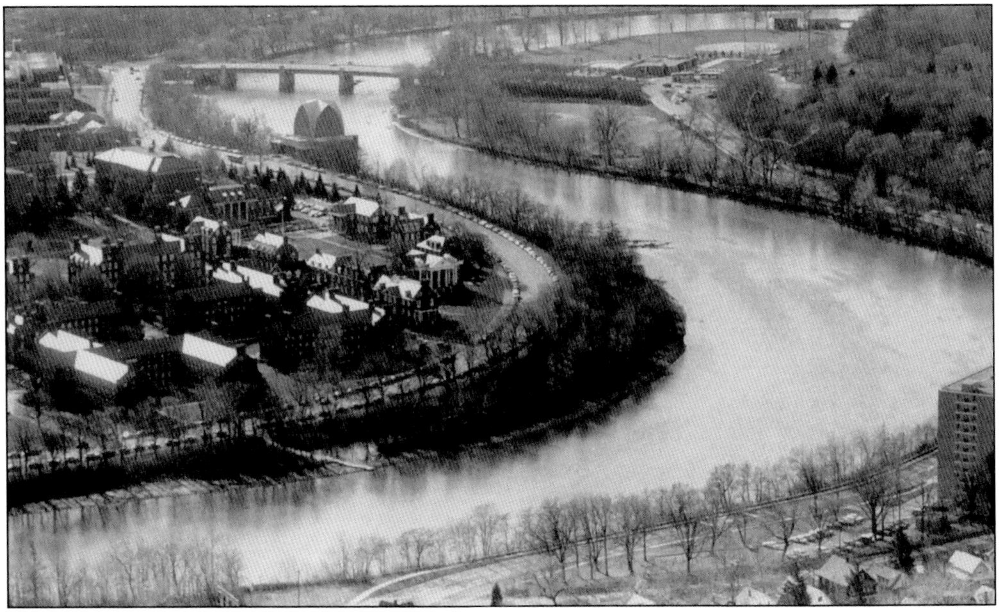

River Campus. The University of Rochester was founded in 1850 along with Rochester Theological Seminary by a group of Baptists in the United States Hotel on West Main Street. Largely due to women's rights advocate Susan B. Anthony, women were admitted to the college in 1890. During Rush Rhees's presidency from 1900 to 1935, George Eastman became a major donor and the Eastman School of Music and the School of Medicine and Dentistry were founded. The university moved to the River Campus in 1930 and was well established by the time of this aerial view looking southeast, in 1984. (Courtesy City of Rochester Photo Lab.)

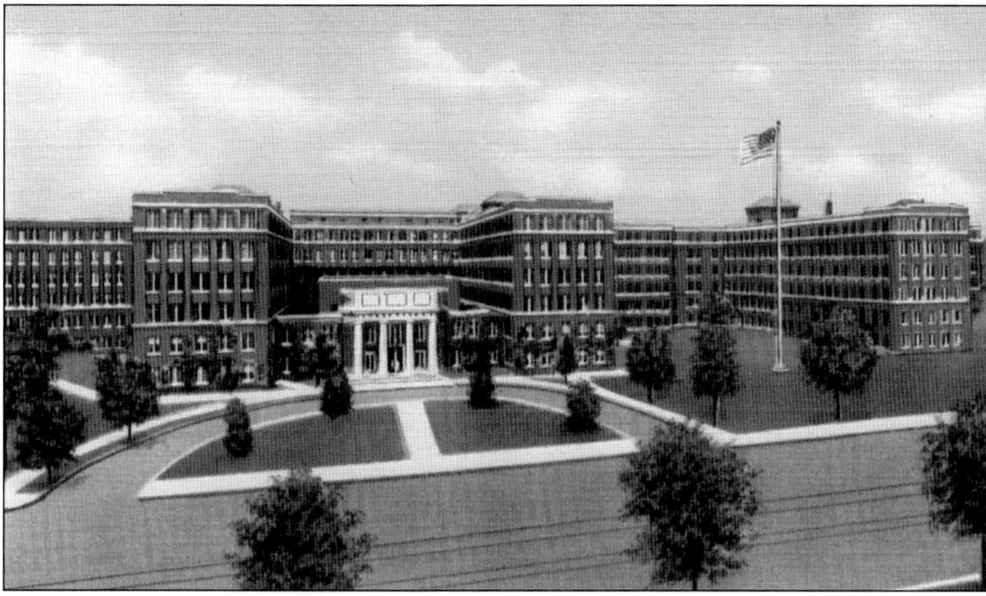

STRONG MEMORIAL. George Eastman and Henry A. Strong had formed the Eastman Dry Plate Company together, with Strong putting up the funds and Eastman the expertise. After the success of the Eastman Kodak Company, Strong made generous donations to the Red Cross, the YMCA, and the University of Rochester. Eastman paid one-third of the building costs of Strong Memorial Hospital, named in memory of his friend and business partner. Rush Rhees, (1860–1939) third University of Rochester president, sought George Eastman's support to establish an engineering department. Eastman helped with the expansion of the liberal arts program, the establishment of a school of medicine, and a music school. Rhees dedicated a new River Campus before retiring in 1935. The postcard shows the new facility at its very best; confident kitchen staff members are shown in 1926. (Above, courtesy Ellwanger and Barry Neighborhood Association; below, courtesy City of Rochester Photo Lab.)

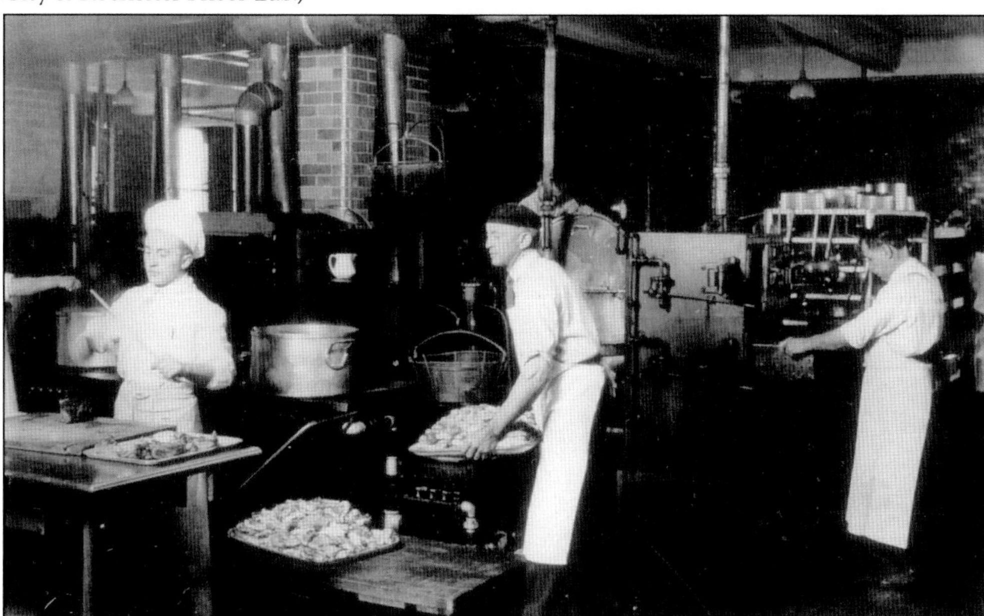

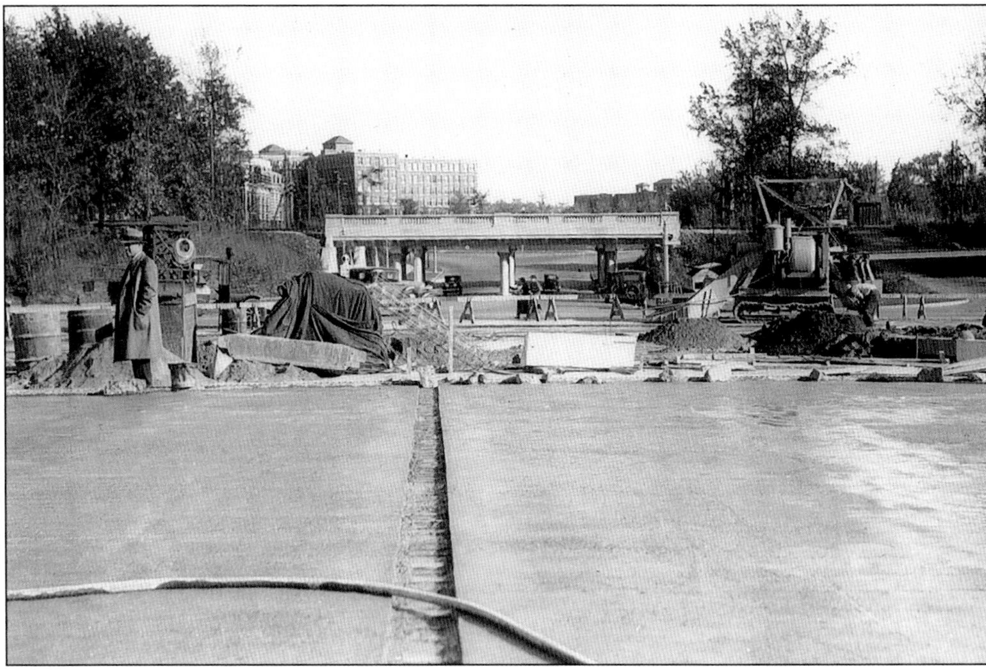

PROGRESS REPORT. This visual report on the Elmwood Avenue underpass reconstruction, dated October 16, 1935, also shows the Medical Center in the background. (Courtesy City of Rochester Archives.)

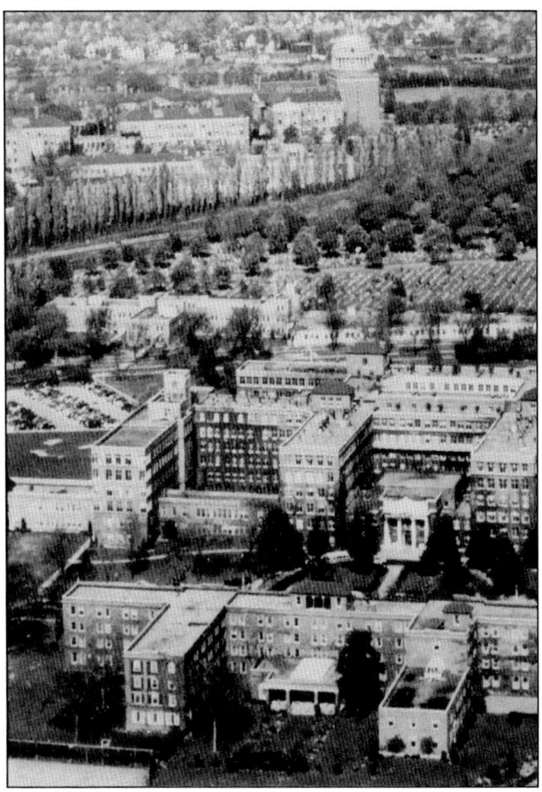

MEDICAL CENTER. The University of Rochester Medical Center is shown in the winter of 1950. (Courtesy City of Rochester Photo Lab.)

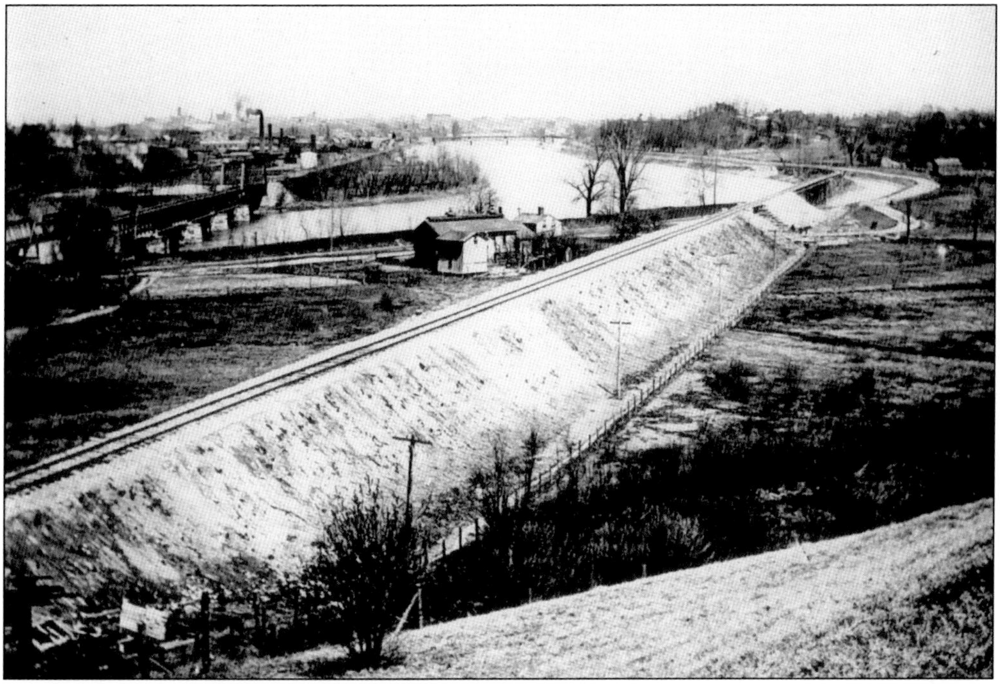

Pest House. Hope Hospital was opened on River Road in 1869 by the city to contain infectious diseases. It was built on the river flats in back of the cemetery and maintained for three decades. Dr. George Goler protested conditions there and warned of a smallpox epidemic, which began in February 1902. More than 100 out of 1,000 who got smallpox died. The hospital was equipped for 18 patients. In early December 1902, there were 143 smallpox cases put up in tents. The hospital was burned in 1903. The land was bought by the University of Rochester in 1966. (Above, courtesy City of Rochester Photo Lab; below, courtesy Rochester Photo Images.)

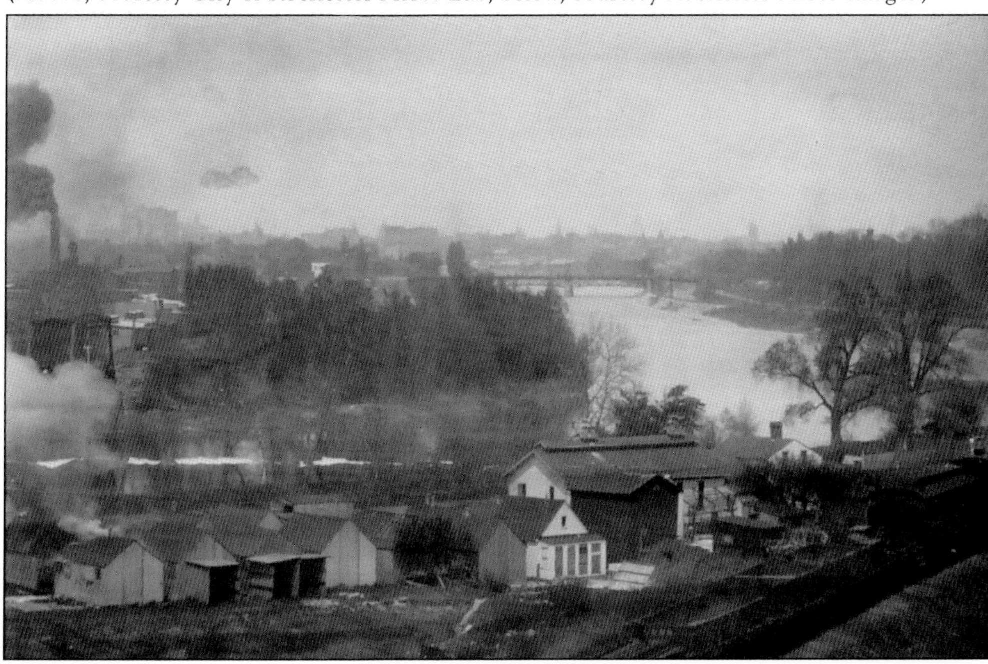

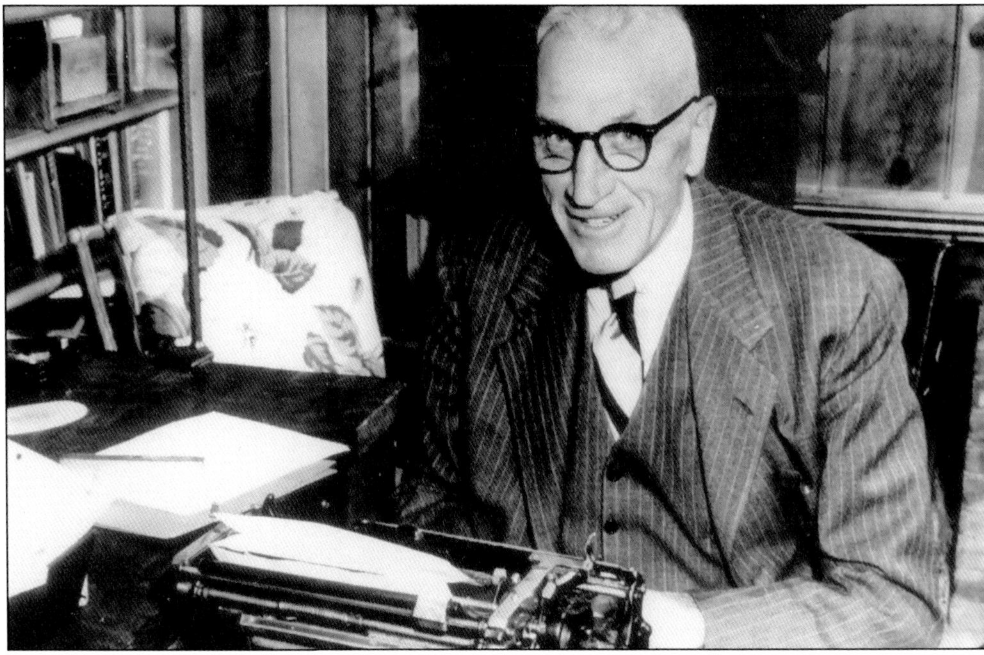

HENRY CLUNE. Henry Clune (1890–1995) was a popular newspaper reporter and historian who grew up on Linden Street. He described Hope Hospital around 1900 as a converted farmhouse on the east bank of the Genesee, close to stagnant Erie Canal waters and by a railroad bridge. It was a two-ward, one-room, 16-bed hospital with one water tap in the kitchen and no sewer. Staff used a weathered, unpainted shack for isolation cases, an old grocery wagon for an ambulance, and had to rent the horse. (Courtesy City of Rochester Photo Lab.).

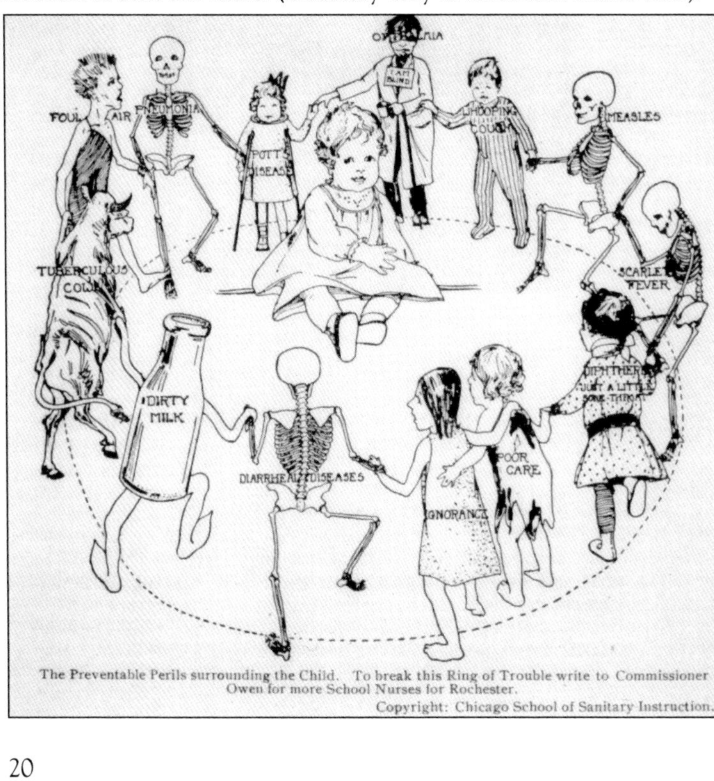

RING AROUND THE ROSIE. This grim poster was part of a campaign to break the cycle of infant deaths from drinking infected milk, foul air, measles, scarlet fever, poor care, and ignorance. Readers were encouraged to write the commissioner for more school nurses in the city of Rochester. As more was understood about how germs spread diseases, the practice of hauling ice in garbage trucks during off hours was stopped in 1893. (Courtesy City of Rochester Photo Lab.)

Two

BETWEEN THE BRIDGES

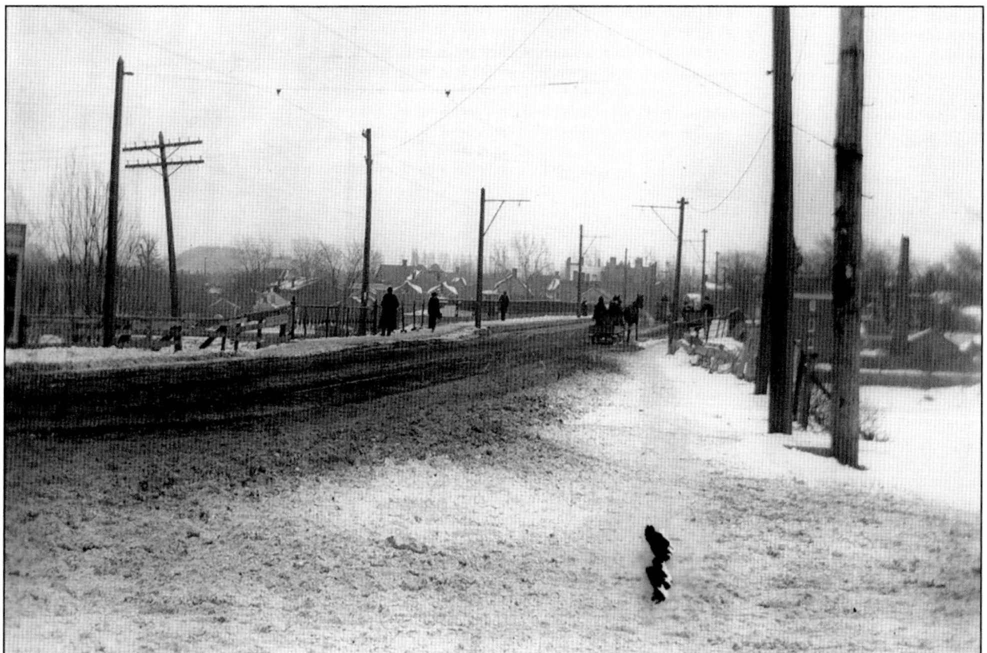

OVER THE RIVER. The horse knows the way to carry the sleigh over the river on the Clarissa Street Bridge. This photograph is dated December 7, 1892. (Courtesy City of Rochester Archives.)

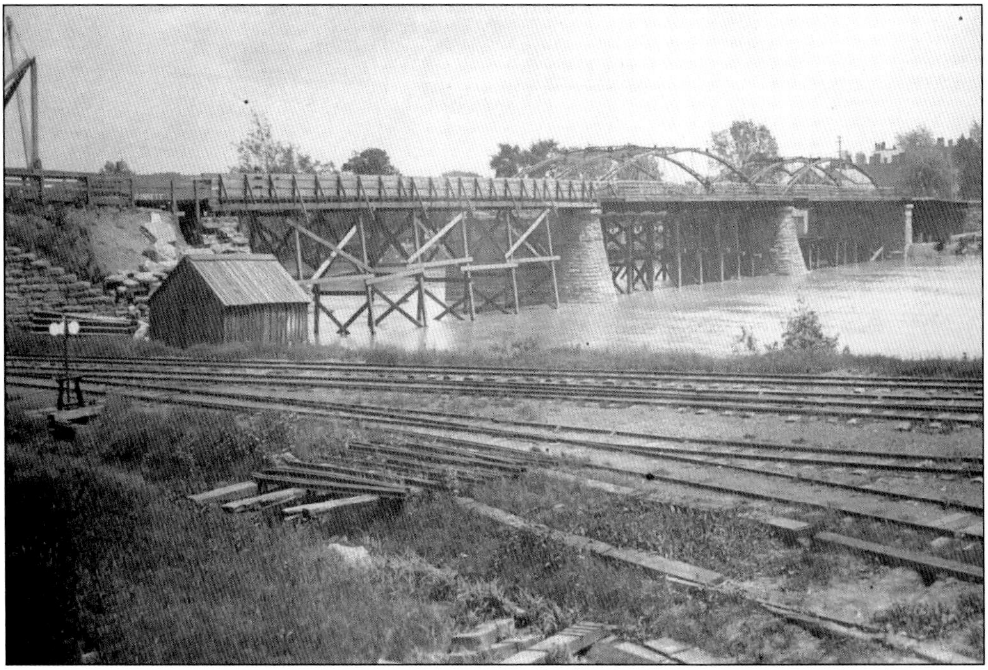

CLARISSA STREET BRIDGE. The original wooden bridge built in 1844 was replaced in 1862, 1892, and 1918. The 1918 bridge was remodeled and renamed the Ford Street Bridge in 1980. This undated view is most likely from the 1890s. (Courtesy City of Rochester Photo Lab.)

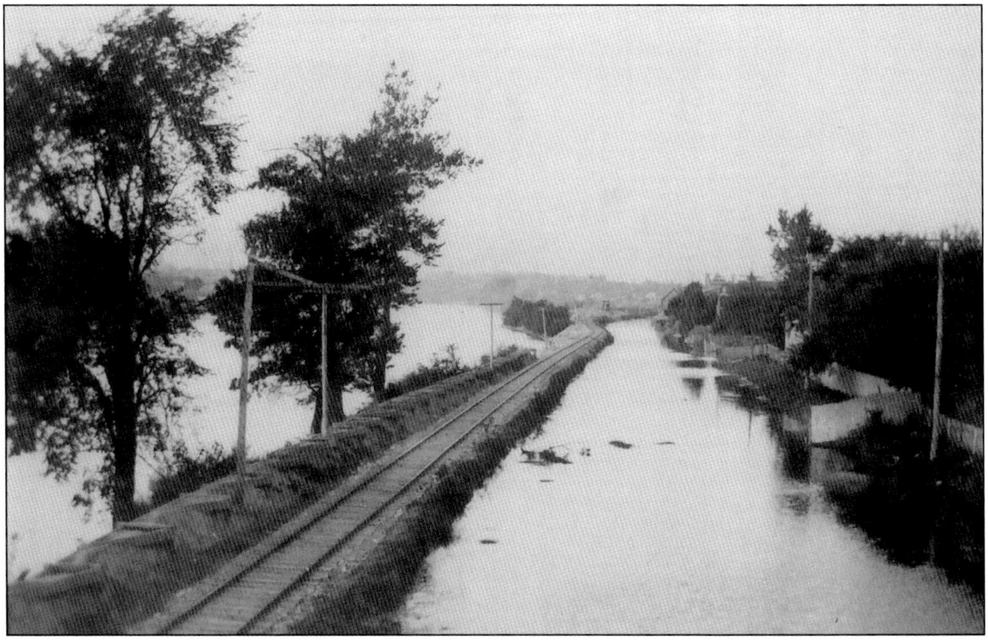

HIGH WATER. This view of the Erie Canal feeder, Lehigh Valley train tracks, and the Genesee River are shown in high water on September 2, 1892. The view is looking north towards the city from the Clarissa Street Bridge. The feeder (on the right) began south of Elmwood Avenue and flowed to a junction with the canal near St. Paul Street and Griffith Street (later South Avenue). (Courtesy City of Rochester Photo Lab.)

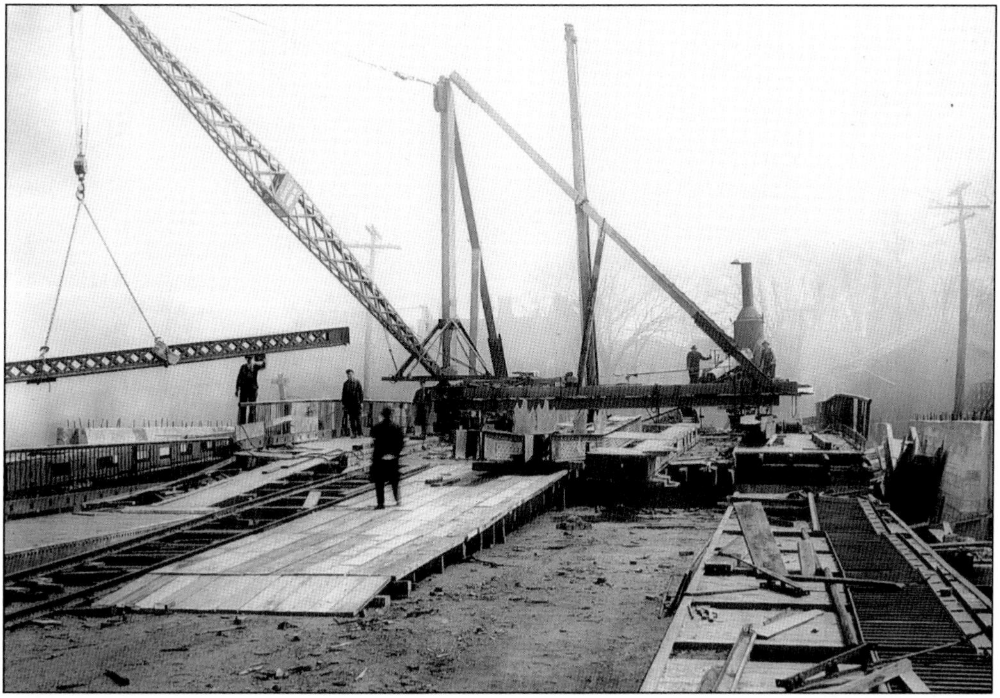

MAJOR OVERHAUL. Work is well underway to reconstruct the Clarissa Street Bridge. Both photographs are dated April 30, 1919. In the bottom photograph, men get ready to move a board, most likely by the Wolcott Distillery. (Courtesy City of Rochester Archives.)

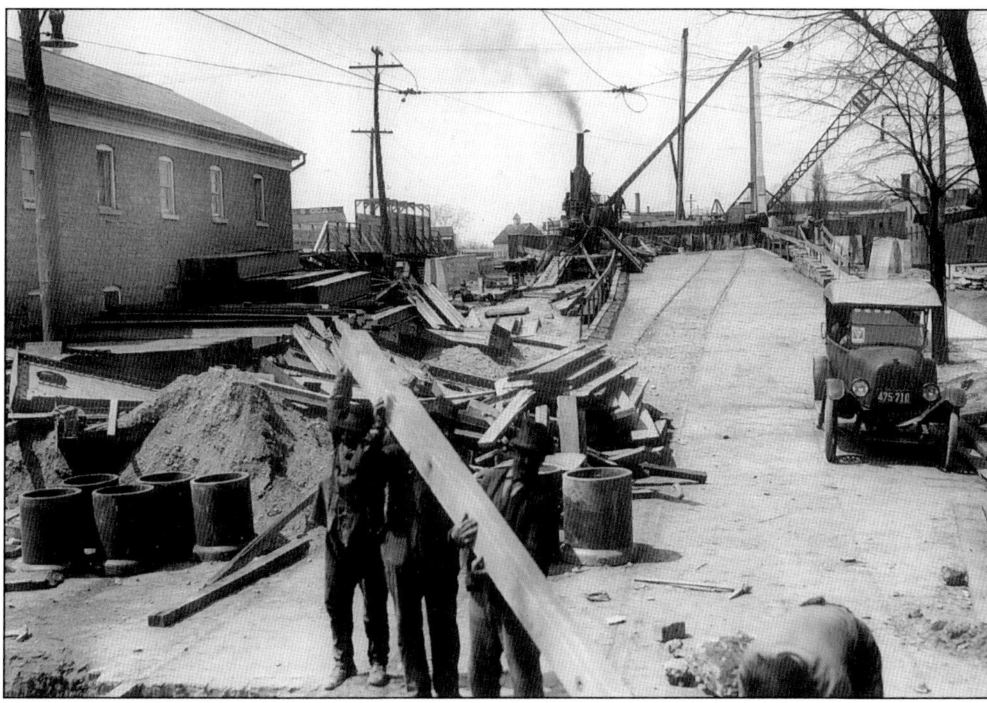

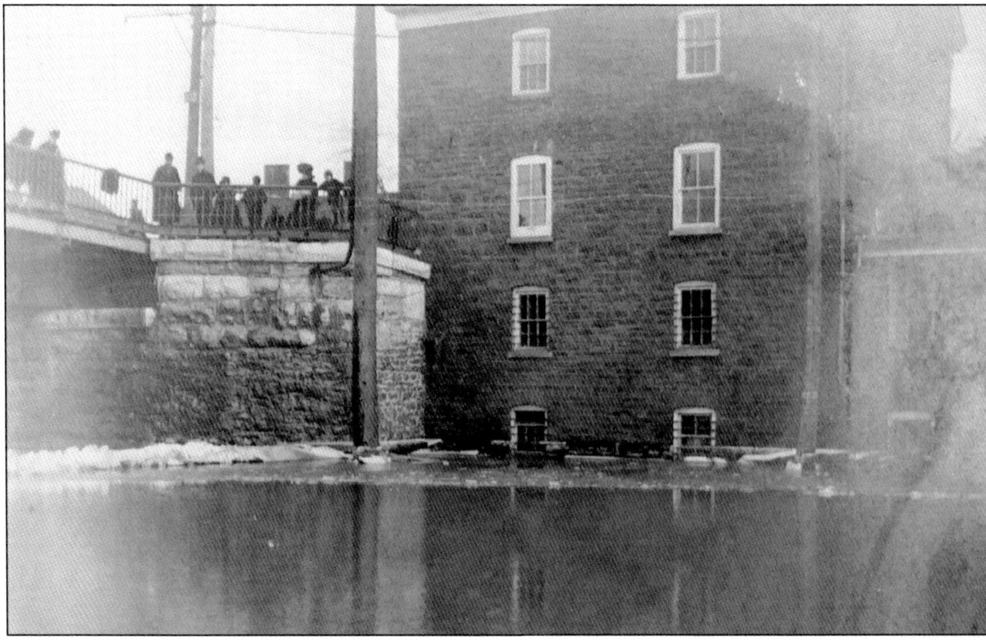

Flooding by Wolcott's Distillery. A crowd gathers on the bridge on March 4, 1902, to check out the flood. High water caused by snow melt damaged many basements along the river. This old picture is captioned: "Looking E. From L.V.R.R. tracks across feeder just S. of Clarissa St. Bridge showing high water marks on Wolcott's distillery." The Wolcott distillery produced a popular whiskey called Corn Hill. John Wolcott is listed in the 1844 city directory as a barkeeper at the corner of South St. Paul and Clarissa Streets; Epaphras is listed as a distiller at 175 South St. Paul Street. In 1851, Wolcott is listed as the proprietor of Mount Hope Avenue House; Anson F. and George P. are listed as distillers and manufacturers of saleratus, a leavening agent, with a business on Mount Hope Avenue and home at 179 Mount Hope Avenue. (Courtesy Rochester Photo Images.)

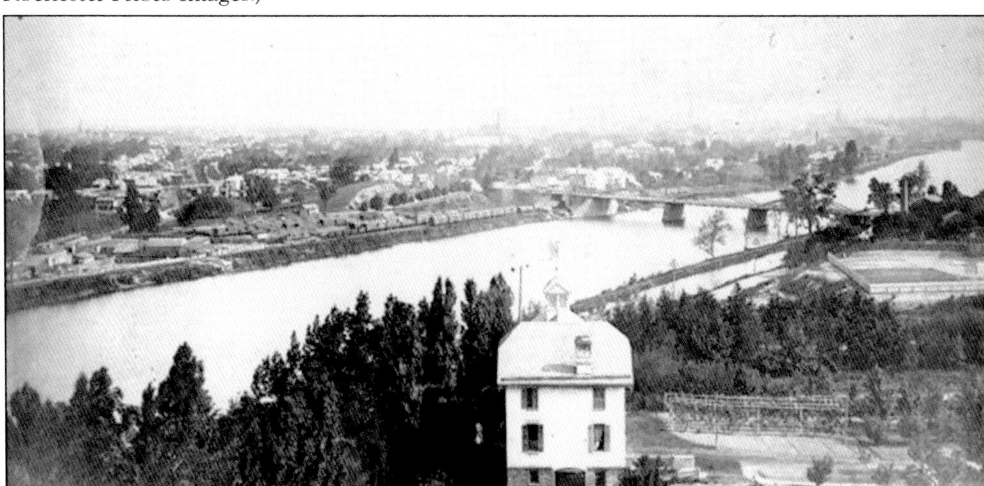

Original Clarissa Street Bridge. This view looking northwest from Mount Hope Cemetery was made from a negative of a photograph dated 1854. It shows the original bridge built in 1844, which was replaced in 1862, 1892, and 1918. The 1918 bridge was remodeled and renamed Ford Street Bridge in 1980. (Courtesy Rochester Photo Images.)

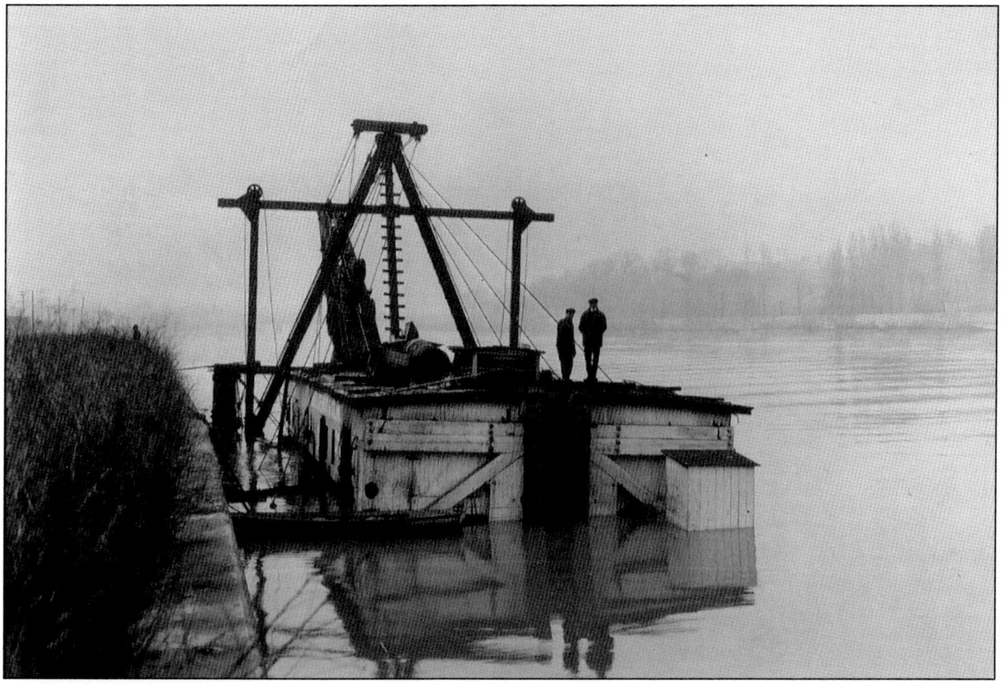

DREDGE BY BRIDGE. Construction from 1905 to 1923 linked the Erie Canal to the New York State Barge Canal. The Genesee River was connected to the new canal system a mile south of the city near Genesee Valley Park. This view of a dredge at work was taken in 1923 near the Clarissa Street Bridge. (Courtesy Rochester Photo Images.)

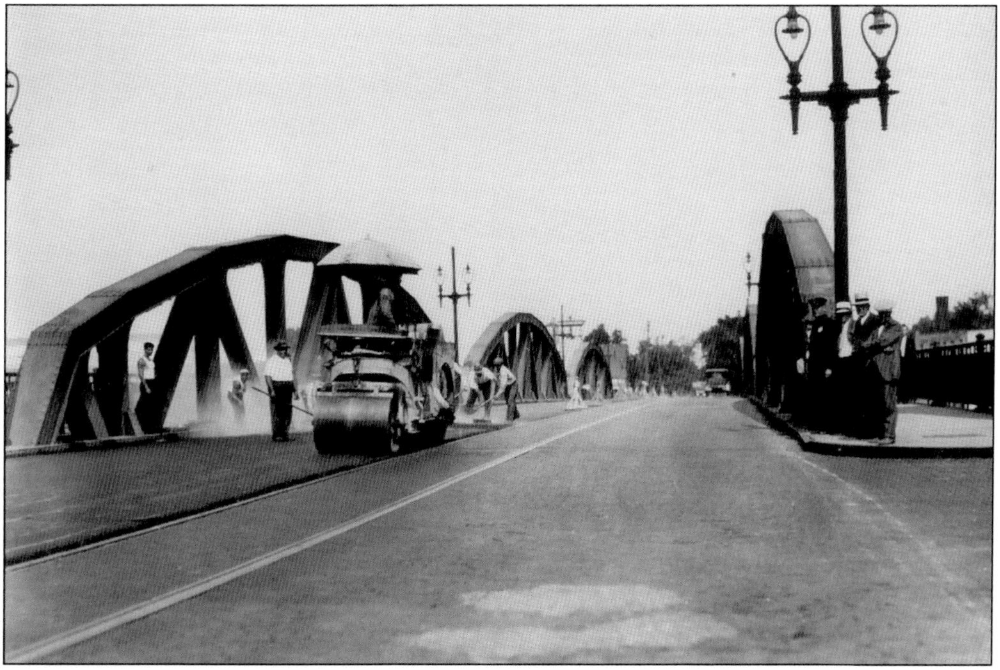

CLARISSA STREET BRIDGE, 1931. Paving crews give the bridge a fresh smooth surface. (Courtesy City of Rochester Photo Lab.)

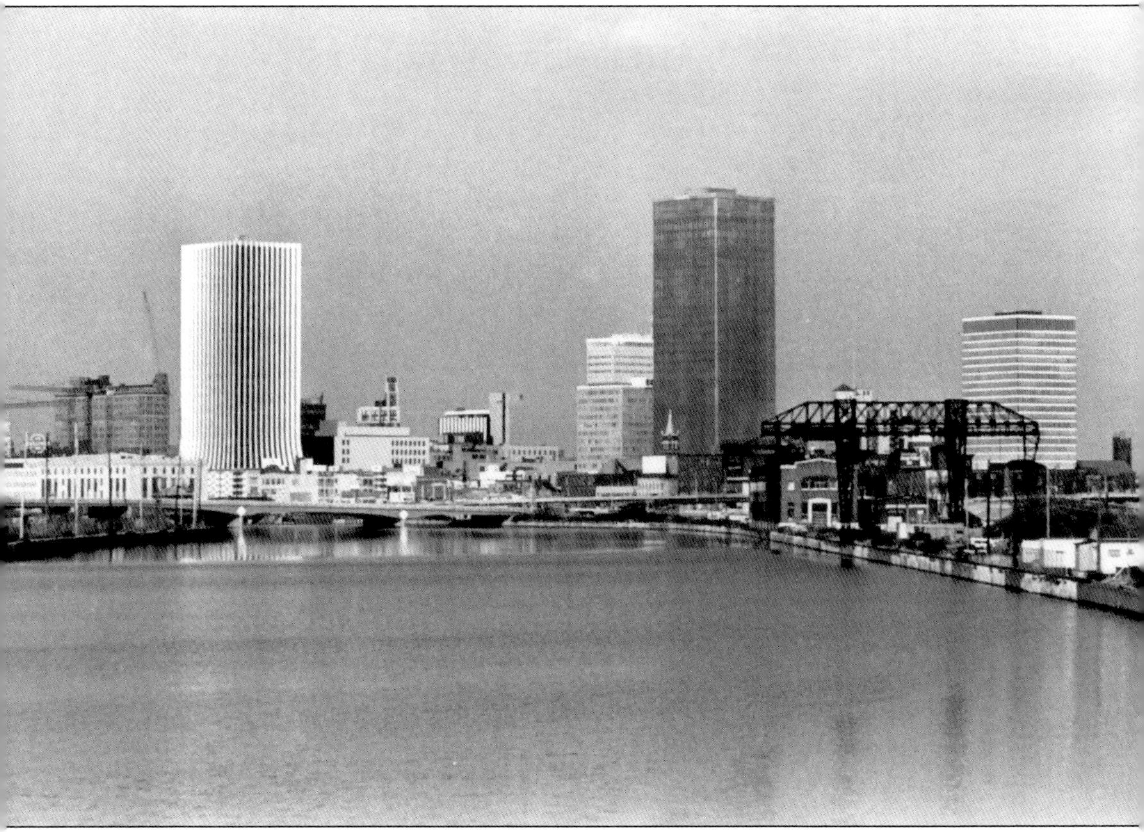

DOWNTOWN SKYLINE. The large gantry crane is visible on the east side of the river in 1973. The Xerox and Midtown Towers are in the background. The old gantry crane still dominated the railroad yards before construction of the River Park Commons, first called Genesee Gateway, townhouses and high rise. (Courtesy City of Rochester Photo Lab.)

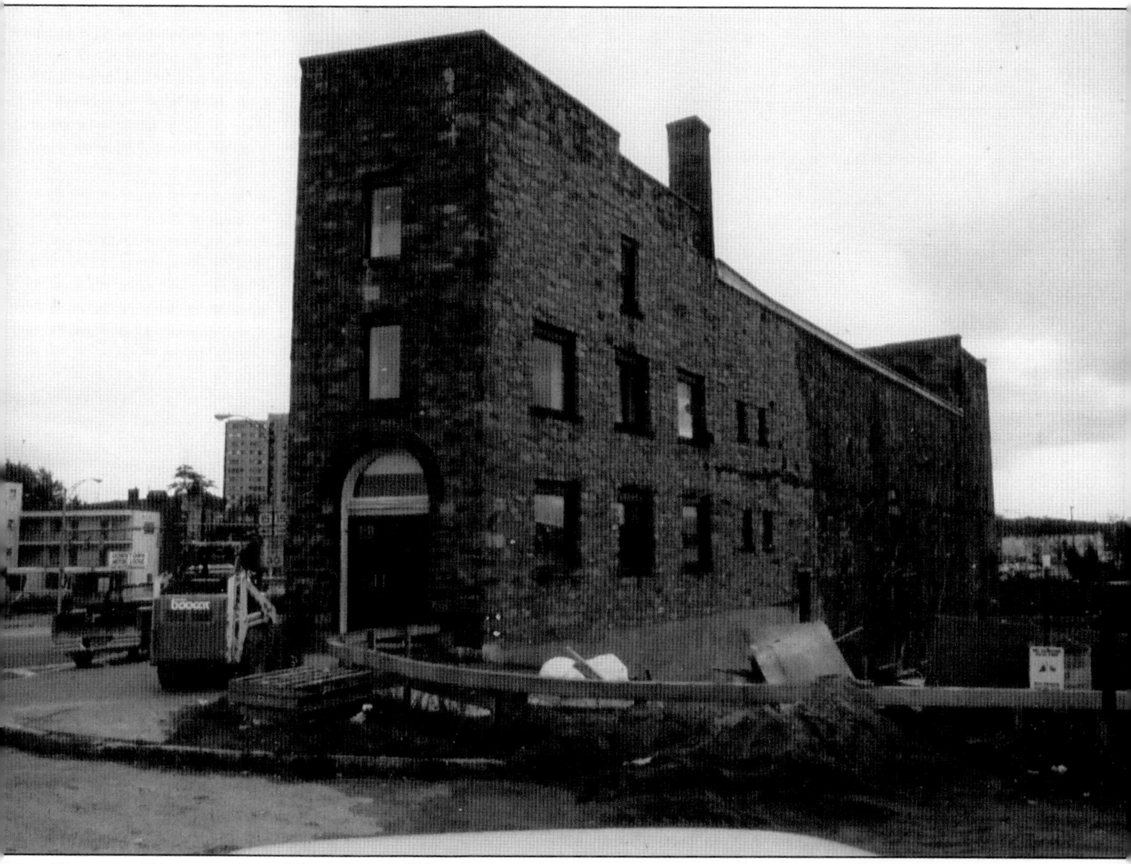

CANAL WAREHOUSE. The Stone Warehouse at the junction of the original Erie Canal and the feeder was also called Gilbert's Warehouse. It was built by John Gilbert between 1821 and 1822 and was the second warehouse along the canal. It became vacant as business moved to Child's Basin on the west side of the city. In 1838, William H. Cheney rented the skeleton of the building for a furnace and a foundry from the owner, Dr. John Elwood. Cooking-stoves made there were the first in this part of the country. Henry Oothout bought the building in 1864 and used it to store malt. Samuel Oothout expanded the warehouse to its present size in 1869 for brewing. It was bought by the Bartholomay Brewing Company in 1889. The Stone Warehouse's most productive time was from 1864 to 1905, when Oothout owned it and operated the country's largest malt house. In 1905, Rochester Carting Company bought the building and owned it until 1968. The interior was heavily damaged after a fire in 1975. Several options were considered without success until developer Ben Kendig bought the building for $1 in 1986, for offices. Kendig sold the building to ABVI-Goodwill Industries in 2005. It is the oldest complete canal warehouse still standing in Rochester. This photograph, taken on October 9, 1986, also shows the Downtown Motor Lodge (left) that was torn down in 2005. (Courtesy Rochester Photo Images.)

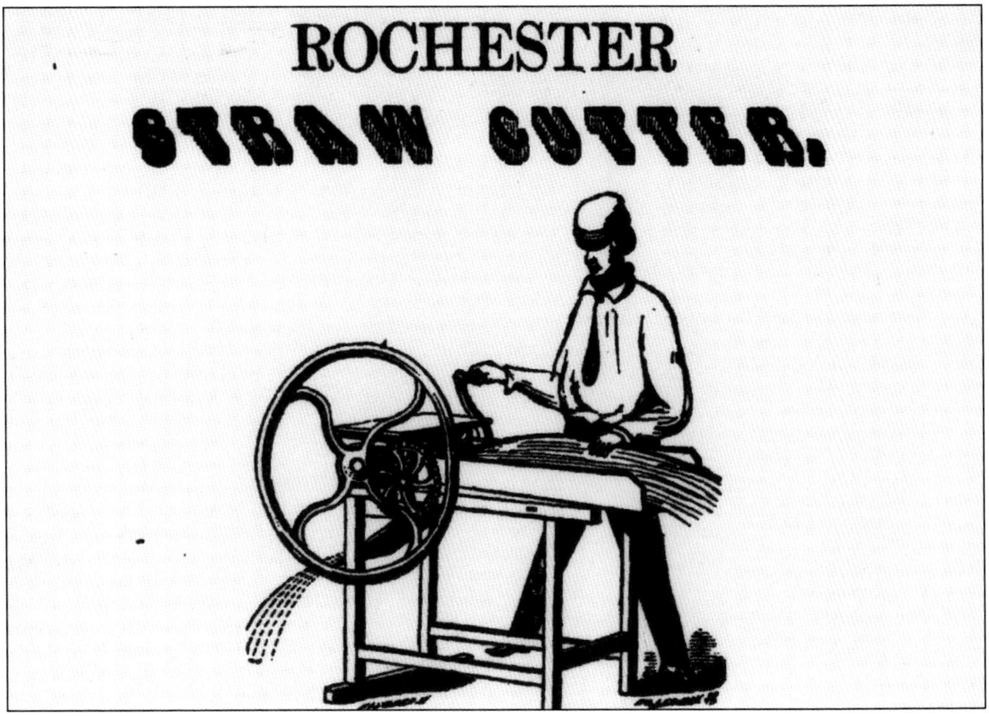

STRAW CUTTER AND AGRICULTURAL WORKS. The 1851 and 1853 city directories list William H. Cheney, "stove foundry, 68 South St. Paul." This straw cutter advertisement for the Alexander Gordon Company in the 1853 directory is at the same address. The new and improved cutter for hay, straw, and corn stalks sold for $12. By the 1861 directory, the company was renamed Rochester Agricultural Works and promoted plows, feed cutters, and threshing machines for "eight and ten horse powers."

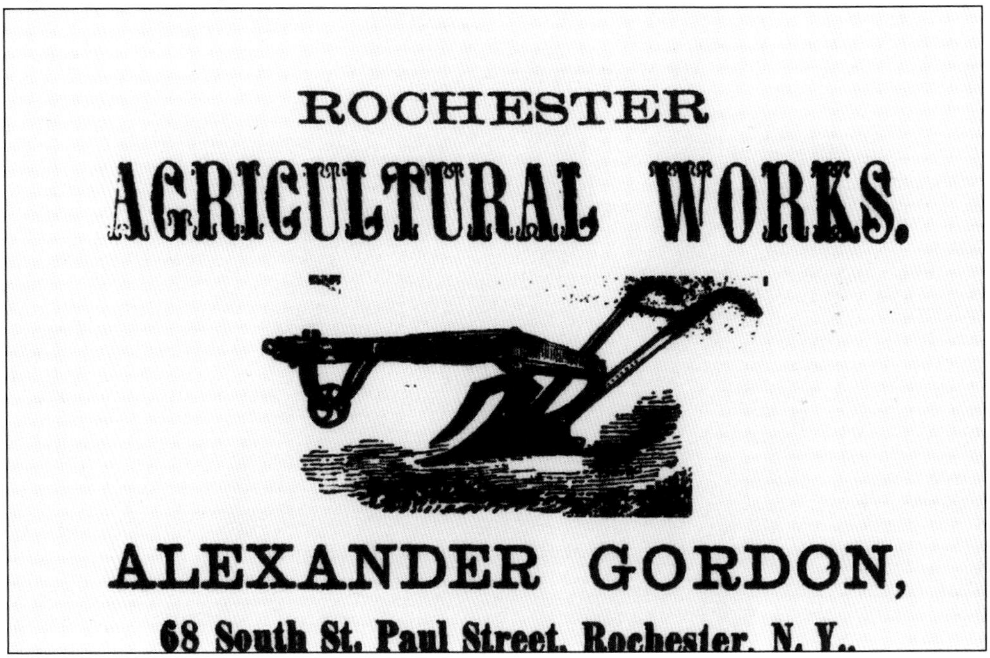

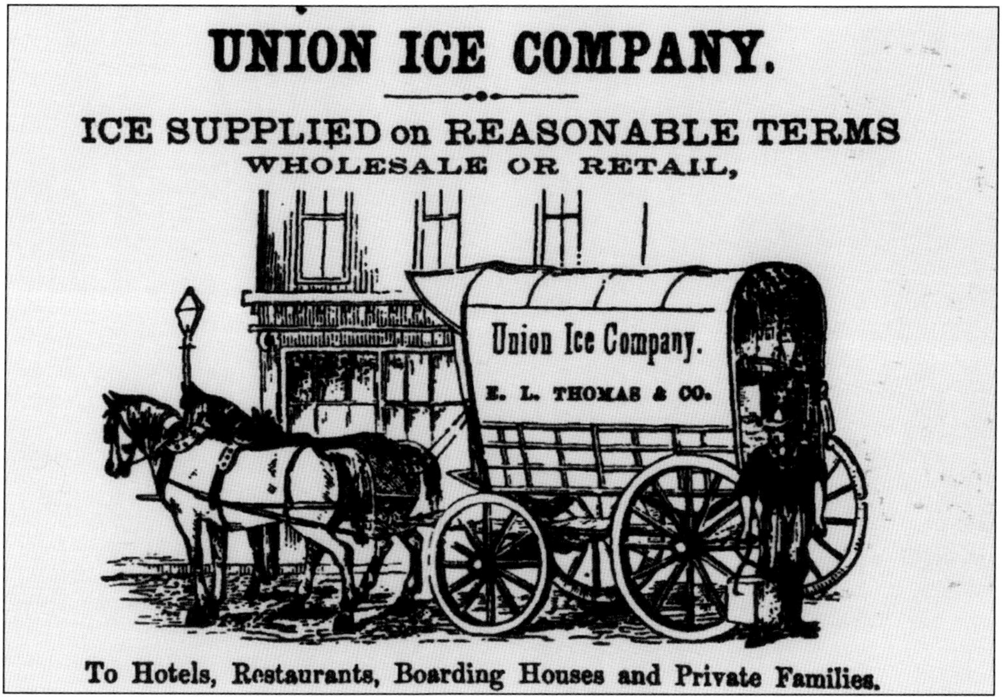

UNION ICE. Some business and home addresses still had no street numbers in the early 1860s. The Union Ice Company, which served hotel, restaurants, boarding houses and homes, was listed in the 1861 city directory at "Depot, Mt. Hope Ave."

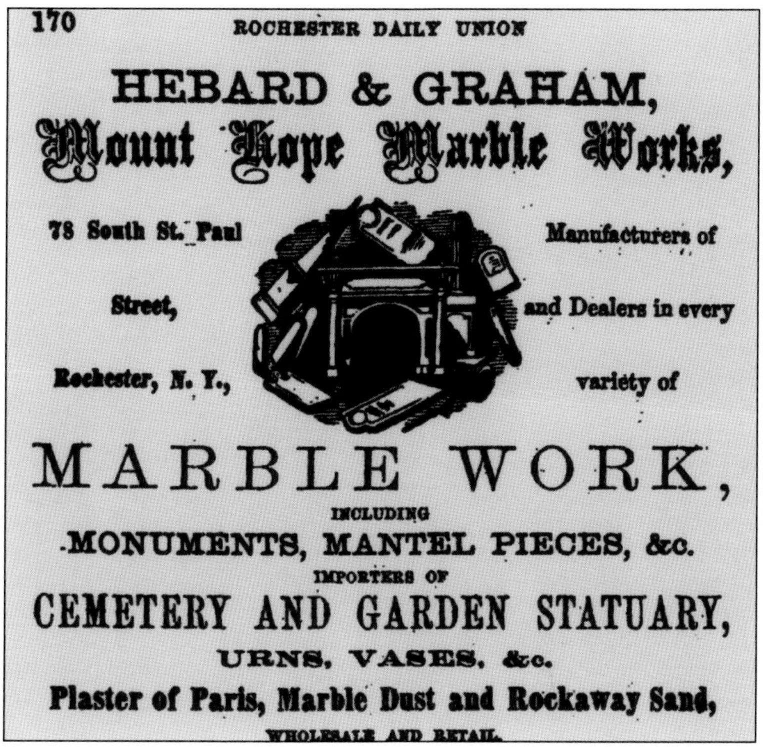

MOUNT HOPE MARBLE WORKS. Hebard and Graham had both a plain and a fancy advertisement in the 1855 city directory and this one in 1861, all at 78 South St. Paul Street.

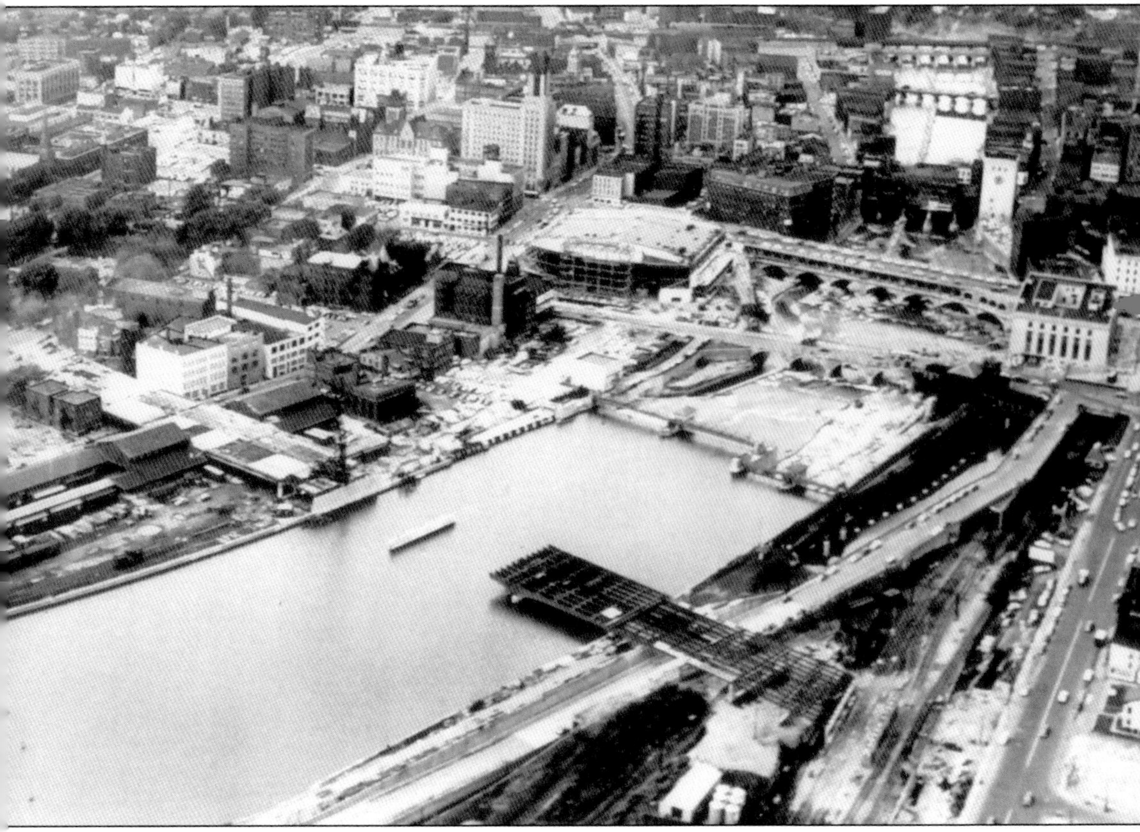

TROUP-HOWELL BRIDGE. Although there are several Howells listed on the southeast side in early city directories, Howell Street was named from Nathaniel W. Howell, (1770–1851) of Canandaigua who was attorney general of western New York from 1799–1802. By the late 1830s there were six year-round boat yards in the city including, W. W. Howell and Brother at Gilbert's Basin by the Old Stone Warehouse. In the city directory of 1847, Richard D. Howell is listed as "superintendent W. W. Howells's Boat Yard, h. 86 S. St. Paul" and William W. is "Boat Yard Proprietor, S. St. Paul, h. corner Jackson and S. St. Paul." This photograph shows the bridge between Troup and Howell Streets under construction in 1952. Troup Street was named for Robert Troup, a New York lawyer who was a pioneer land agent. (The village of Charlotte was named for his daughter.) After the construction of the Inner Loop, both Troup and Howell Streets became much shorter than they used to be. (Courtesy City of Rochester Photo Lab.)

Three

The Original Erie Canal

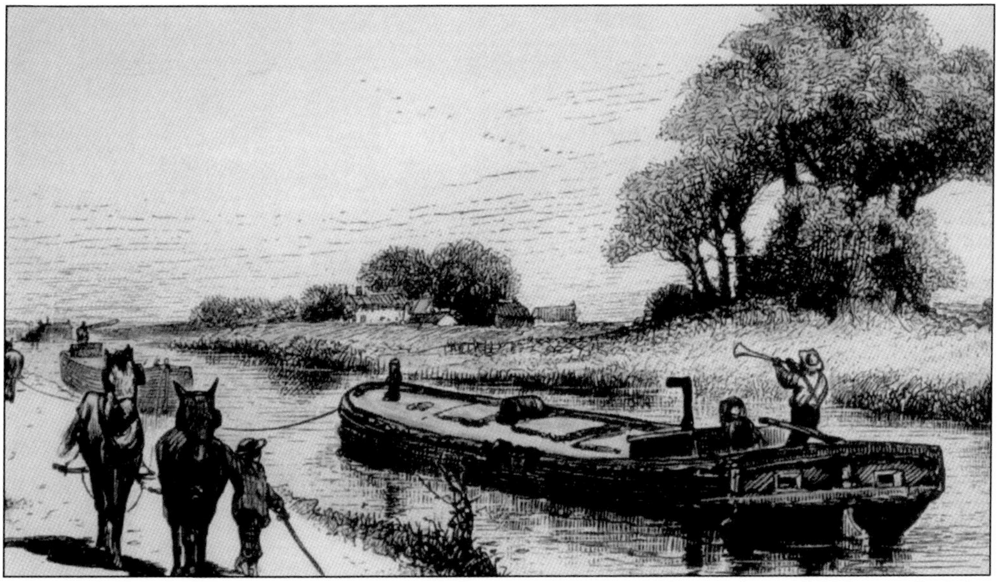

A Slower Pace. The caption on this illustration is "Hoggees drove the mules that pulled the boats in the Erie Canal, which at first was four feet deep and seven feet wide." A hoggee was a boy between the ages of 10 and 18 who had the sometimes thankless job of keeping the mules moving. (Courtesy City of Rochester Photo Lab.)

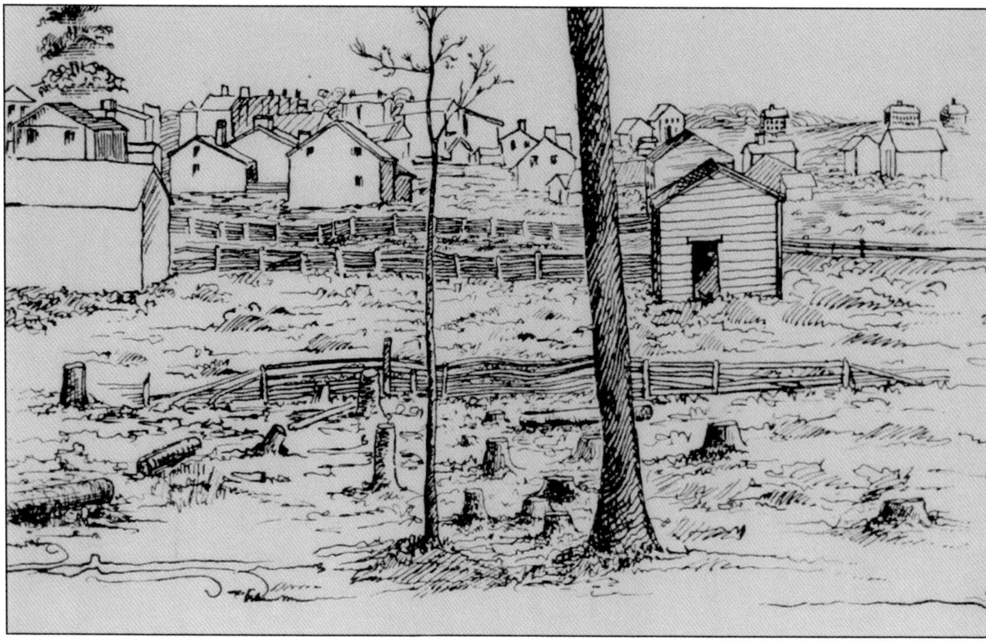

ROCHESTER, 1820. At the time of Rochester's beginning, western New York was considered the far west of the United States. To get around the Appalachian Mountains, travelers from northern Alabama to the province of Quebec had to sail around Florida to reach the Mississippi. This illustration of Rochester in 1820 is a realistic view of rough clearings around modest dwellings. Most of the early settlement in the new village was west of the Genesee River. The construction of the Erie Canal, which reached the city in 1819, turned it into a boomtown called "The Young Lion of the West." From that time, southeast Rochester also expanded quickly. (Courtesy City of Rochester Photo Lab.)

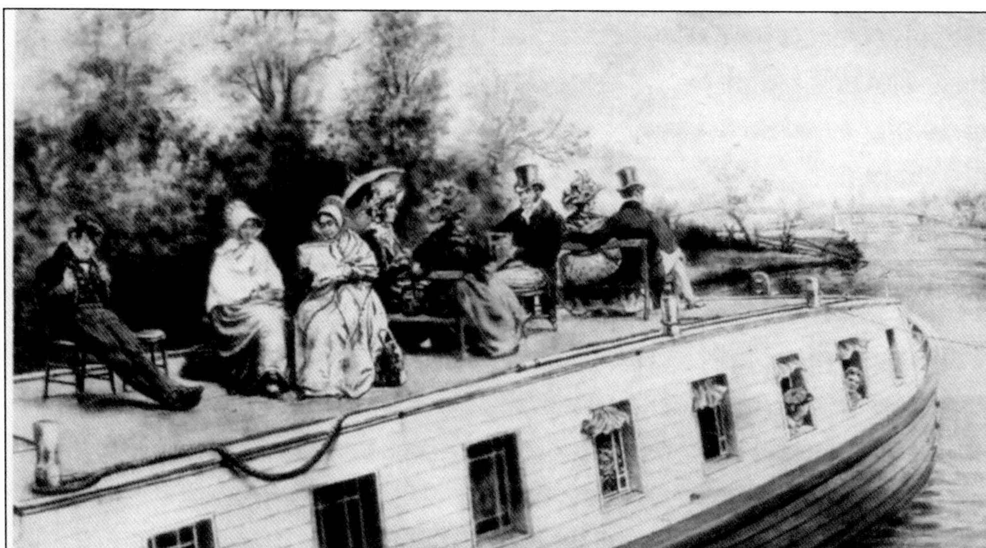

DECEPTIVELY QUIET. The caption for this illustration is: "Fugitive slaves often escaped on passenger boats accompanied by an abolitionist or they hid in the cargo holds of canal boats. There was less secrecy as the Civil War neared." (Courtesy City of Rochester Photo Lab.)

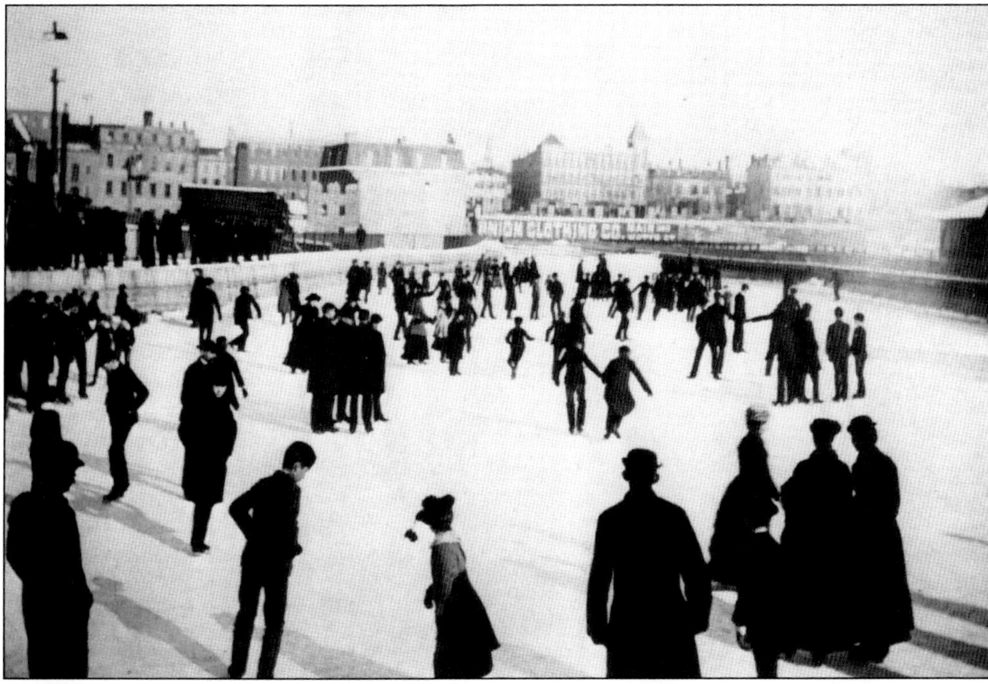

Skating on the Old Canal. There seems to be as much chatting as skating in this *c.* 1880 photograph. (Courtesy City of Rochester Photo Lab.)

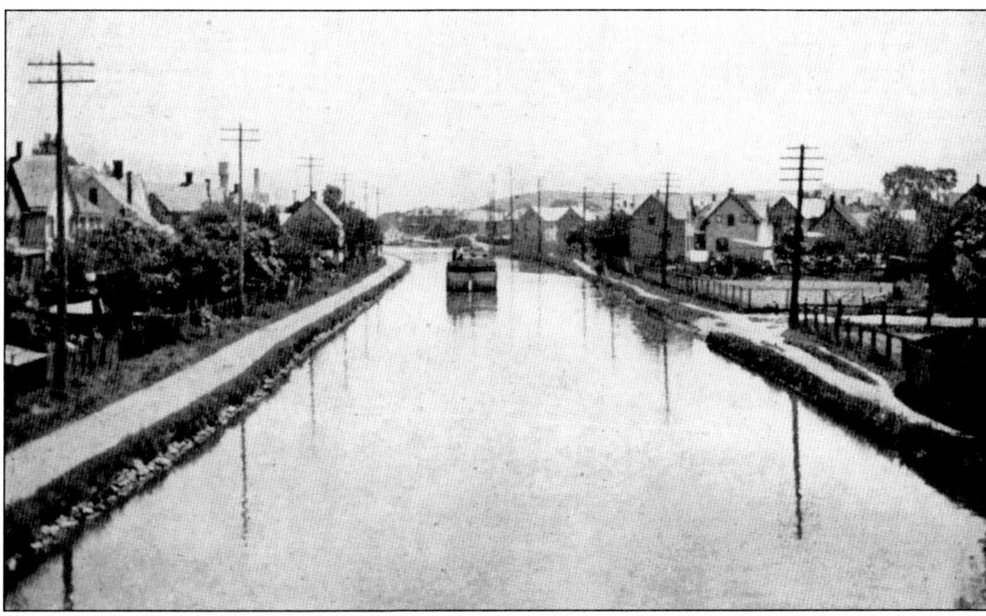

Old Canal. By the time this serene view of the canal was taken in 1919, the city had not allowed dumping of any and all garbage in the canal and river for several decades. In the 1880s, by order of the Board of Health, excess garbage was dumped in the Genesee River. The city also sold garbage to pig farmers. These practices were halted when health pioneers better understood how contagious diseases spread. (Courtesy City of Rochester Photo Lab.)

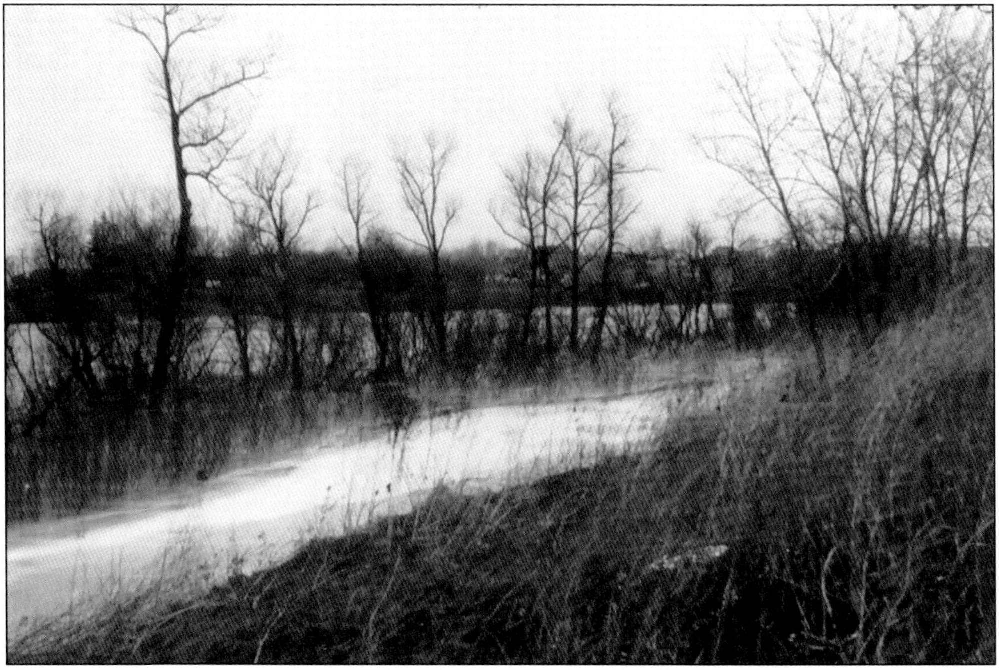

CANAL FEEDER. Before the Erie Canal was completed from Rochester to Buffalo, there was a feeder to the Genesee River that had a guard lock at its head on the east side. It was near rapids down stream from the present University of Rochester Interfaith Chapel. The rapids were at the bend in the river where Brooks Avenue joins Plymouth Avenue. After the feeder was built, the canal was filled from Rochester to Pittsford. This picture captioned "Sta. 5 looking north" is dated March 2, 1903. (Courtesy Rochester Photo Images.)

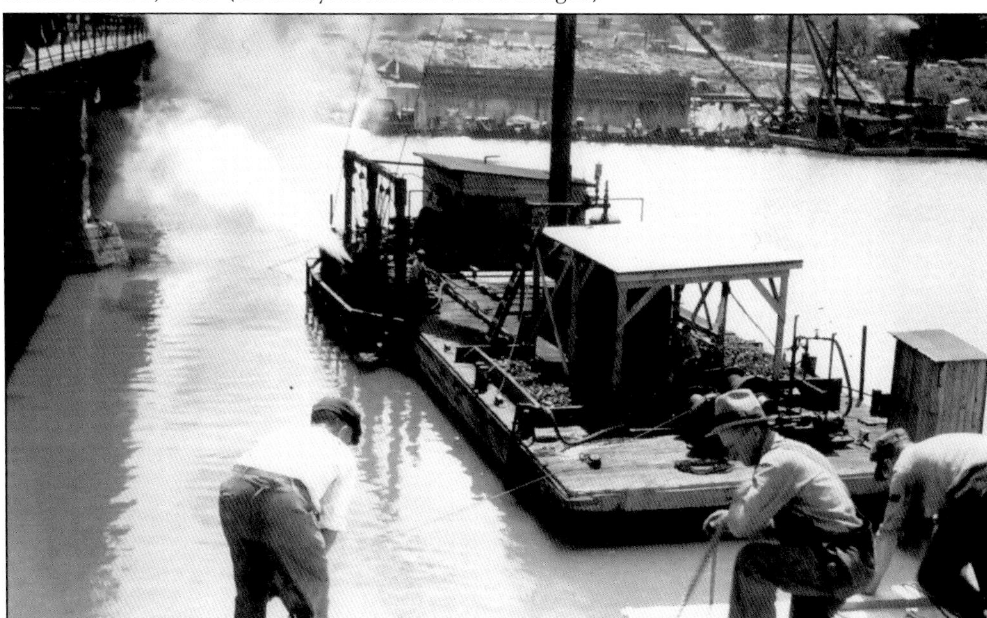

BARGE WORKERS. Construction from 1905 to 1923 linked the Erie Canal to the New York State Barge Canal. This photograph is from around 1935. (Courtesy City of Rochester Photo Lab.)

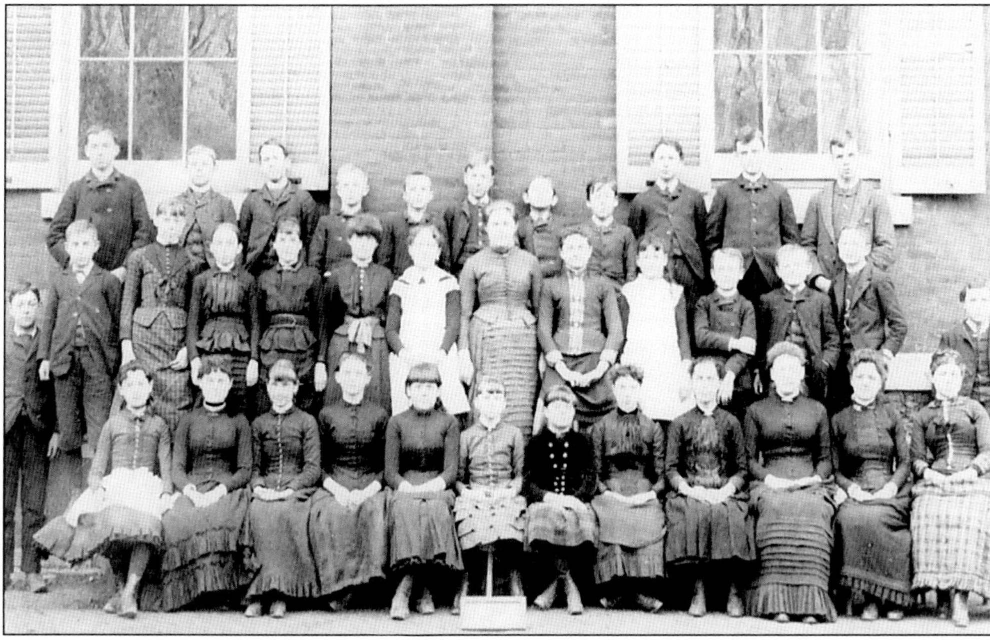

CLASS OF 1886. No. 12 School opened on Marshall Street in 1842 and was known as the General Wadsworth School after the general who donated the land for it. The school was rebuilt in 1856 and 1899, and closed in 1932. It reopened in 1973 at 999 South Avenue as the James P. Duffy School. The names of all the children of this class are listed on the back of the photograph, which was a gift of Blanche Castleman Link in 1953. (Courtesy Rochester Photo Images.)

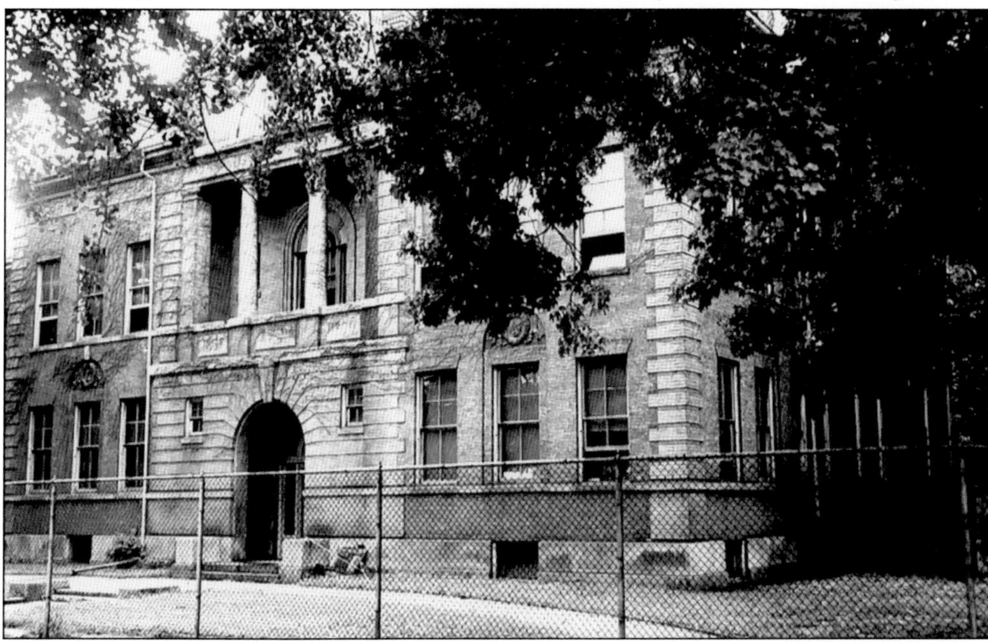

NO. 12 SCHOOL. This brick school building was built on Clinton Avenue between Howell and Marshall Streets in 1899. It was closed as a school in 1932. When this photograph was taken in 1950, it was the location of the City of Rochester's Health Bureau and Department of Public Welfare. The building was torn down around 1968. (Courtesy Rochester Photo Images.)

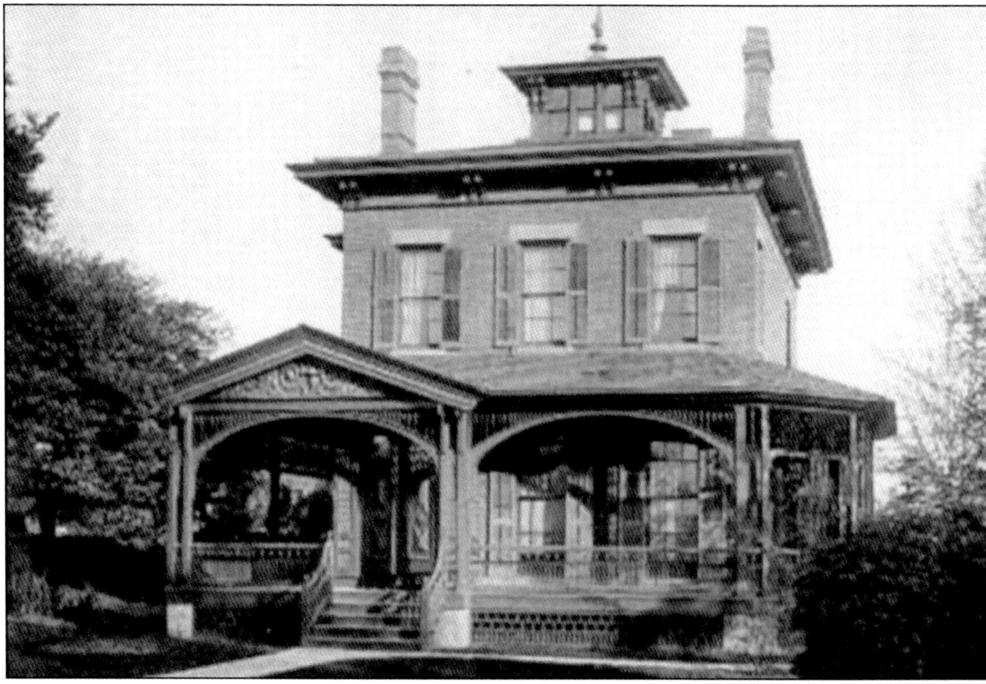

MEYER HOME. On the city map of 1900, Charles C. Meyer, owner of C. C. Meyer and Son, had a home on Meigs Street between Pearl Street and the Erie Canal. This picture was published in a magazine in 1890. The Meyer family traveled from Germany in 1836 and came to Rochester on the canal. They ran several boatyards that specialized in building lakers, steamboats, and bullheads—a canal boat used for grains and other dry products. An 1850s city directory lists a Caleb J. Meyer as a boat builder, with his home on South St. Paul Street. The 1861 directory lists John A. Myers, a boat builder at Mount Hope Avenue, with his home at 71 West Alexander Street, and Myers and McQuatters boat builders, at Cayuga Street (South Clinton Avenue). (Courtesy Rochester Photo Images.)

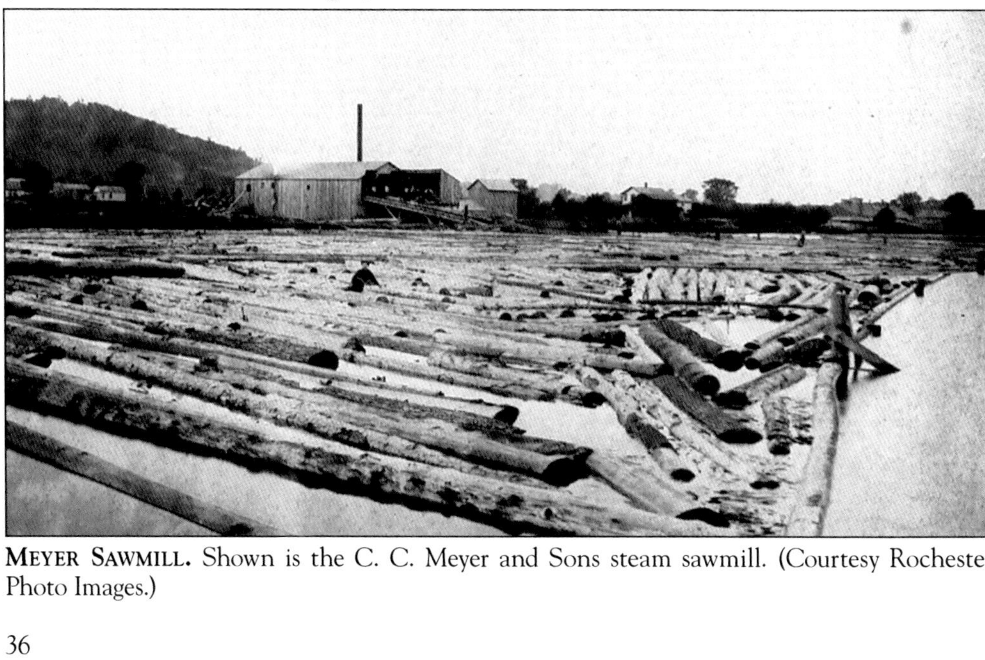

MEYER SAWMILL. Shown is the C. C. Meyer and Sons steam sawmill. (Courtesy Rochester Photo Images.)

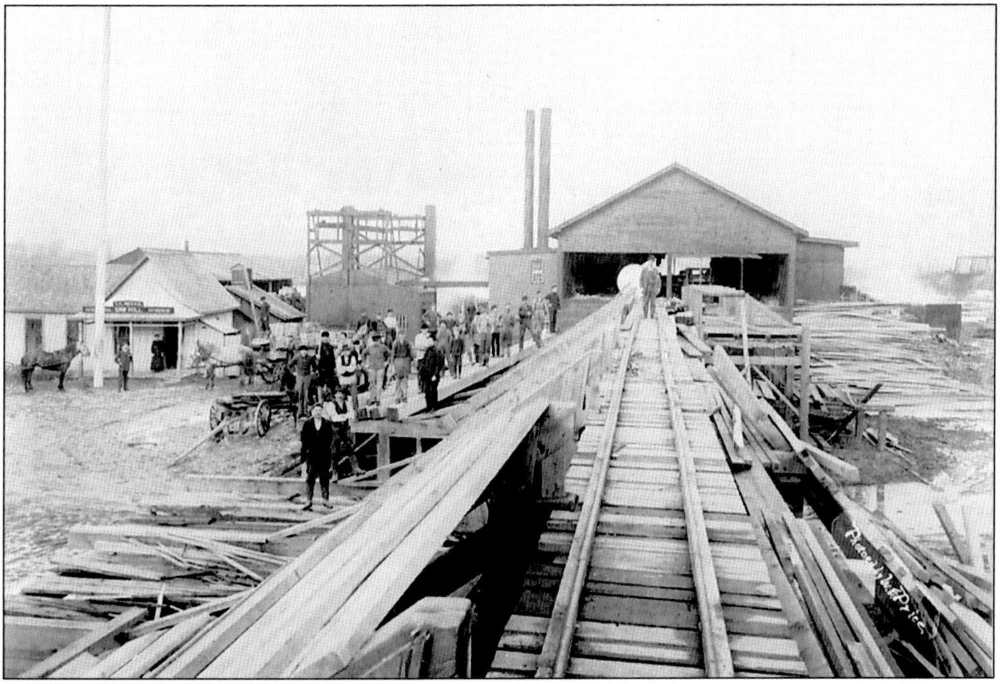

STEAM SAWMILL. The C. C. Meyer and Sons steam sawmill opened along the canal near Monroe Avenue and Culver Road around 1883. The Meyer family also had a boatyard. (Courtesy Rochester Photo Images.)

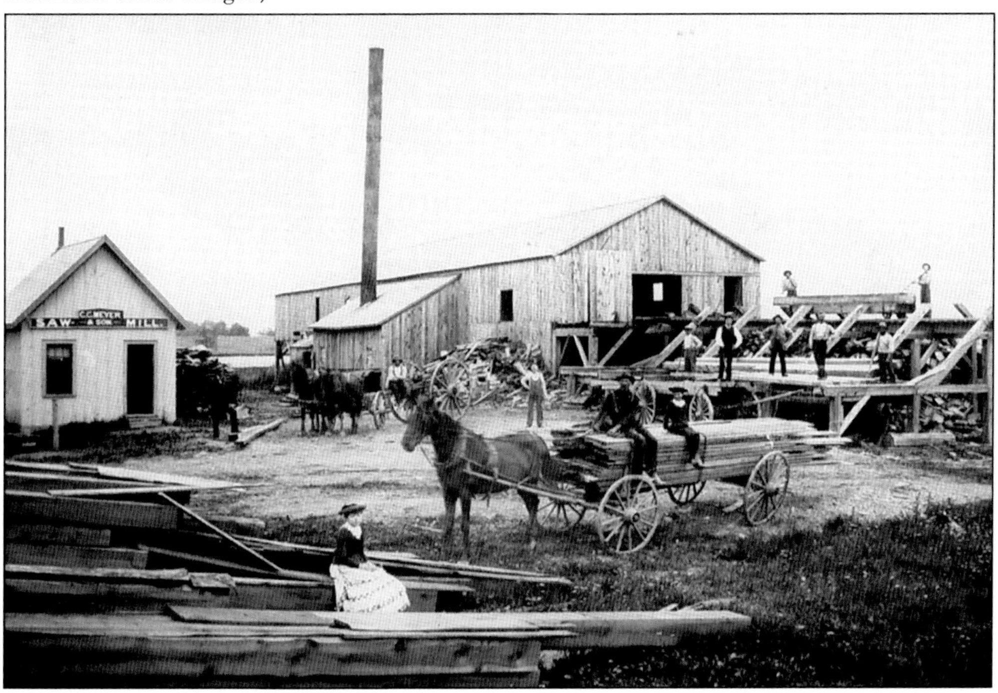

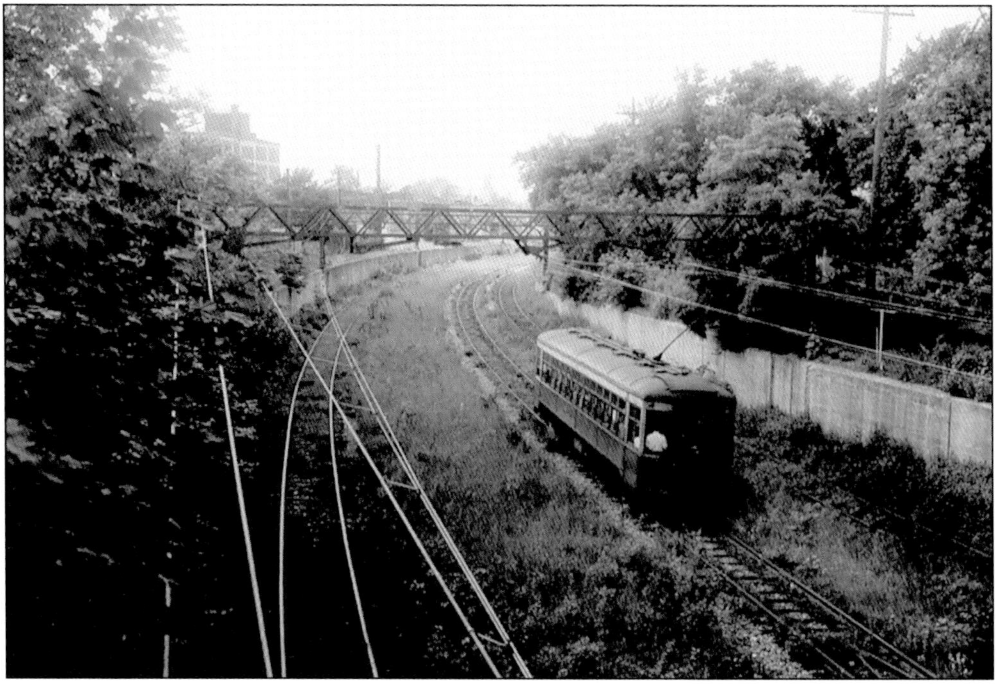

SUBWAY CAR. This photograph of a westbound subway car, west of Meigs Street, was taken in June 1956. (Courtesy City of Rochester Photo Lab.)

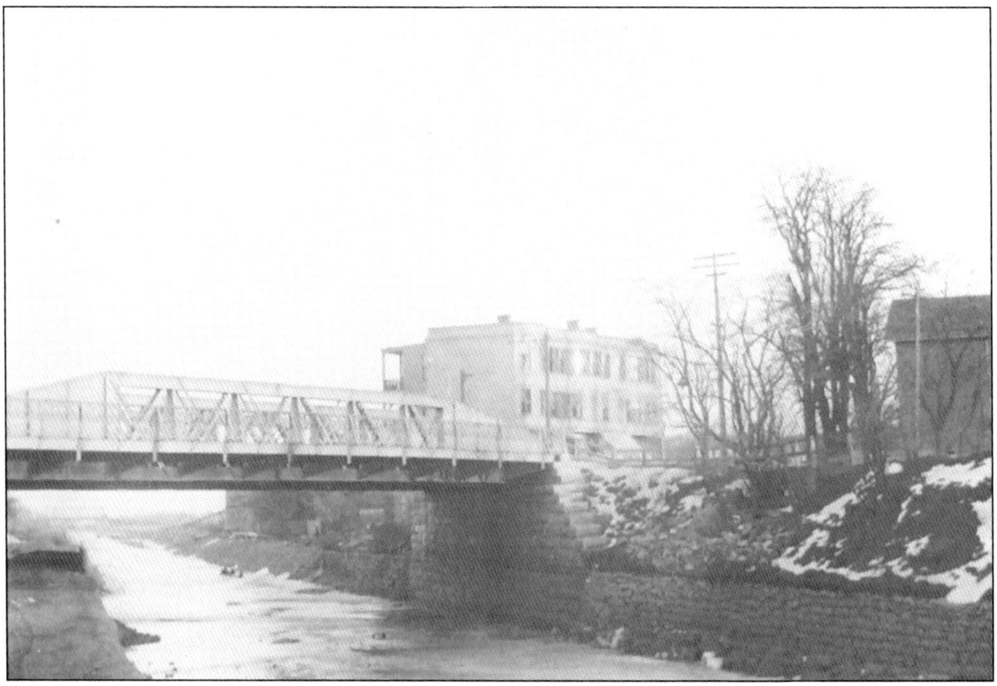

MONROE AVENUE BRIDGE. This picture of the bridge over the Erie Canal at Monroe Avenue, facing southeast, was taken between the time it was built, in 1899, and 1906. (Courtesy Rochester Photo Images.)

PLAY CLOTHES. What boy has not worn jeans and a T-shirt? These two boys hold still for the camera on a sunny day, September 22, 1950. The footbridge over the subway was west of the Monroe Avenue station near Adwin Place. (Courtesy Rochester Photo Images.)

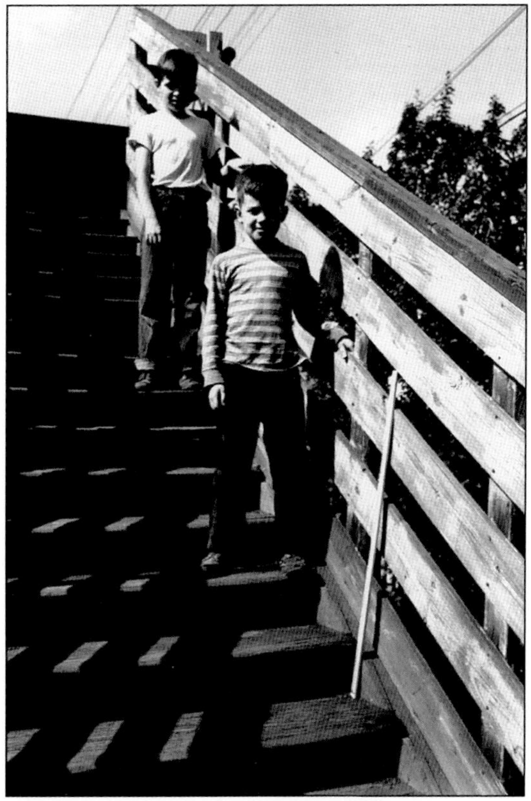

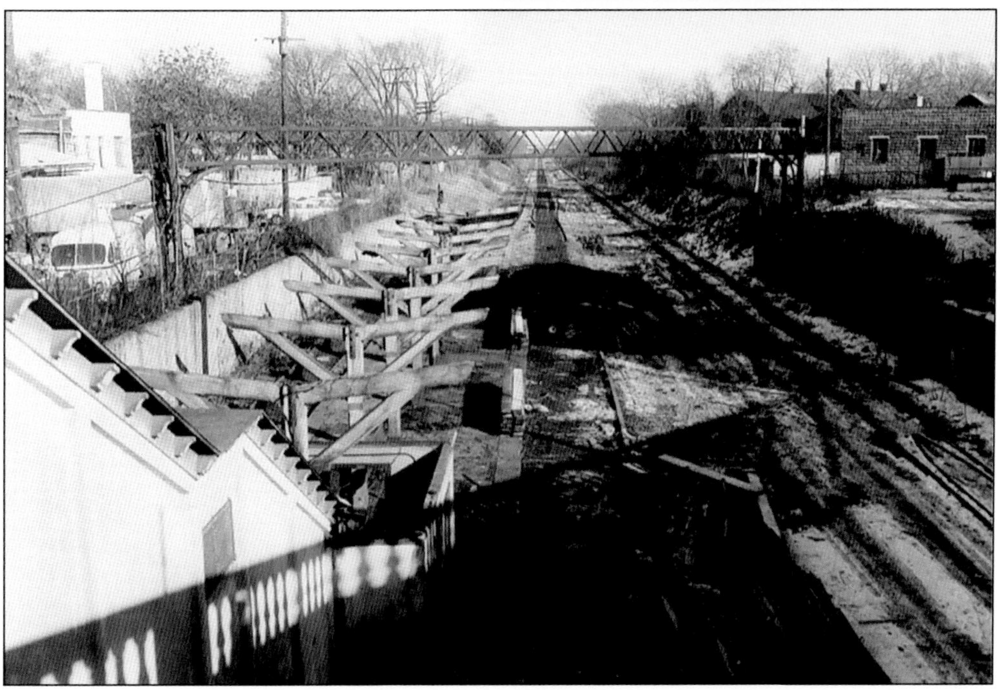

DISMANTLING THE SUBWAY. The subway was partially dismantled in 1957 when this photograph was taken looking east from the Monroe Avenue Bridge. (Courtesy Rochester Photo Images.)

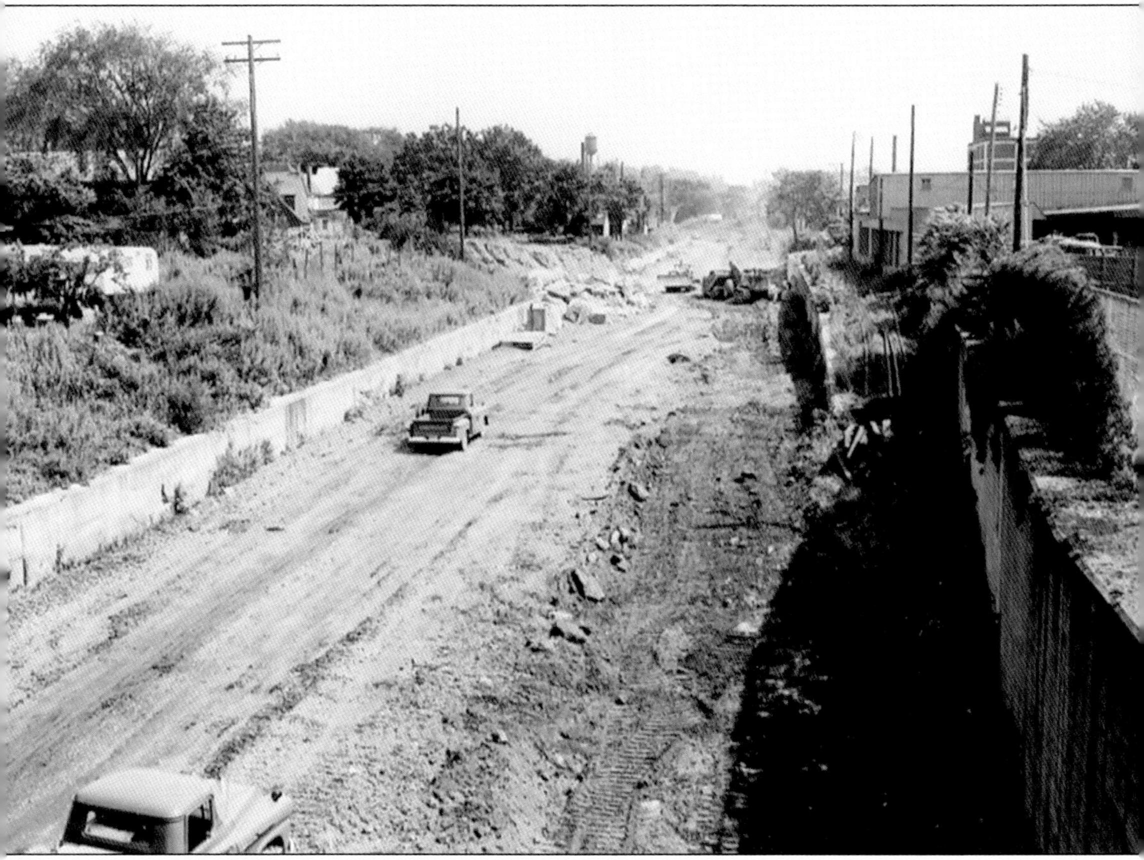

INTERSTATE 490 CONSTRUCTION. It may be hard to imagine that where the expressway is now six modern traffic lanes wide, the original Erie Canal was four feet deep and seven feet wide. This photograph of the construction of Interstate 490 was taken near Alexander Street in July 1956. (Courtesy Rochester Photo Images.)

Four

ALONG MOUNT HOPE AVENUE

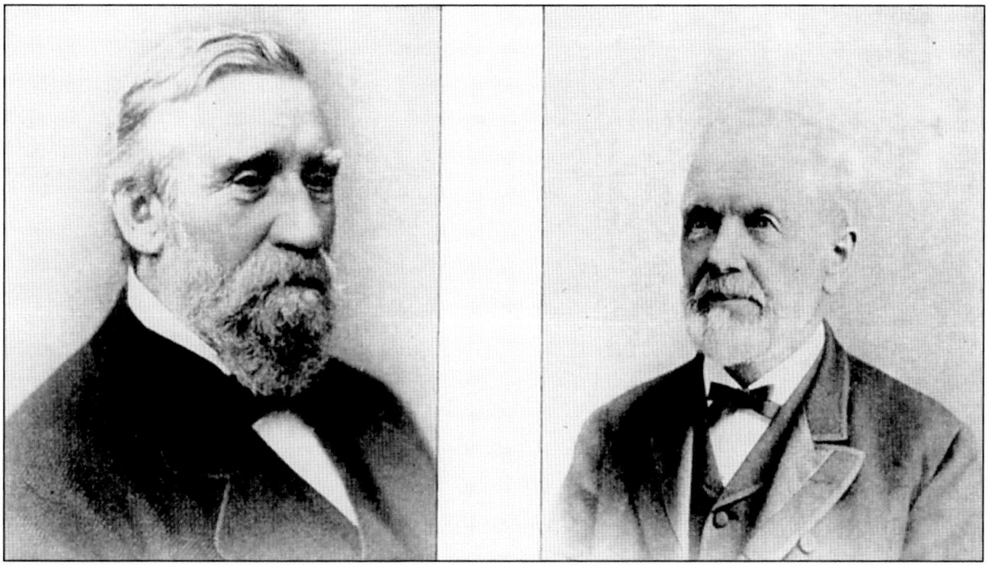

NURSERYMEN AND FRIENDS. George Ellwanger (right) (1816–1906) and Patrick Barry (left) (1816–1890) were not only leading horticulturists for decades, they were also good friends at a time when Protestants and Catholics did not usually mingle. (Courtesy City of Rochester Photo Lab.)

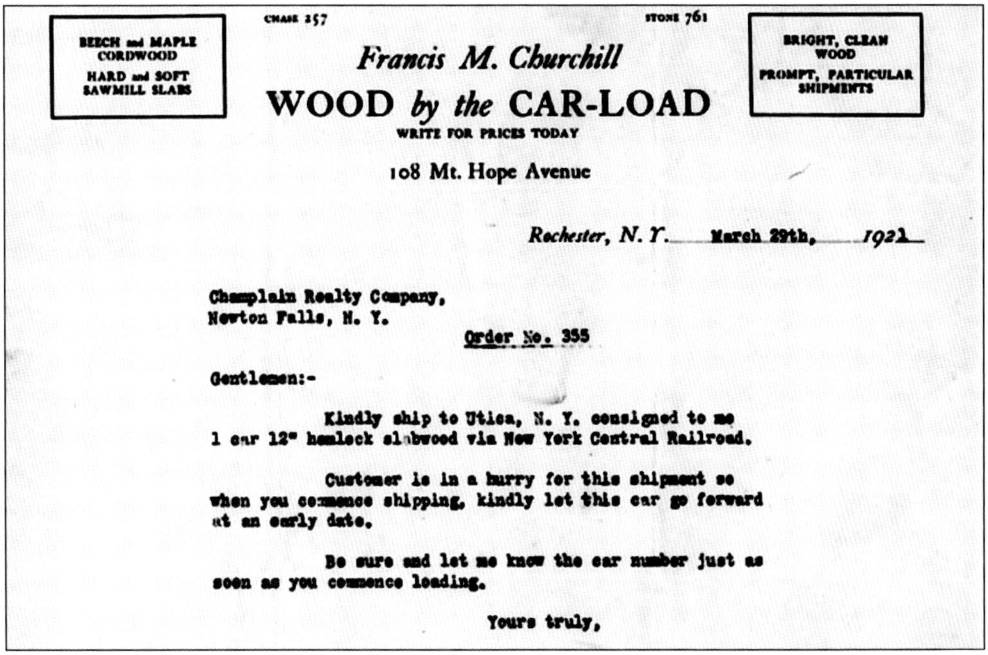

CHASE 257 | STONE 761

BEECH and MAPLE CORDWOOD
HARD and SOFT SAWMILL SLABS

Francis M. Churchill
WOOD *by the* CAR-LOAD
WRITE FOR PRICES TODAY
108 Mt. Hope Avenue

BRIGHT, CLEAN WOOD
PROMPT, PARTICULAR SHIPMENTS

Rochester, N. Y. March 29th, 1921

Champlain Realty Company,
Newton Falls, N. Y.

Order No. 355

Gentlemen:-

Kindly ship to Utica, N. Y. consigned to me 1 car 12" hemlock slabwood via New York Central Railroad.

Customer is in a hurry for this shipment so when you commence shipping, kindly let this car go forward at an early date.

Be sure and let me know the car number just as soon as you commence loading.

Yours truly,

HOW MUCH WOOD? Many businesses on the east side have come and gone including that of Francis M. Churchill (d. 1944) who ran a lumber yard at 108 Mount Hope Avenue that was a division of the International Paper Company from 1906 through 1926. This letter is dated March 29, 1921. One of Francis Churchill's sons ran a used car dealership at 110 Mount Hope Avenue in 1947. (Courtesy Ellie Cameron.)

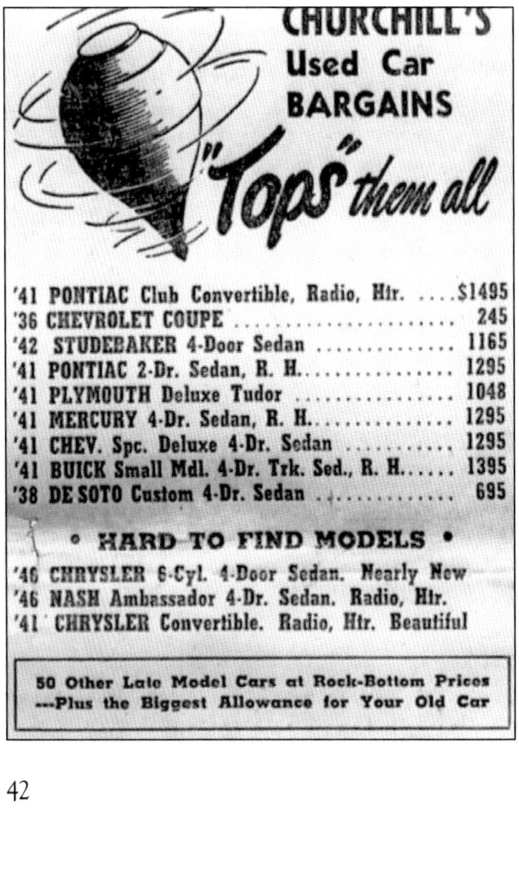

CHURCHILL'S
Used Car
BARGAINS
"Tops" them all

'41 PONTIAC Club Convertible, Radio, Htr.	$1495
'36 CHEVROLET COUPE	245
'42 STUDEBAKER 4-Door Sedan	1165
'41 PONTIAC 2-Dr. Sedan, R. H.	1295
'41 PLYMOUTH Deluxe Tudor	1048
'41 MERCURY 4-Dr. Sedan, R. H.	1295
'41 CHEV. Spc. Deluxe 4-Dr. Sedan	1295
'41 BUICK Small Mdl. 4-Dr. Trk. Sed., R. H.	1395
'38 DE SOTO Custom 4-Dr. Sedan	695

• HARD TO FIND MODELS •
'46 CHRYSLER 6-Cyl. 4-Door Sedan. Nearly New
'46 NASH Ambassador 4-Dr. Sedan. Radio, Htr.
'41 CHRYSLER Convertible. Radio, Htr. Beautiful

50 Other Late Model Cars at Rock-Bottom Prices
---Plus the Biggest Allowance for Your Old Car

CAR BARGAINS. Winston Churchill (d. 1967), a son of Francis Churchill, owned Churchill Motors for 40 years. He was named after American novelist and historian Winston Churchill (1871–1947). Winston's brother Raymond (d. 1974) worked there as a salesman for 35 years. This advertisement for Churchill's Used Cars 110 Mount Hope Avenue advertised cars from a 1941 Pontiac Club convertible to a 1938 De Soto custom four-door sedan. It appeared in the *Democrat and Chronicle* in April 1947. (Courtesy Josh Canfield.)

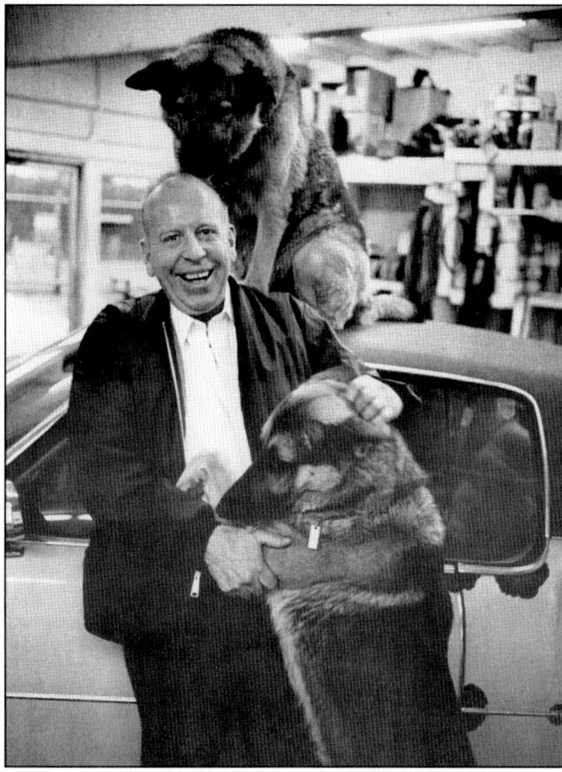

JOHN AMES AND HIS DOGS. In a 1979 interview, John "Jack" Ames said, "I believe I'm the best liked used car dealer in the country." He had several lots in the South Wedge for 20 years, including Mount Hope Avenue at Gregory Street; Mount Hope Avenue at Averill Avenue, and later, on South Clinton Avenue. (Courtesy Jon Elmer, *Genesean, Vol. 8*, a year-long project by Rochester Institute of Technology photography students.)

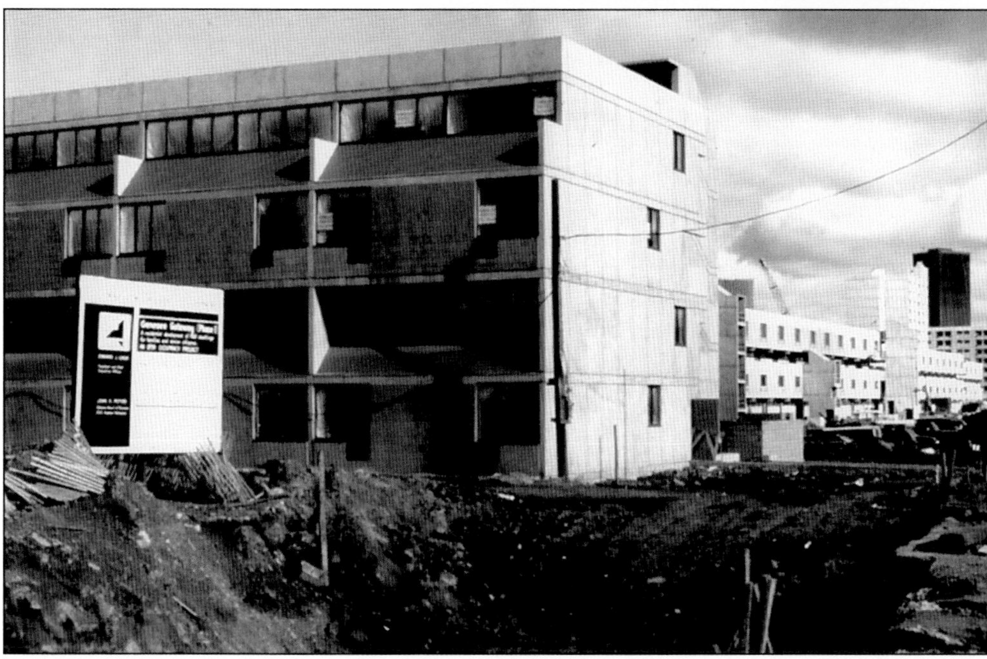

NEW TOWNHOUSES. The innovative design of the Genesee Gateway won an award in its day. This photograph, looking north toward the townhouses, was taken in 1973. Some families have lived there for decades. The River Park Commons high rise is scheduled for renovations in 2006 and the townhouses for eventual replacement. (Courtesy City of Rochester Photo Lab.)

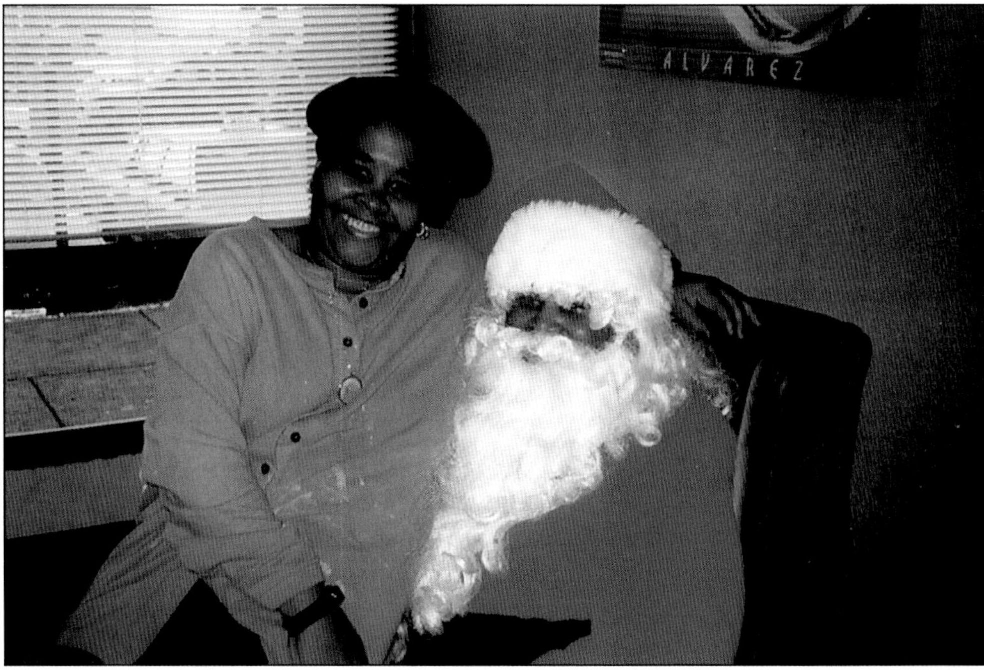

HOME FOR 28 YEARS. Because her two sisters, Brenda Cotton and Jacquie Cotton, had moved into Genesee Gateway shortly after it opened, JoAnn Thomas moved in as well, in 1977, and raised her daughter Latasha there. JoAnn is shown here, on the lap of one of Santa's helpers, Tony Martin, at a 2004 Christmas party. (Courtesy JoAnn Thomas.)

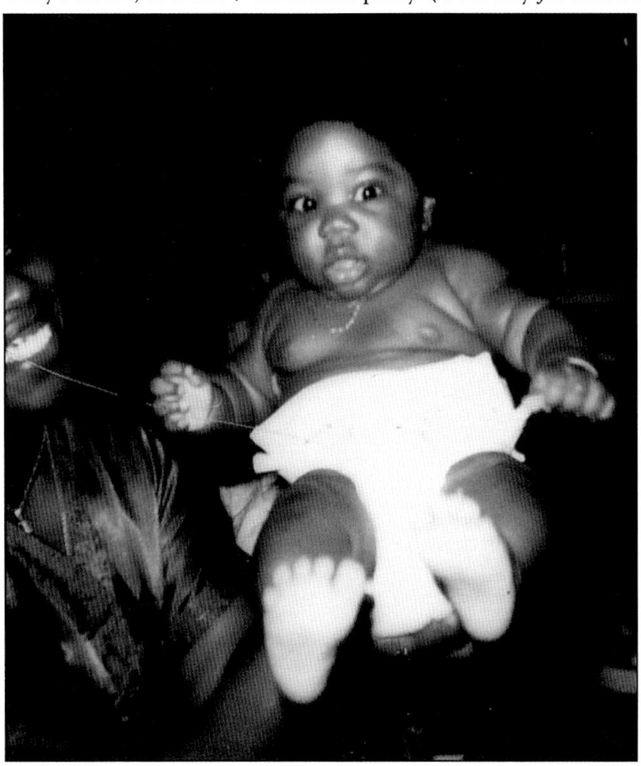

DAUGHTER'S DELIGHT. Marva Corbin's daughter, Erica Evans, beams at her new baby Walter Jr. Marva has lived in the Genesee Gateway townhouses since 1987. Erica was living with Marva when little Walter was born in 1996. At the time, Marva's children, who all grew up there, were Erica, 27; Eurica, 26; and Ricky, 22. (Courtesy Marva Corbin.)

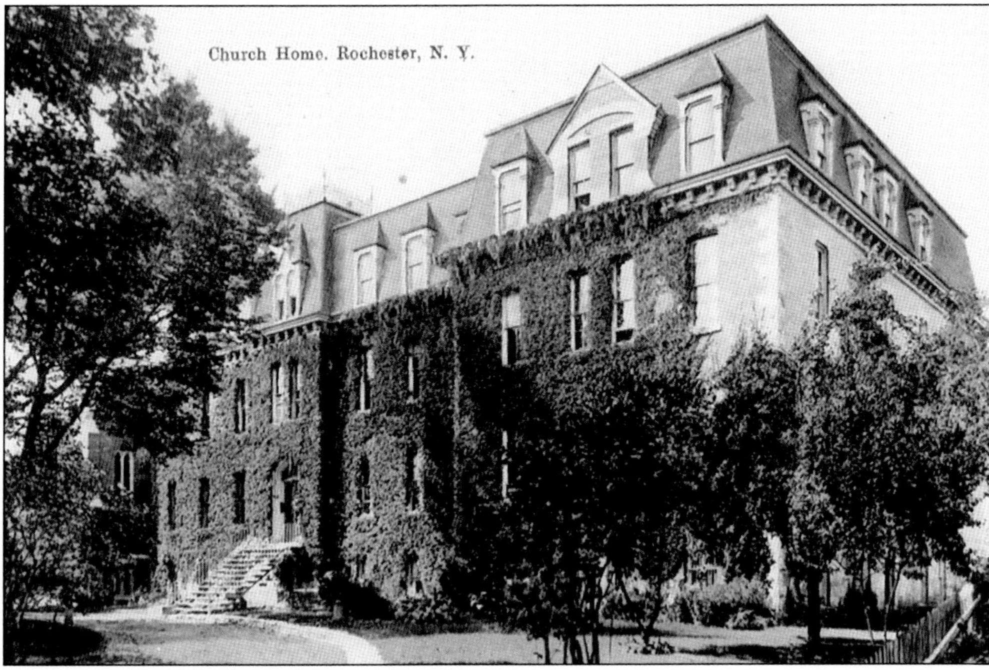

OLD CHURCH HOME. The Episcopal Church Home for the elderly, destitute, and orphaned children started in a house along the Genesee River, near the Clarissa Street Bridge, in 1868. Land for the home was donated in 1869 by George E. Mumford and George R. Clark. The house was replaced by a larger building in 1869.

CORNET AND QUADRILLE BAND. George Sanford and Julius M. Sanford are listed as a carpenter and boat builder at separate locations in the 1841 city directory. Both are listed as "Joiner, h. Mt. Hope Avenue, op.- Clarissa" in 1847. In the 1851 directory, George and Julius are "joiner, b. Mt. Hope Avenue," on the same page as John Sauer "boat builder, h. Gregory." In 1853, George Sanford, "builder, Mt. Hope Avenue" is on the same page as John C. Sauer, "boat builder, h. 17 William" (around Howell Street). This advertisement for a band is from the 1859 directory.

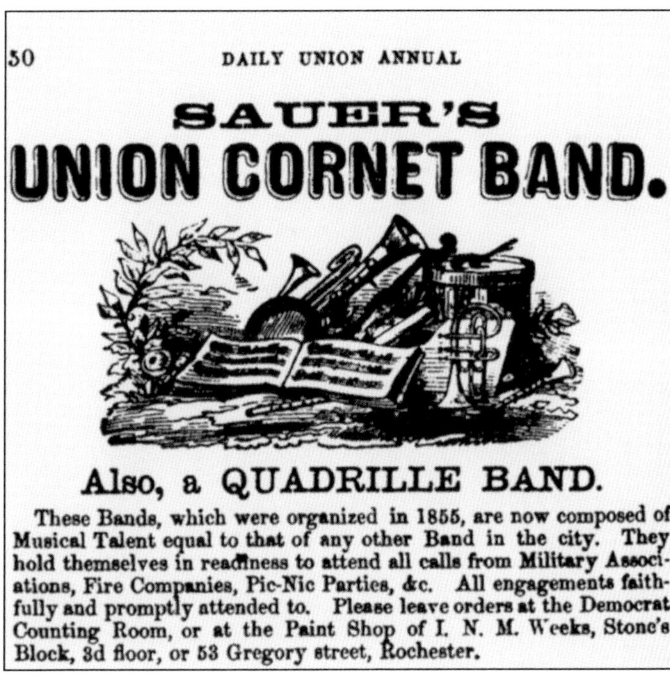

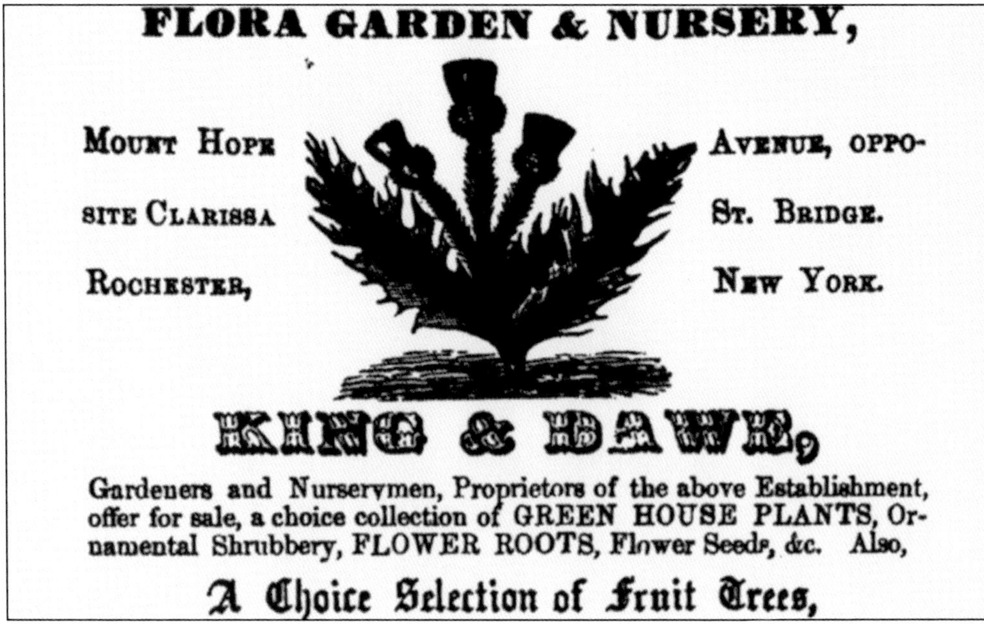

KING AND DAWE. The 1847 city directory listing for William King is, "Gardener and Florist, Nursery and h. 7 Monroe." In 1851, the King and Dawe Flora Garden and Nursery on "Mount Hope Avenue opposite Clarissa Street Bridge," offered a choice selection of fruit trees. In 1853, the Flora Garden and Nursery at the same address only listed William King. His home address was Prospect Hill in 1853, and in 1861, the advertisement changed to Prospect Hill Nurseries, William King Proprietor, fruit and ornamental trees.

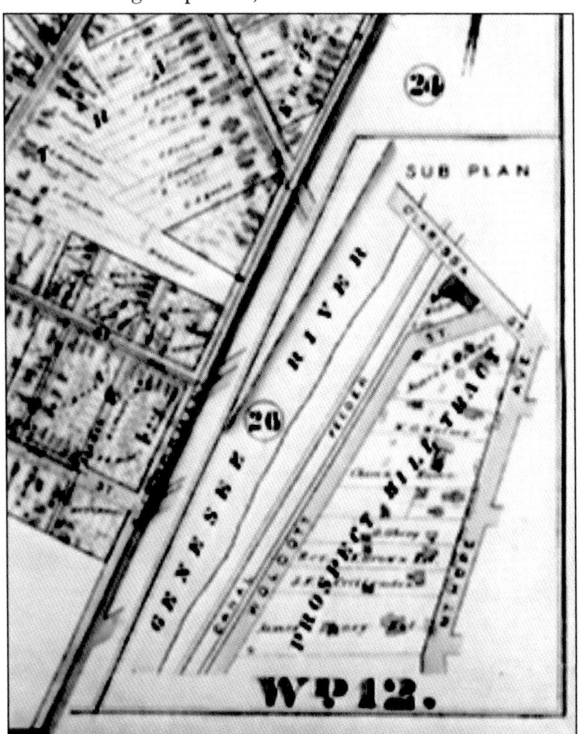

PROSPECT HILL, 1888. The Ellwanger and Barry and Prospect Hill tracts are included in the larger city map. This subsection shows the Prospect Hill Tract as the land between Mount Hope Avenue and Wolcott Street, south of the bridge. On the 1900 map, the Prospect Hill Tract is the entire block from Mount Hope to South Avenue between Sanford and Cypress Streets. (Courtesy Rochester Photo Images.)

Central Library of Rochester and Monroe County · City Directory Collection · 1844

FRUIT AND ORNAMENTAL TREES, &C.

MT. HOPE BOTANIC GARDEN & NURSERIES,

South St. Paul-street, nearly opposite the Cemetery,

ROCHESTER, N. Y.

MOUNT HOPE BOTANIC GARDEN. George Ellwanger was listed in the 1841 city directory as a "horticulturist, b. Arcade." Advertisements in the 1844 and 1845 city directories list the Mount Hope Botanic Garden and Nurseries on "South St. Paul-street, nearly opposite the Cemetery." Ellwanger and Barry have a full advertisement for Mount Hope Garden and Nurseries in the 1851 and 1853 city directories, with no specific address. Ellwanger was an authority on roses who also introduced dwarf apple and pear trees and the German tradition of Christmas trees. Patrick Barry was a horticultural writer whose 1862 *Catalogue of Fruits* became the authority for fruits grown in America.

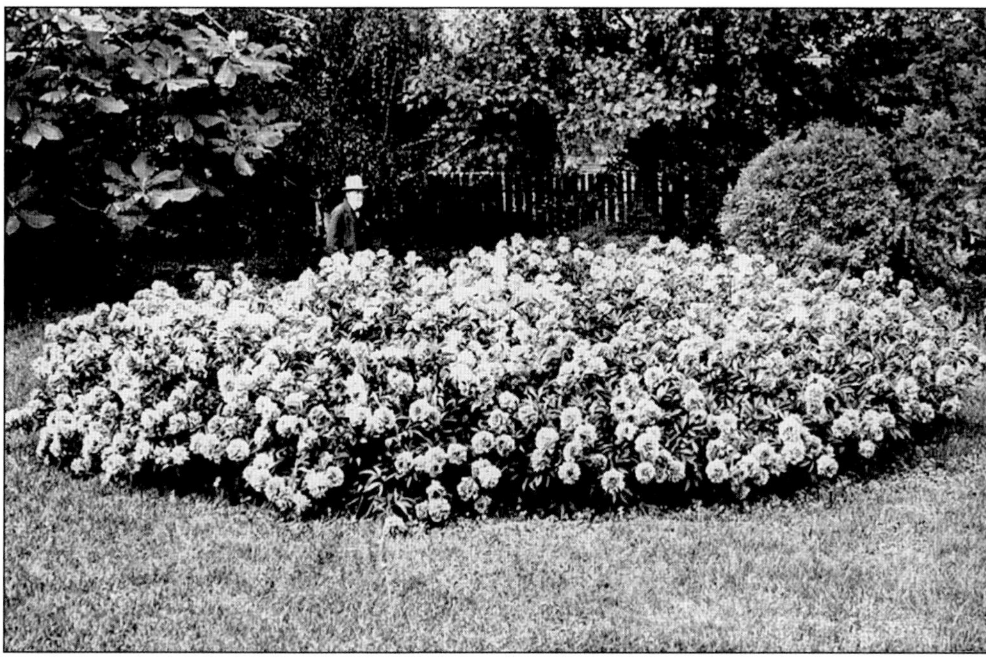

HEAVEN ON EARTH. No doubt this bed of Chinese peonies in full bloom was a delight for the eyes and a feast for the soul. Despite strong competition, Mount Hope Nurseries were unrivaled in range and quality of selection. By 1859, the original seven acres had grown to 400, with a third in pear trees—then the most popular fruit tree in America. Besides the acreage devoted to apples, cherries, plums, deciduous trees, berries, evergreens, and magnolias, they also nurtured 5,000 sequoia trees. Ellwanger once said their nurseries provided the original stock for every nursery in California. By 1880, three-quarters of their sales were overseas. Helen C. Ellwanger, who was the granddaughter of George Ellwanger, founded the Landmark Society. Upon her death at age 96 in 1982, her house at 625 Mount Hope Avenue was donated to the society. (Courtesy City of Rochester Photo Lab.)

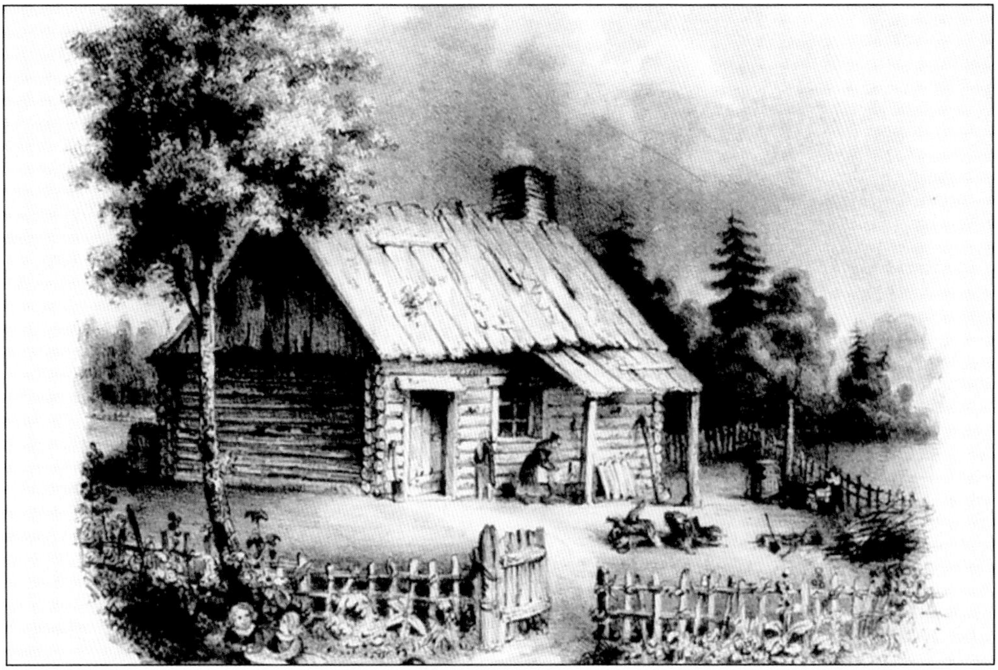

HOME SWEET HOME. The date on this depiction of a cozy cabin, titled *Rochester, 1812*, masks how long it took for settlers to clear thick forests and remove tree stumps. Nancy Harris Quackenbush (1818–1900), one of the first residents in primitive Brighton, was born in a cabin that her grandfather Jacob Miller built in 1810 in dense woods. They had to barricade the door at night to keep out bears, wolves, and wildcats. After her death, Nancy was buried on the site of that cabin, now near the north entrance of Mount Hope Cemetery. (Courtesy City of Rochester Photo Lab.)

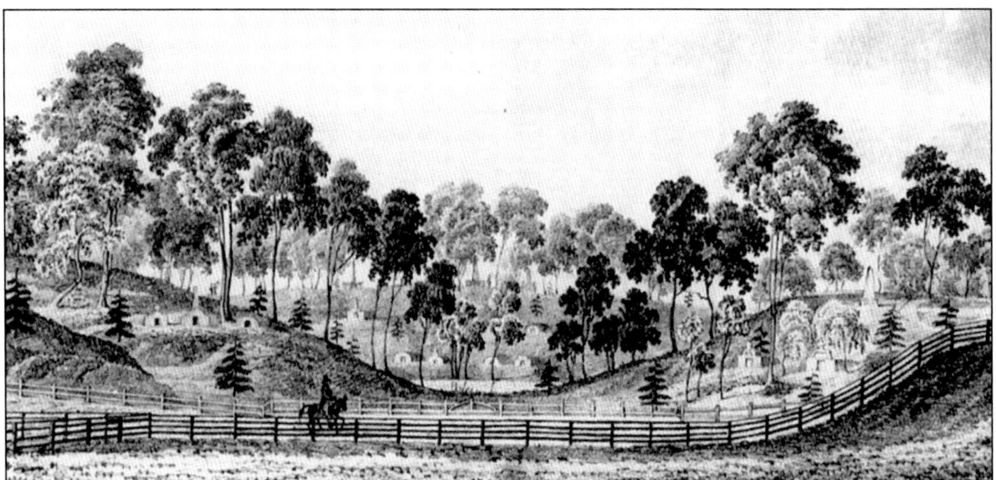

NEW CEMETERY. When city planners sought a burial site away from the crowded downtown area, a controversy erupted over spending funds for a cemetery in an untamed wilderness. Mount Hope Cemetery, the first municipal Victorian cemetery in the United States, was dedicated October 3, 1838. It was modeled after early 19th century rural garden cemeteries in Europe. This flattering engraving by J. E. Young was done around the time of the cemetery's dedication in 1838. (Courtesy Rochester Photo Images.)

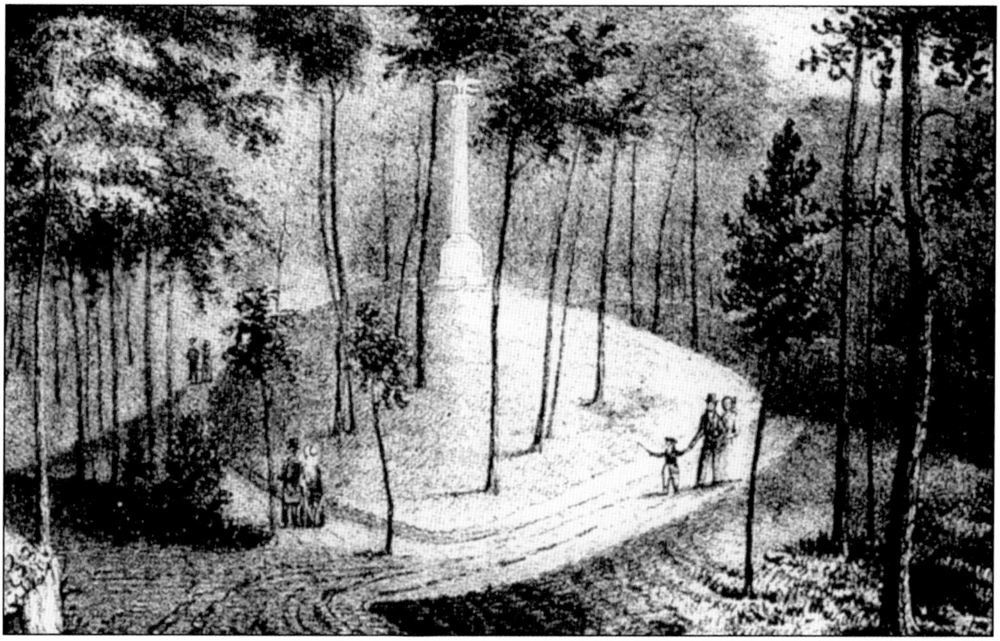

A Sunday Stroll. There is not a mosquito in sight to mar these leisurely strolls in 1842 in Mount Hope Cemetery. A Gothic Revival chapel, designed by local architect Henry Robinson Searle, was built in 1862. The Florentine Fountain was cast in 1875. (Courtesy City of Rochester Photo Lab.)

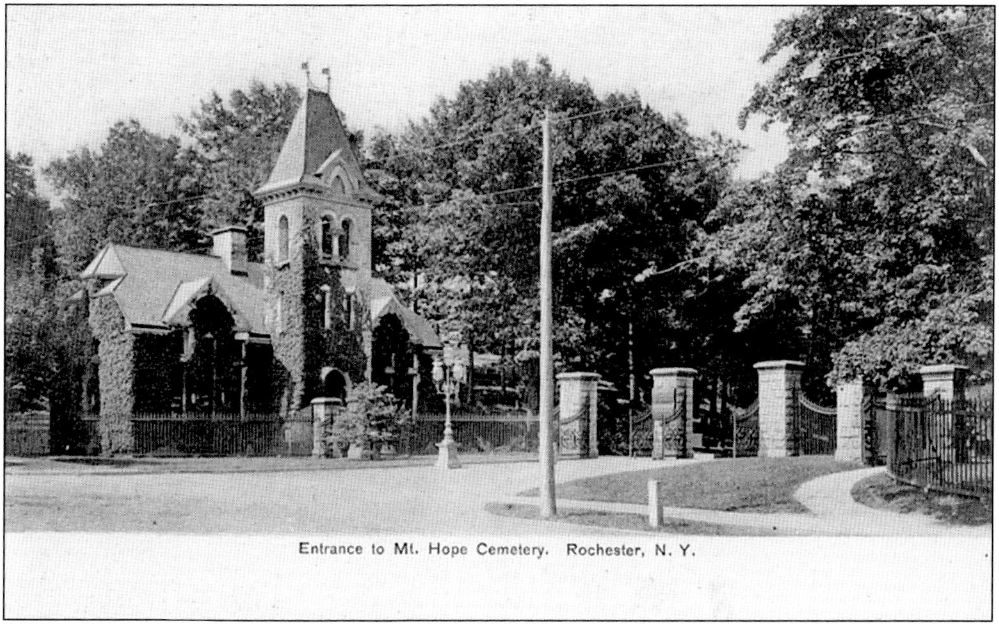

North Entrance. The first gatehouse was a wooden, Egyptian-style structure that was replaced in 1859 with a stone one. It was too narrow and was demolished around 1872. The current entrance gate and gatehouse were built in 1874. (Courtesy Josh Canfield.)

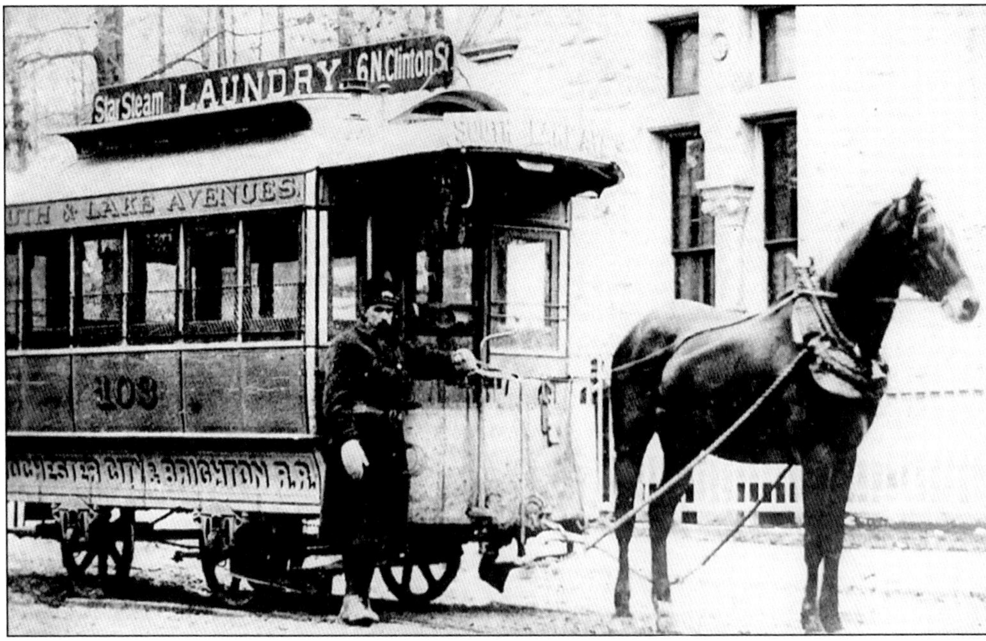

Last Horse-Drawn Streetcar. The nurseries and cemetery on Mount Hope Avenue created a demand for a trolley line. George Ellwanger and Patrick Barry helped establish the Rochester-Brighton Street Railroad in 1863, the first in the city. This picture, taken in 1889, is of the last horse-drawn streetcar in front of a stone building at Mount Hope Cemetery. (Courtesy Rochester Photo Images.)

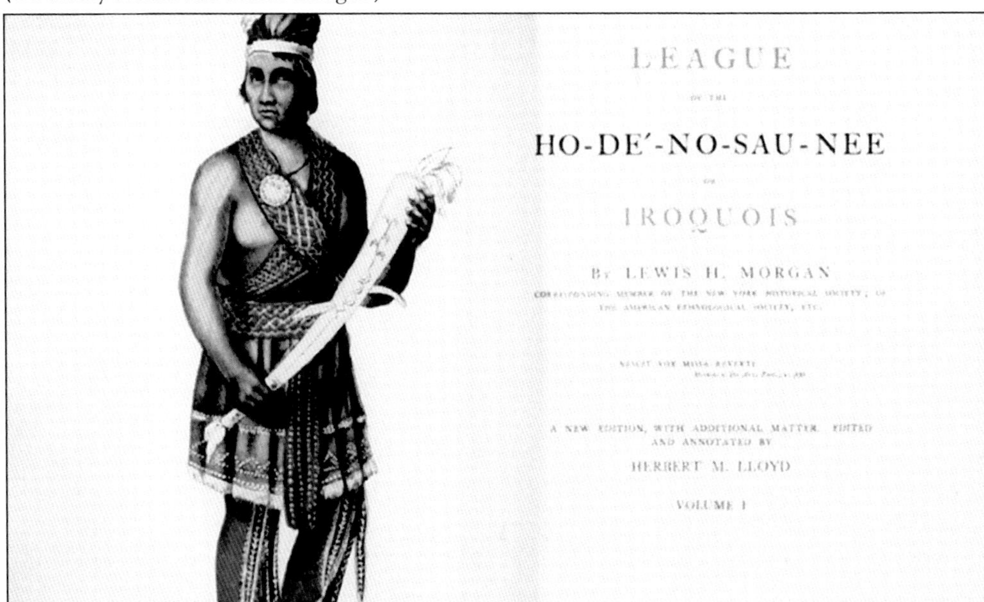

League of the *Ho-De-No-Sau-Nee*. Lewis H. Morgan, who is considered the father of American anthropology, wrote Seneca Ely Samuel Parker's account of the Iroquoian way of life in *League of the Ho-de-no-sau-nee*, in 1851. He was a Corn Hill neighbor who died in 1881. Attendees of a Six Nations conference in Rochester, in November 1920, held a memorial service at Morgan's mausoleum on November 16, 1920. (Courtesy Rochester Photo Images.)

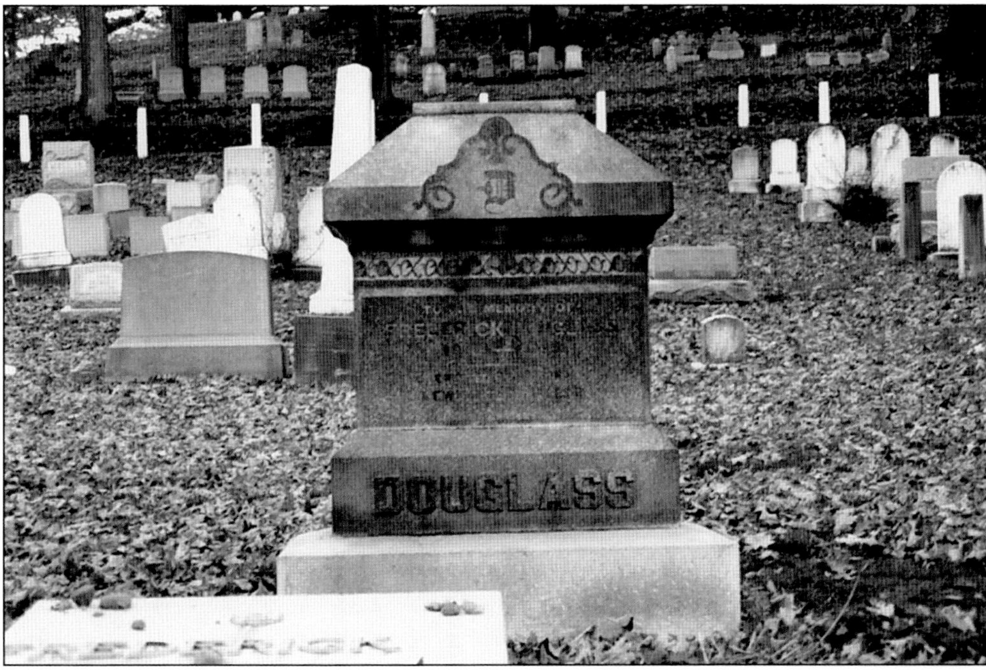

Cemetery Notables. Two of the most famous groups at rest in the cemetery are the Frederick Douglass and Susan B. Anthony families. Although the Douglass family had moved to Washington D.C. in 1872, Frederick Douglass chose to be buried in Rochester, where the family had lived from 1847 to 1872, because he considered it home. Susan B. Anthony (1820–1906) was a tireless advocate for women's political, social, economic, and educational rights, who proposed the 19th Amendment, giving women the right to vote. (Courtesy Robert P. Meadows.)

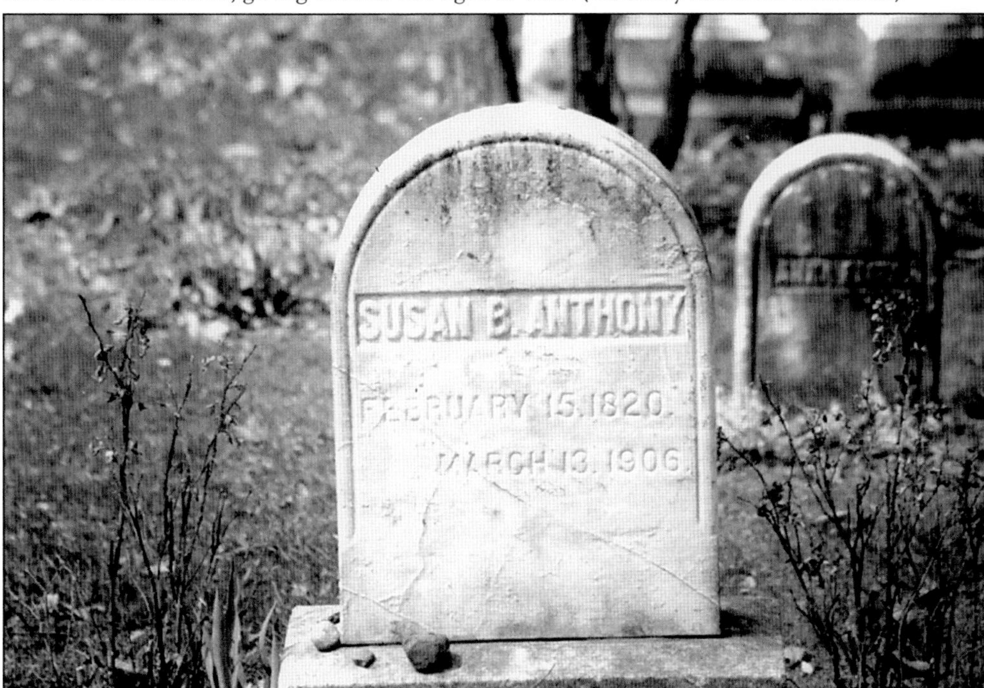

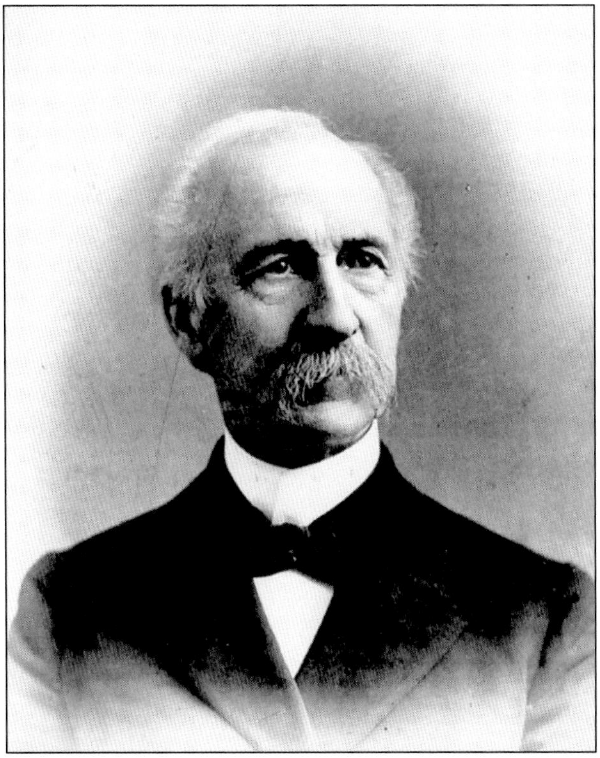

J. W. STEBBINS. John W. Stebbins (1819–1905) was an accomplished baseball player, umpire, attorney, and Odd Fellows grand master. Stebbins Street in the South Wedge is most likely named for him. He organized the Rochester Mutual Health Association to supply cooperative health insurance in the city in the 1850s. His advertisement in the 1851 city directory stated: "attorney and counselor . . . where all business of a legal character will receive prompt attention." Stebbins Street was first called Jefferson Park. (Courtesy City of Rochester Photo Lab.)

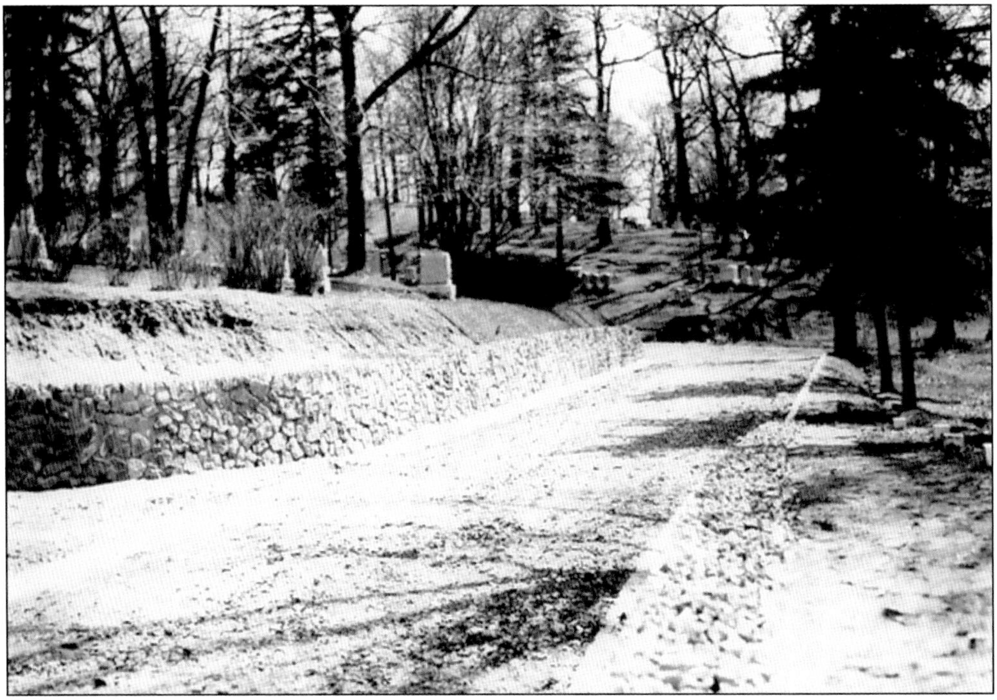

CEMETERY ROADWORK. Much of the beautiful stonework in the cemetery was done as part of Works Progress Administration projects during the Depression. This photograph was taken on April 20, 1933. (Courtesy City of Rochester Photo Lab.)

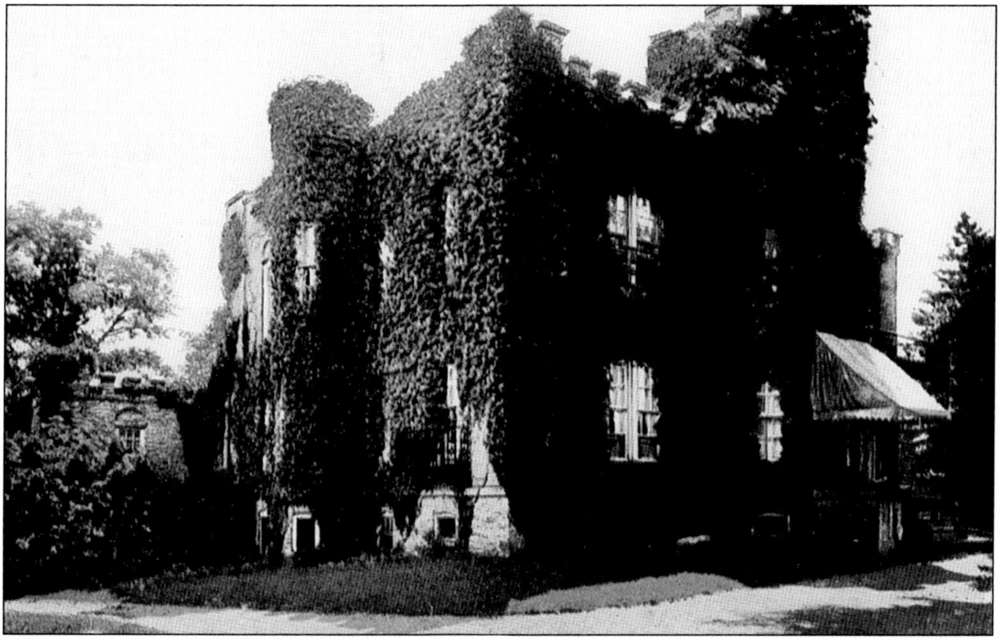

WARNER CASTLE. Horatio Warner is listed in the 1844 city directory with a home address of Mount Hope Place. He was a judge, newspaper publisher, and banker, as well as an anti-abolitionist who made the drawings for this English-style castle built in 1854. According to the *Landmark Society House and Garden Tour* 1993 booklet, the castle has 22 rooms, black walnut woodwork, and thick stone walls. It is home to the Rochester Civic Garden Center. (Courtesy Ellwanger and Barry Neighborhood Association.)

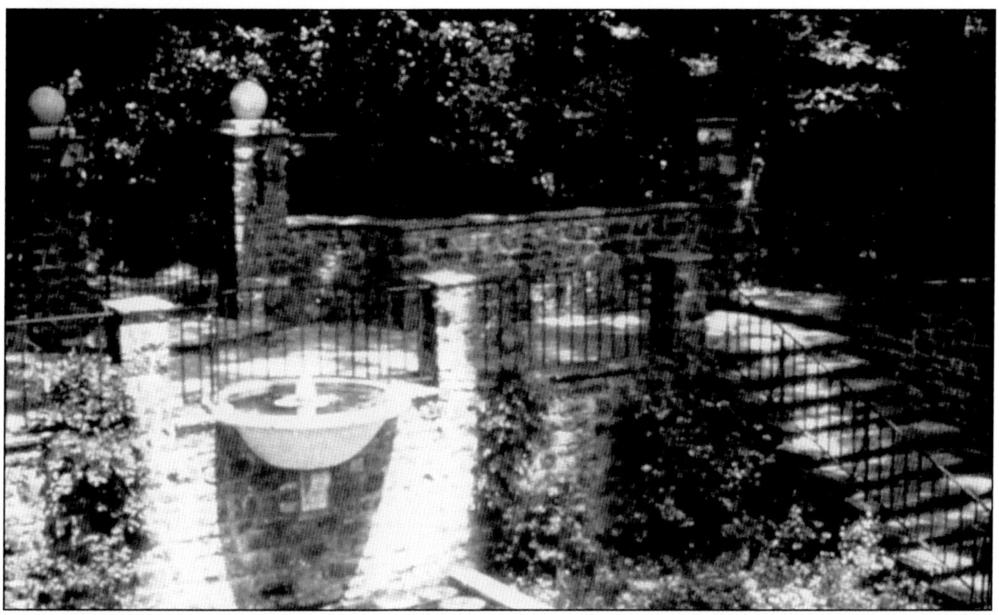

DELIGHTFUL GARDEN. Warner Castle and the sunken garden behind it, which was designed in 1930, were acquired by the city in 1951 and became part of Highland Park. The sunken garden was restored in 1990, according to the *Landmark Society House and Garden Tour* 1993 booklet. (Courtesy City of Rochester Photo Lab.)

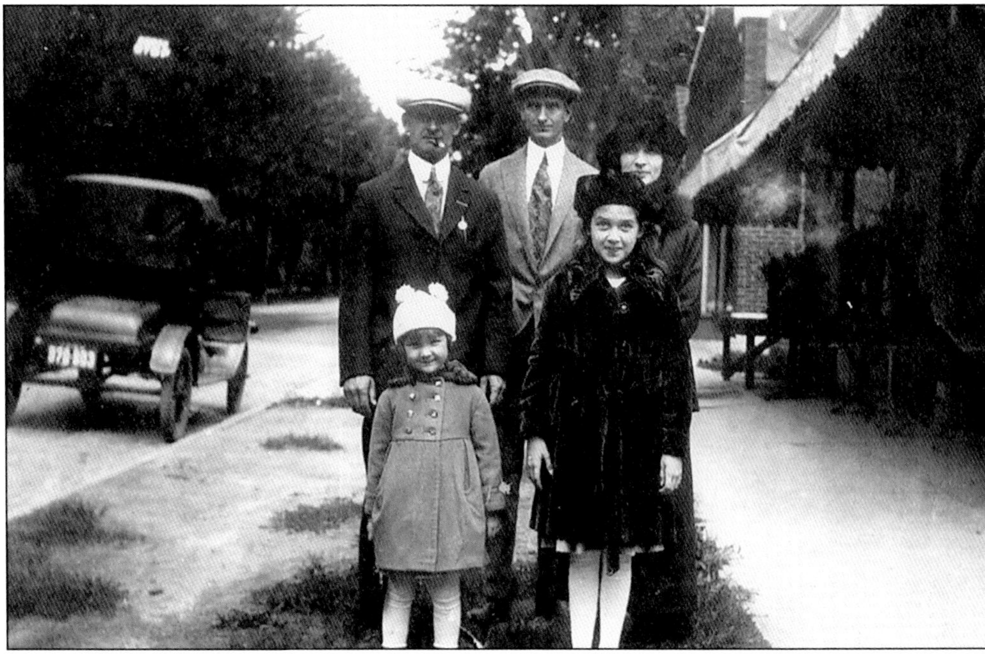

EARLY FLORISTS. Above from left to right are (first row) Ruth Westfall and her sister Helene; (second row) owners William C. Westfall, Bert Elliot, and Grace A. Westfall. They are standing at 1146 Mount Hope Avenue. The cemetery entrance is across the street. The car is probably a Ford Runabout. In the photograph below, Bill Westfall poses in the greenhouse. Westfall Road got its name from the Westfall Farm that a great-uncle owned around the former St. Agnes High School in west Brighton. Norman Road and Helen Road off East River Road, which was originally Westfall Road, are named for family members. (Courtesy Charlie Westfall.)

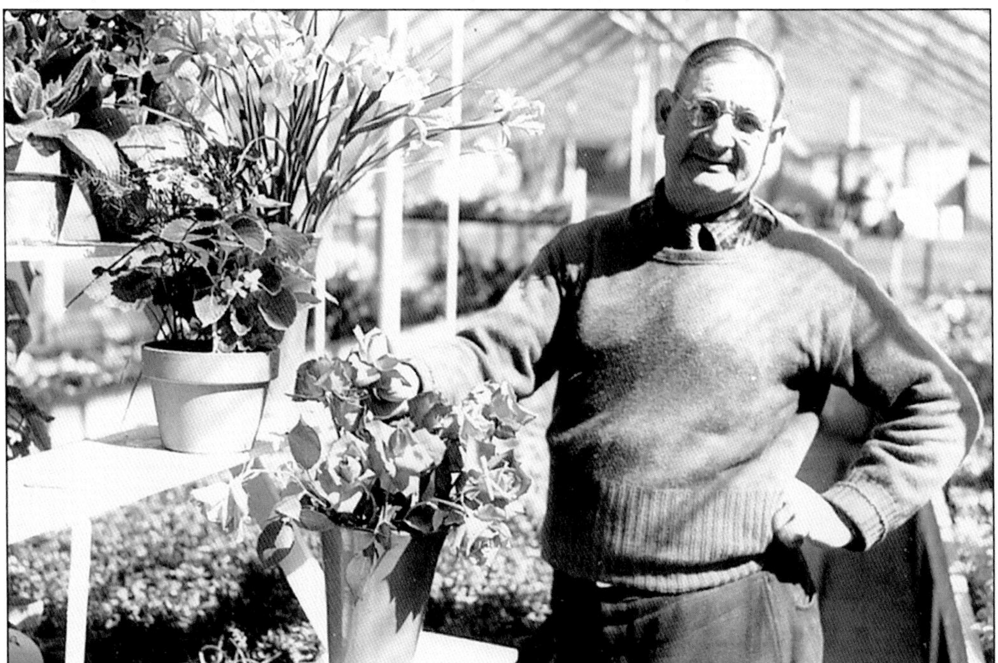

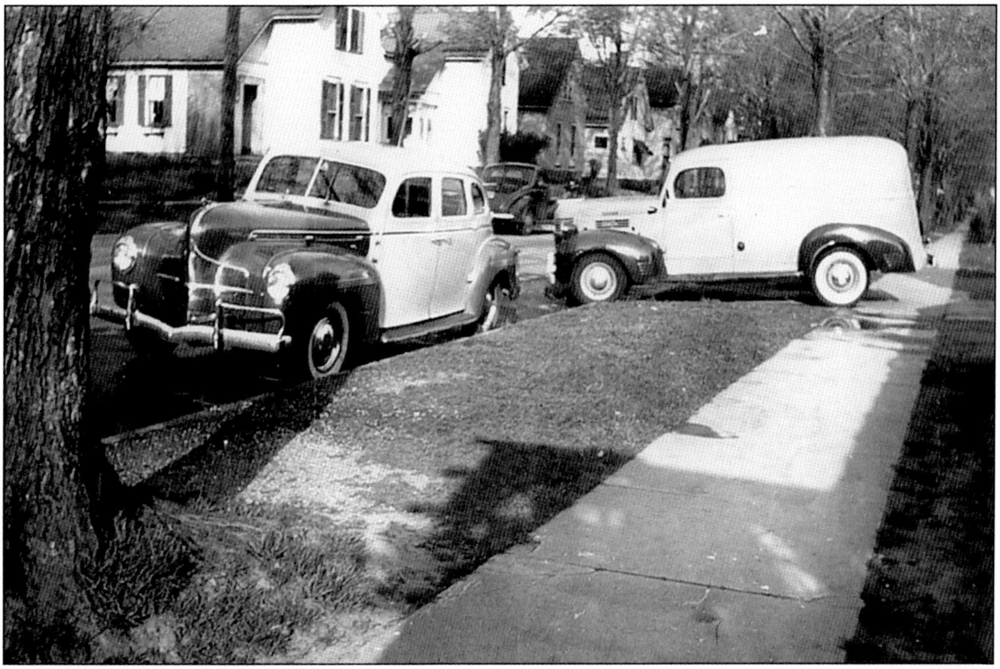

Company Vehicles. These company vehicles parked by Westfall Florist in 1946 on Mount Hope Avenue at May Street are a 1940 Dodge (left) and a 1941 Dodge. (Courtesy Charlie Westfall.)

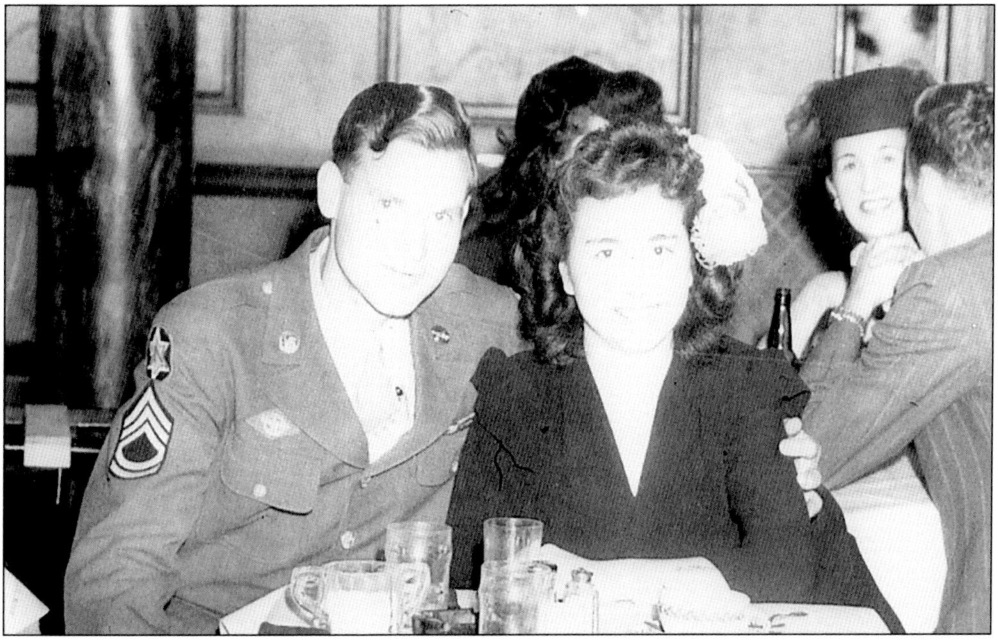

Ready for Civilian Life. At his wife Emily's request, Charlie Westfall wore his uniform for the last time at a celebration party on November 4, 1945, at the Odenbach Restaurant on Main Street. They were married in 1942 before he left on January 1, 1943, to serve with the 25th Infantry Division in the Pacific in Guadalcanal, New Zealand, and Luzon in the Philippine Islands. In addition to running the floral business, he served as Monroe County legislator for 15 years until 1975. (Courtesy Charlie Westfall.)

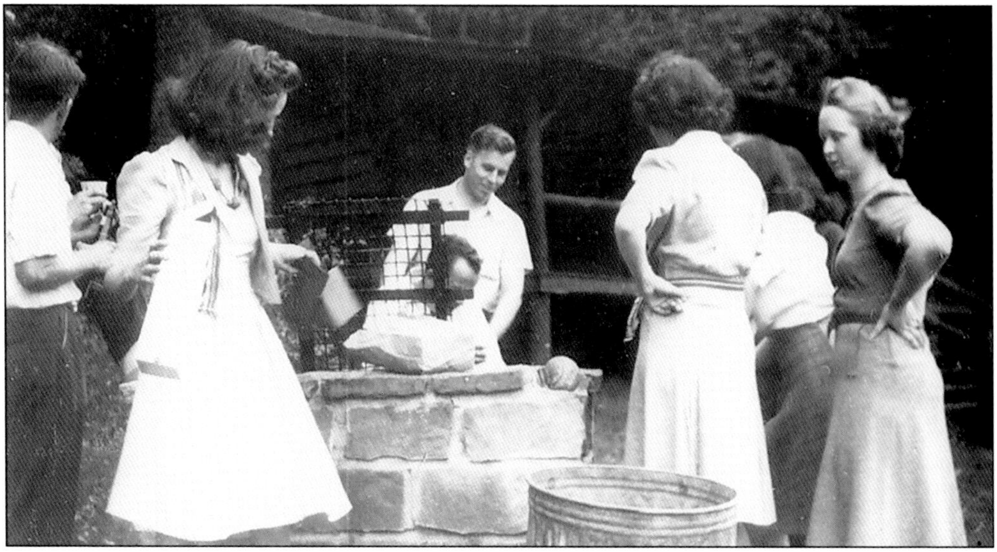

TODD COMPANY PICNIC. Emily Westfall (left) waits her turn near the grill at a Todd Company summer picnic in one of the local parks. Members of the Todd family lived on Gregory Street, near Cayuga Street, and started a business in their garage behind the little house. The Todd Company, which dates from 1899, was the first to make a machine that printed the amount of money on a check and then went into check manufacturing, printing, and imprinting. Emily Westfall's father, George W. Adlam, who is listed at 17½ Whitmore Street in the 1924–1925 city directory and was an expert on check forgery, was secretary to George Todd. He was married to Neva McQuatters Adlam whose family owned several small rental properties on Whitmore Street. The Todd Company played an important role in F. D. Roosevelt's bank reorganization in March 1933. In 1941, they had 591 employees at University Avenue near Culver Road, and 1,000 employees when it merged with the Burroughs Corporation in 1958. (Courtesy Charlie Westfall.)

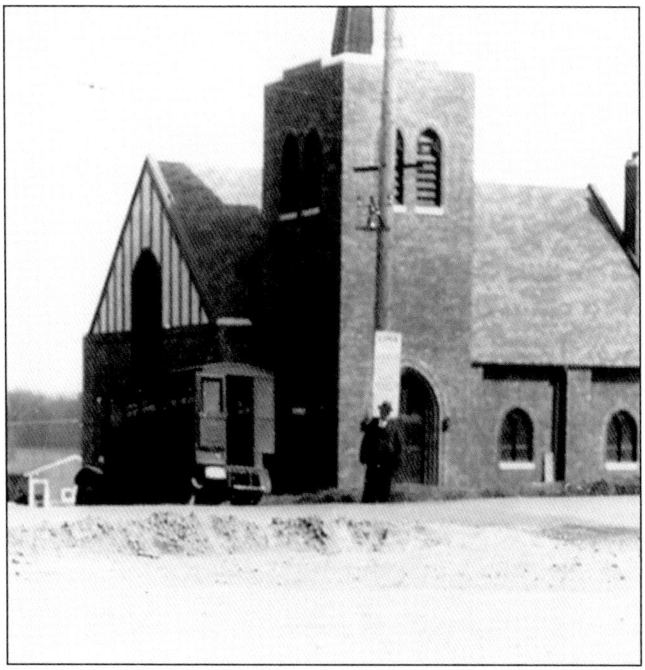

NEW CHURCH. This work progress photograph of "Henrietta Rd. and Stokes St." is dated April 20, 1926. South Presbyterian Church organized in 1895 as the West Brighton Chapel Society. The brick church was built about 1926. Since there were no street numbers at that location, it was not listed on either street in 1928, but under churches at Mount Hope Avenue and Stokes Street. Additions were made in 1954 and 1960. Previously, the congregation had worshiped on Mount Hope Avenue in the wooden building that most recently was Record Archive. (Courtesy City of Rochester Archives.)

Five

Around South Avenue

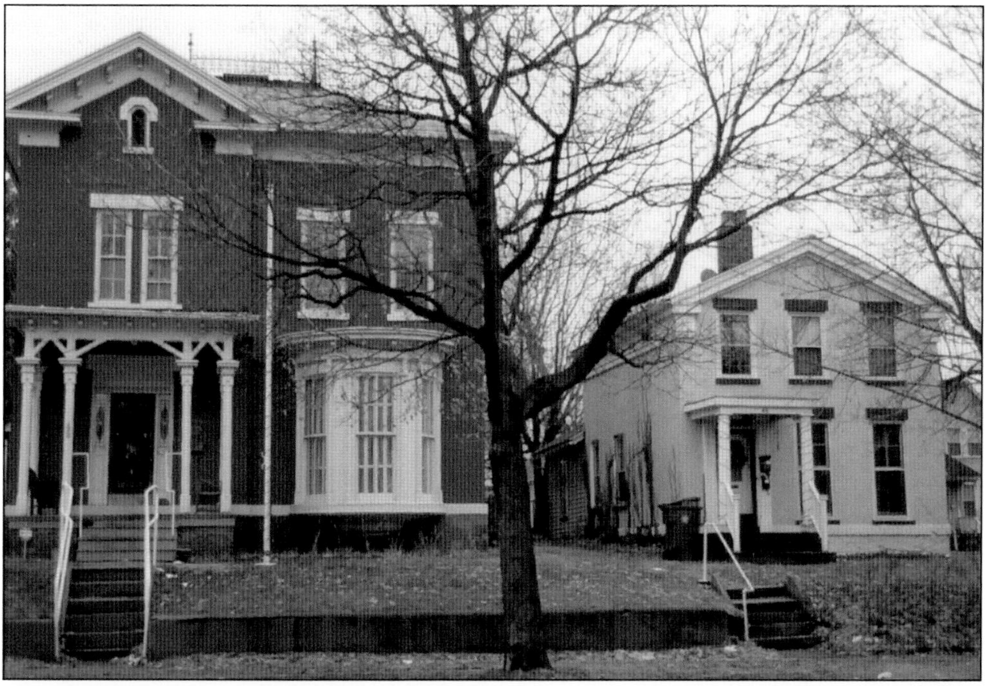

The Old Hibernian Club. James McQuatters Sr. was a mason and brick layer who moved from Ireland to Rochester with his family in 1823. He bought land in 1839, and the house, now numbered 46 Alexander Street, is on the map of 1851. James McQuatters Jr. and Paulina McQuatters moved to their new home in 1872 from the smaller house next door. After James Jr. died in 1896, Paulina remained in this house, with her son-in-law James F. O'Neil and her daughter Julia A. O'Neil, until 1908. At the time of the Landmark Society survey in 1977, it had been the clubhouse for the Ancient Order of Hibernian Club of Monroe County Incorporated since 1952. (Courtesy Robert P. Meadows.)

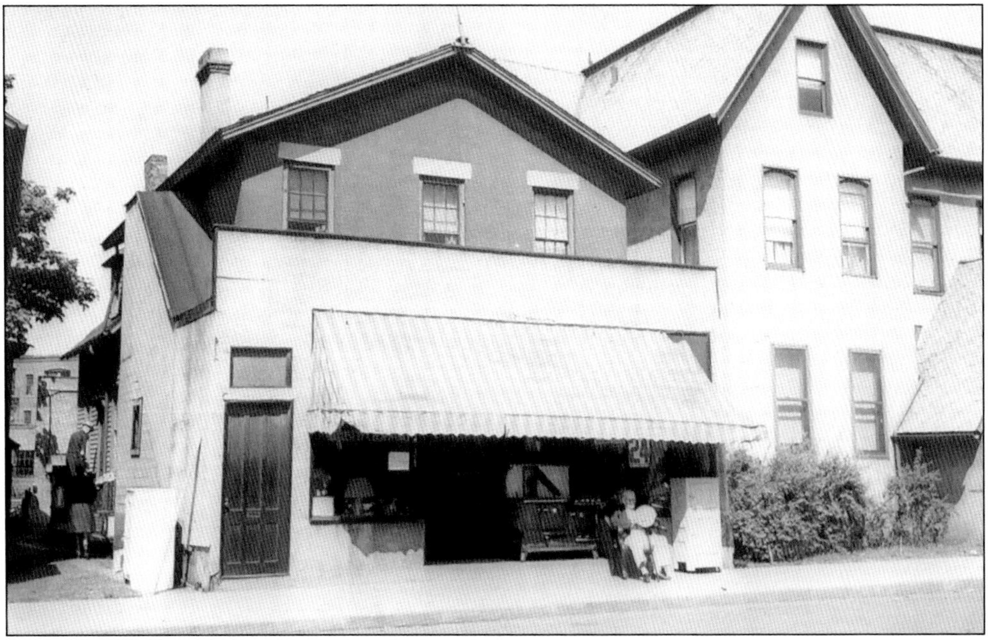

A Sunny Morning. Most likely the strong sun is cutting the cool breeze of a spring day in this photograph of an elderly man with a cane and possibly a straw hat, sitting in a wicker chair, dated April 11, 1944. A used clothing store is listed at 415 South Avenue in the 1944 directory. (Courtesy City of Rochester Archives.)

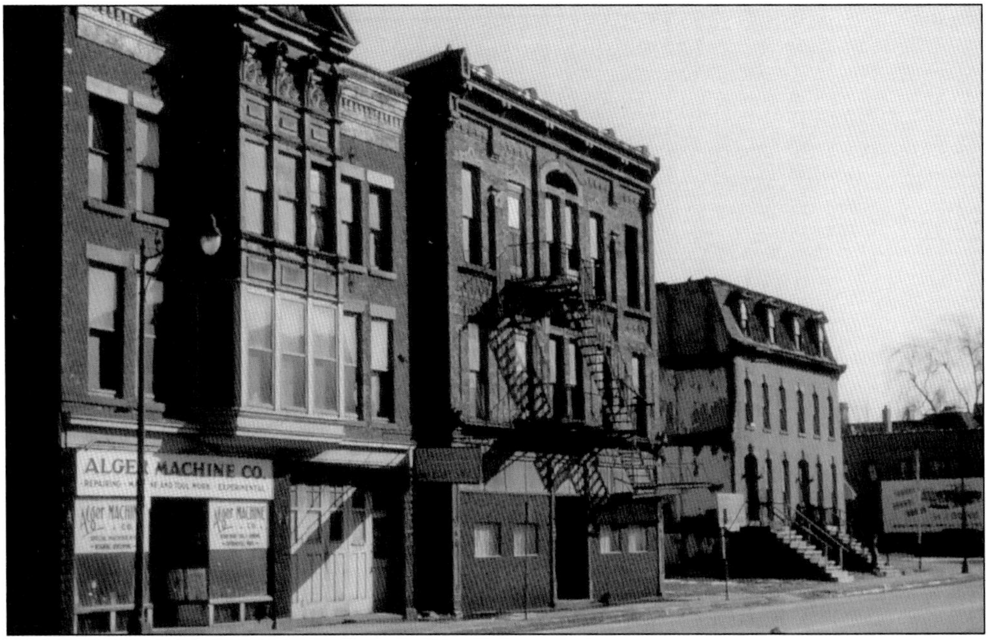

House of Hospitality. St. Joseph's House of Hospitality, which was established in Rochester in 1938, moved to the north end of South Avenue in 1941. In the 1980s, it was one of 50 centers run by the Catholic Worker Movement, an organization dedicated to pacifism and civil rights for indigent people. This photograph, dated January 24, 1954, also shows a brick building to the south. (Courtesy Catholic Diocese of Rochester.)

ALL DRESSED UP. These two happy women look all dressed up and ready to go, standing on the northwest side of South Avenue near Hickory Street. The building across the street lists Ryan's Restaurant and Geck is further south. This is one of four undated, unlabeled photographs from the collection of the late Ruby Murphy of Averill Avenue. (Courtesy Josh Canfield.)

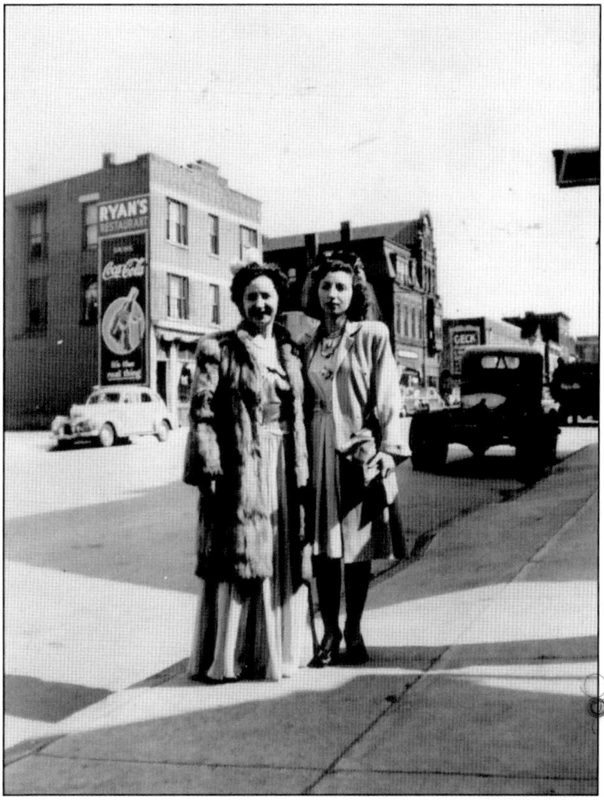

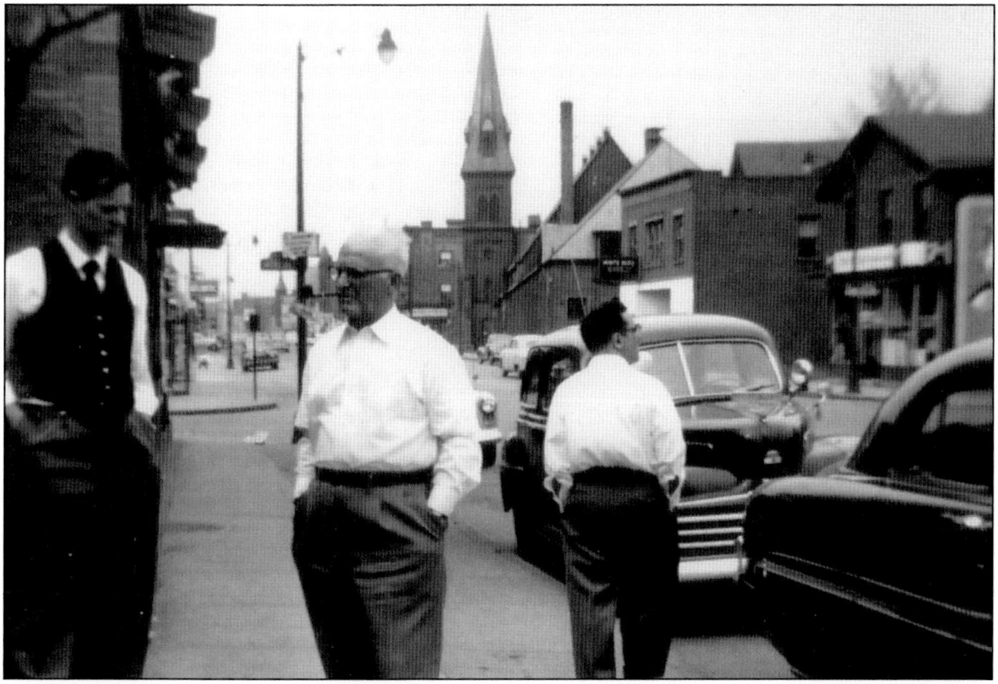

ALONG THE AVENUE. This undated photograph of men along South Avenue shows Calvary Presbyterian Church in the background. (Courtesy Josh Canfield.)

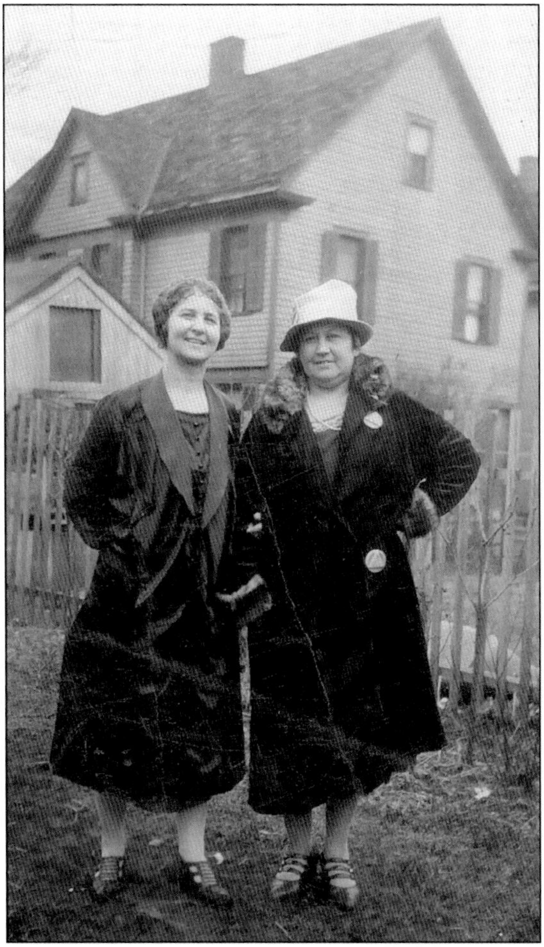

Ruby Murphy and Elizabeth Oliver. According to next-door neighbor Mary Williams, who never knew Mrs. Oliver's first name, Ruby Murphy lived alone on Lake Avenue when her husband Robert was in Iola Sanitarium and after his death. Ruby Murphy was a clerk who had become a member of Edwards 25-year's club in 1925. Mrs. Oliver, who is listed as Elizabeth M., widow of Charles, in the 1955 city directory, invited Ruby Murphy to live with her at 135 Averill Avenue. Oliver deeded the house upon her death to Murphy who also lived there until her death. Seen here in the top photograph, around 1950, Ruby Murphy is on the left and Elizabeth Oliver is on the right. In the bottom backyard photograph, Murphy is in the middle and Oliver is on the right with an unidentified friend. One of their neighbors was Maeva Dobner who wrote teenage romance novels under the pen name of Anne Park. Dobner was interviewed in the *Democrat and Chronicle* in October 1982, after her latest book, *Love Song*, came out in Bantam's Sweet Dreams line. (Courtesy Josh Canfield.)

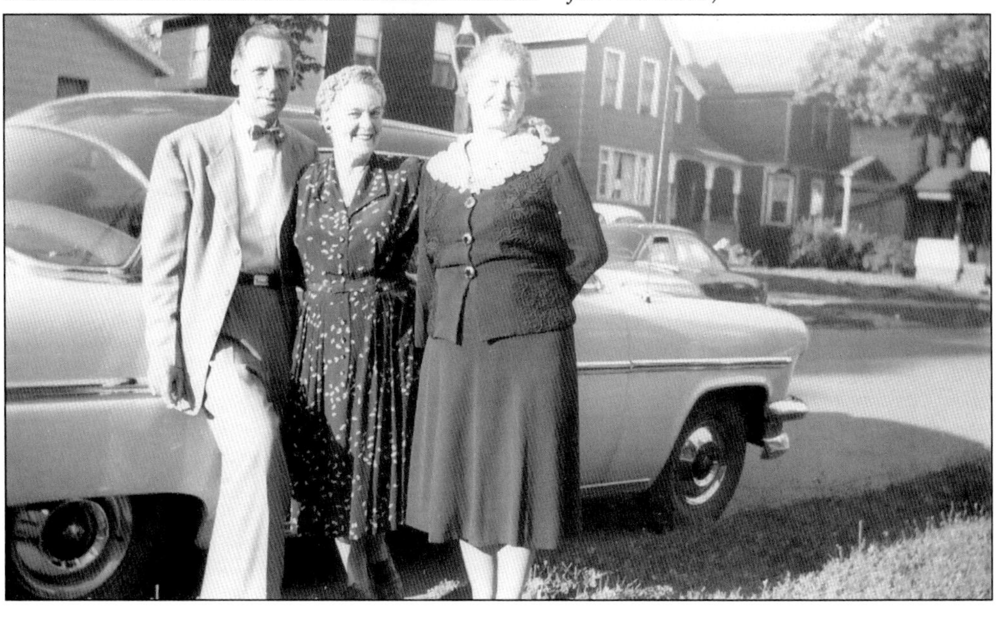

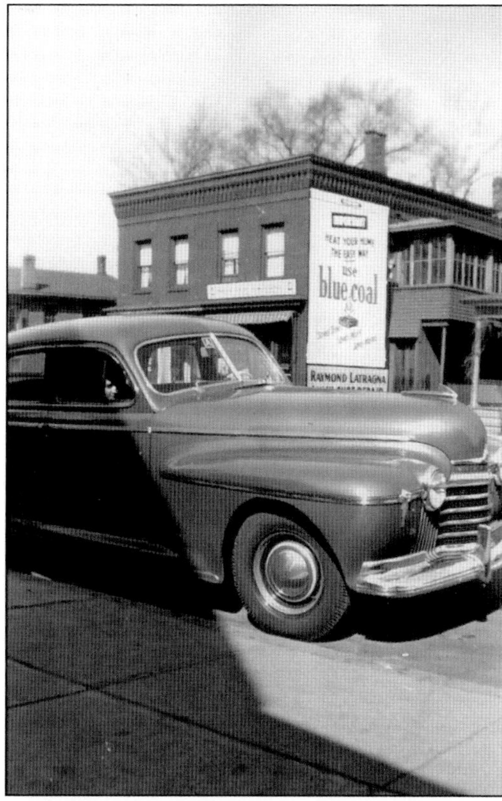

SAME WINDOWS AND CHIMNEYS. These photographs of 602 South Avenue were taken at different dates. The top shows a large building to the north of a bar that was later torn down. There is a "blue coal" advertisement over Raymond Latragna's name by the side porch, and a porch on the house next door. Depending upon the year, the car is parked in front of the Siebert Rambler dealership. The bottom photograph shows Kramer's Korners; the house next door does not have a porch. The Cozy Oak Grill was listed at 602 South Avenue in the 1952 city directory. (Courtesy Josh Canfield, from Ruby Murphy's collection.)

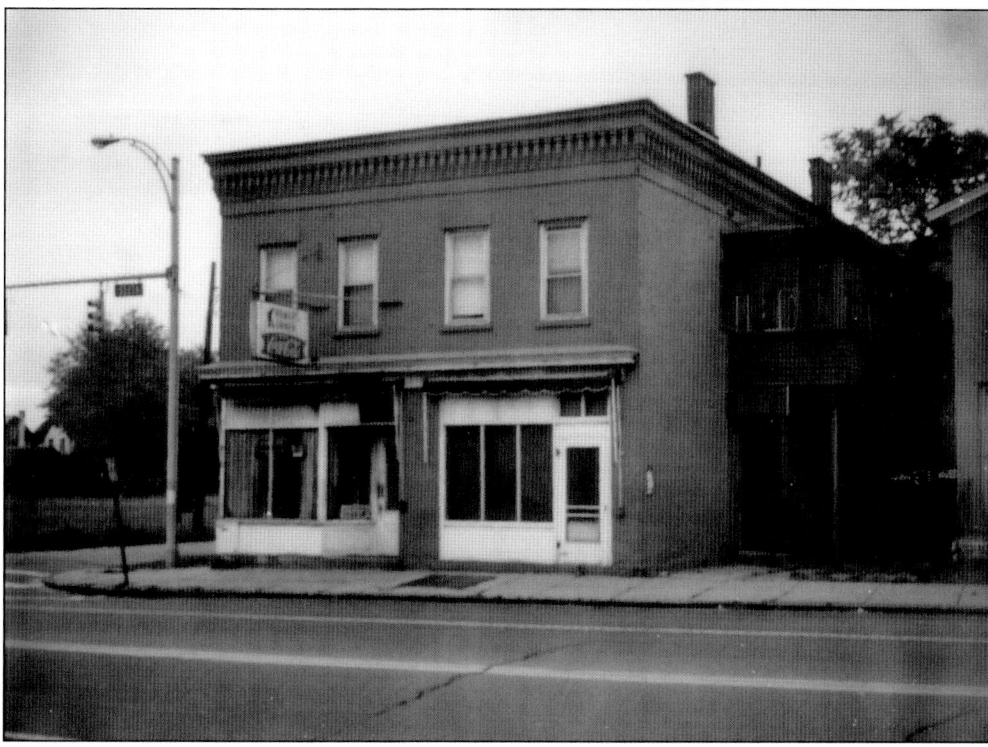

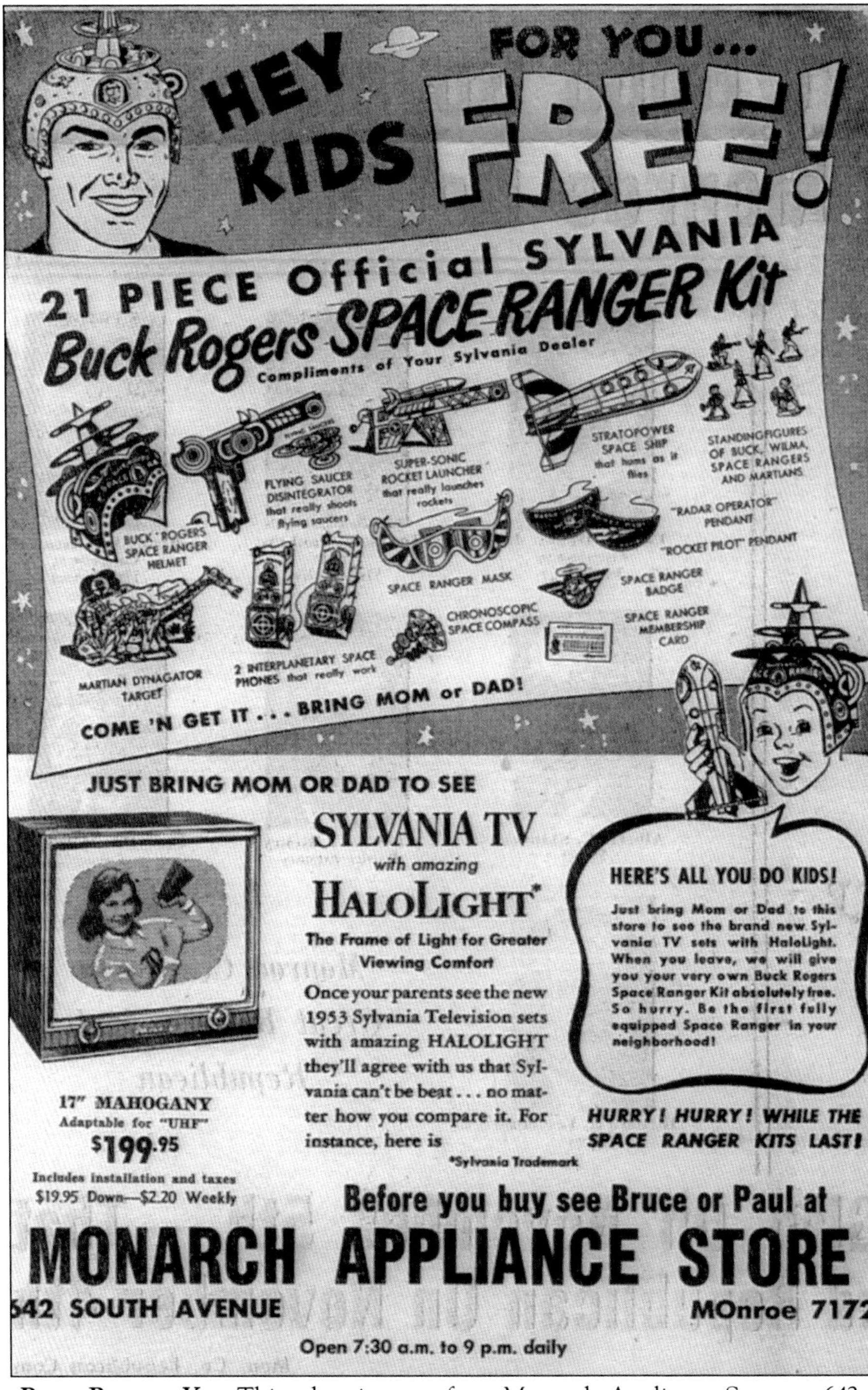

FREE BUCK ROGERS KIT. This advertisement from Monarch Appliance Store, at 642 South Avenue, promised Buck Rogers fans a free, 21-piece, official Sylvania Buck Rogers space ranger kit in a bid for parents' business. It appeared in the October 23, 1952, issue Vol. X, No. 3 of the *South Side News*, whose logo was, "Your Community Newspaper Published in the Interest of Rochester's Southside." (Courtesy Josh Canfield.)

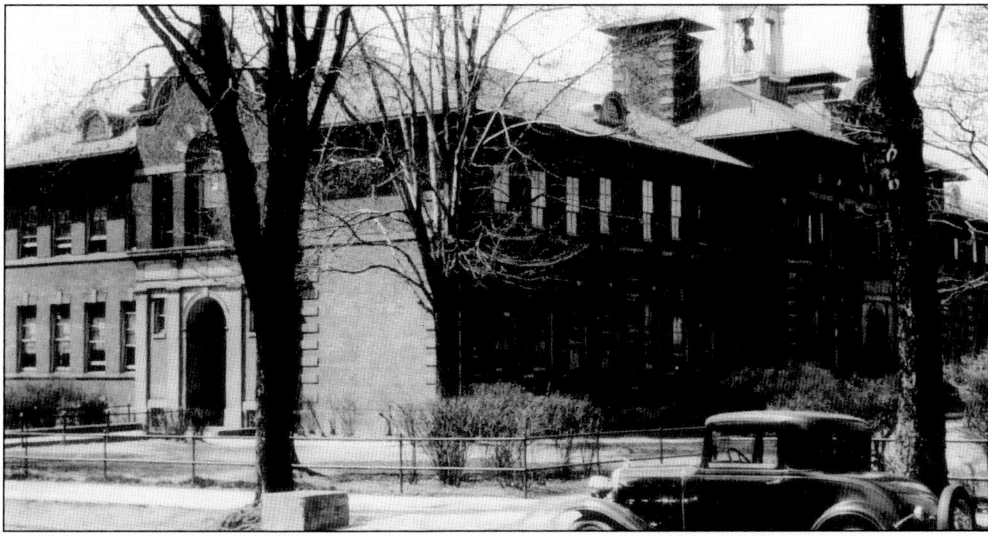

HORACE MANN SCHOOL. Averill Avenue was first called Munger Street. Several Mungers are listed in the 1834 city directory including two farmers and a boat builder at "river, St. Paul St." The first Munger School met in rented rooms on Hickory Street. In 1842, the first wooden schoolhouse built on Hickory Street became Horace Mann School No. 13. A third new school for 250 pupils was dedicated in June 1853. Due to the influence of Frederick Douglass and others, the city school board designated Horace Mann School No. 13 as an integrated school in the 1850s before state-wide integration was in effect in 1857. Frederick and Anna Douglass' younger children attended there for a time. A new school was built in 1893 and another, designed by J. Foster Warner, in 1903–1904. Due to declining enrollment, it was closed in 1979 and converted to Gregory Park condominiums in 1982. This view is from 1935. (Courtesy Rochester Photo Images.)

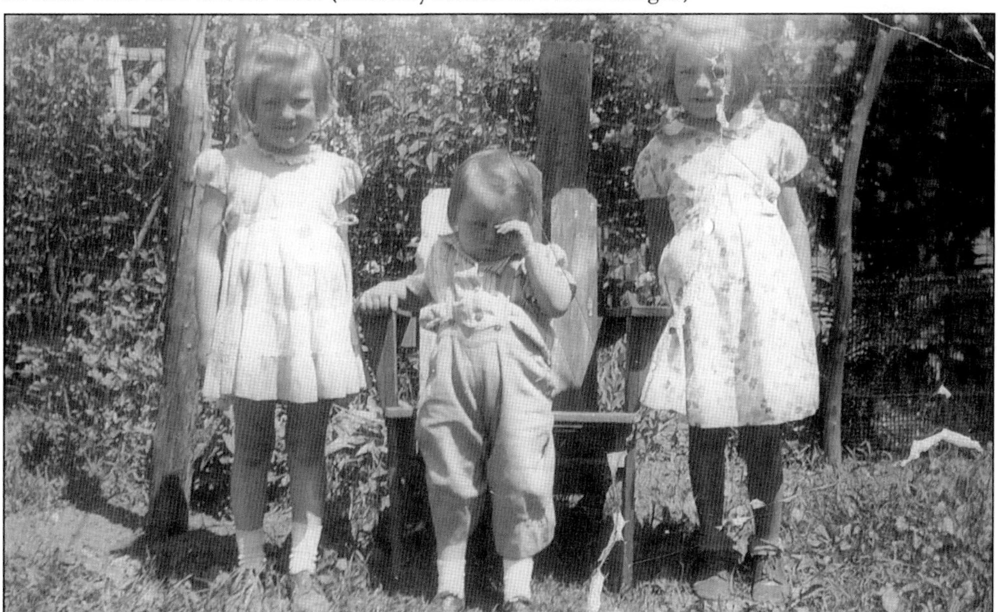

NAP TIME? The Shamp family raised 11 children in the house at 18 Hickory Street, a block west of 13 school. It is hard to tell whether little Grace is sleepy or weepy, standing between Lorraine (left) and Beverly in the backyard in 1943. (Courtesy Tom Page.)

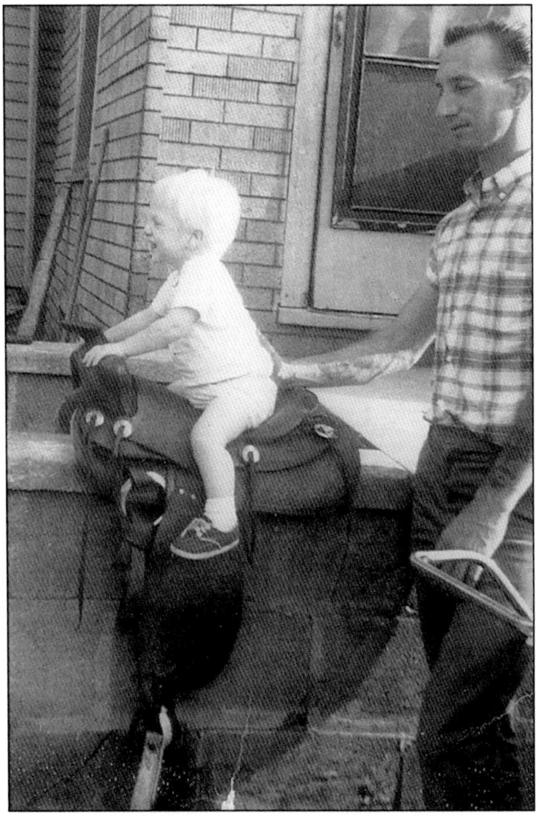

RIDE 'EM, COWBOY! Louie Conti keeps a watchful eye on little Tony, in the backyard at 18 Hickory Street in June 1967. Louie's cousin, Sam Bianchi, had a horse farm for a short time on west Ridge Road. (Courtesy Tom Page.)

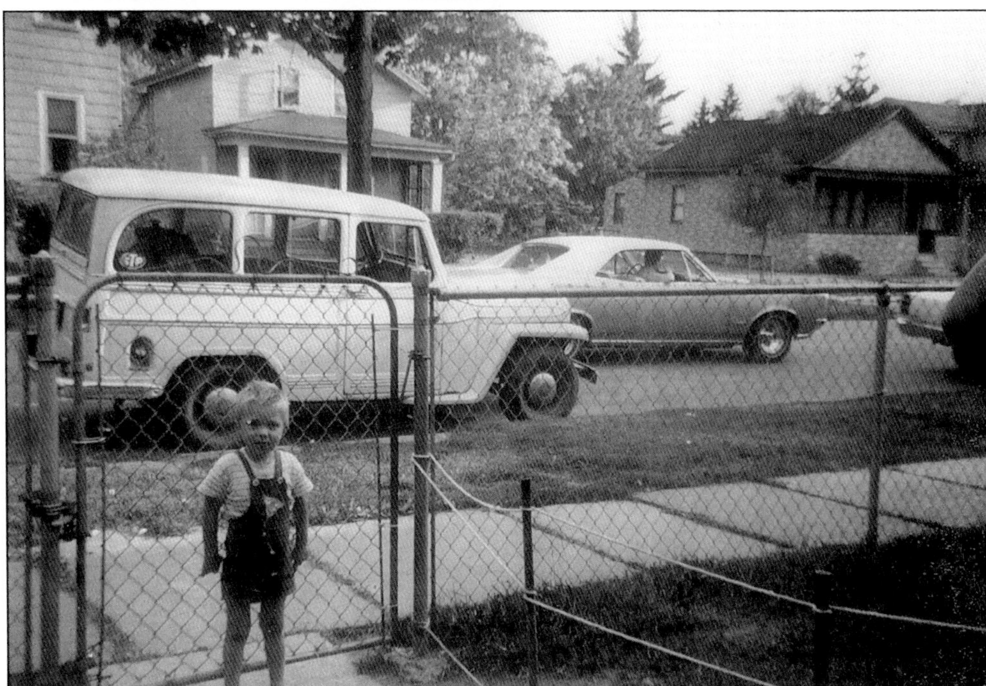

STAY IN THE YARD. Louie Conti Jr. stands by the front fence in 1967. (Courtesy Tom Page.)

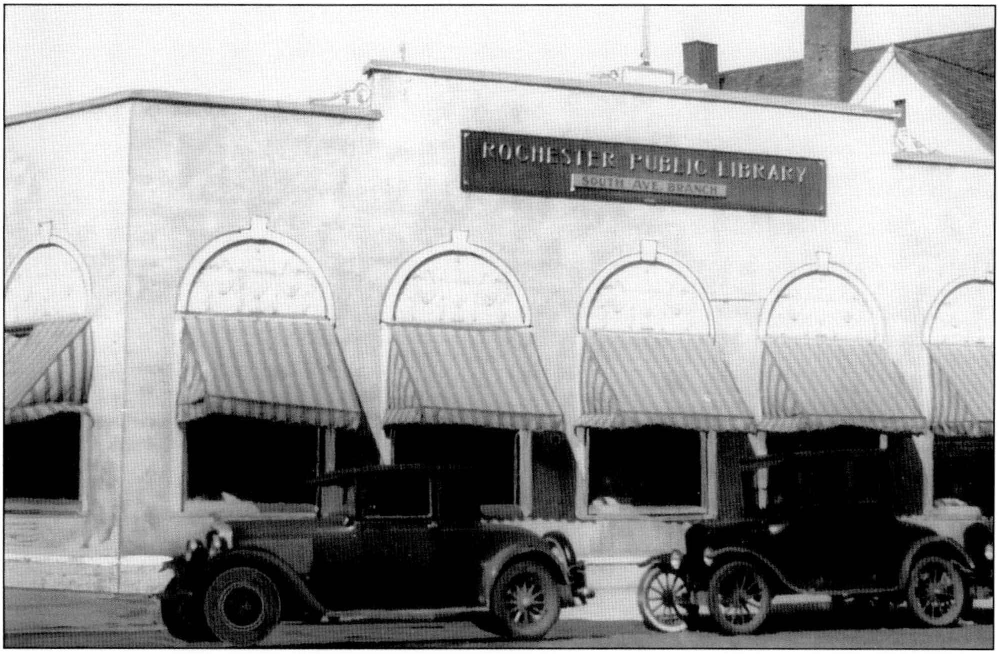

BRANCH LIBRARY. The South Avenue Branch Library opened in 1927 south of Gregory Street. This photograph was taken in 1928. After a fire in the 1980s, it was temporarily in the Abeles Building, on the north west corner of South Avenue and Gregory Street before the new Highland Branch opened next to No. 12 School in 1986. (Courtesy City of Rochester Photo Lab.)

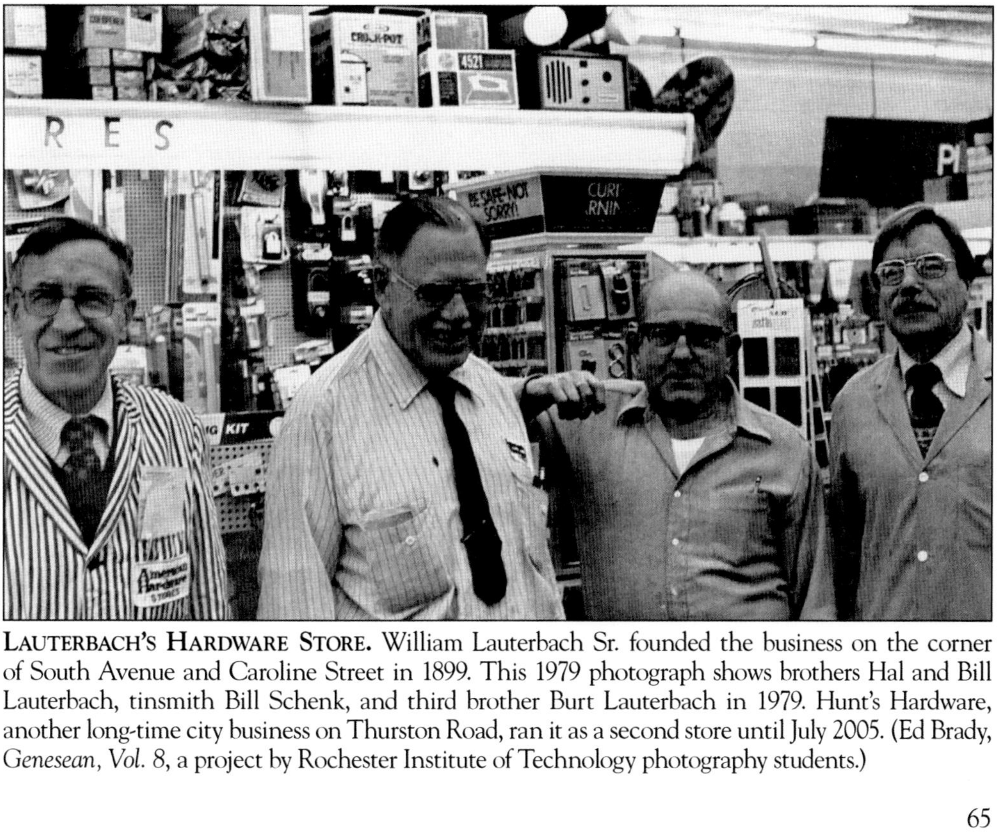

LAUTERBACH'S HARDWARE STORE. William Lauterbach Sr. founded the business on the corner of South Avenue and Caroline Street in 1899. This 1979 photograph shows brothers Hal and Bill Lauterbach, tinsmith Bill Schenk, and third brother Burt Lauterbach in 1979. Hunt's Hardware, another long-time city business on Thurston Road, ran it as a second store until July 2005. (Ed Brady, *Genesean, Vol. 8*, a project by Rochester Institute of Technology photography students.)

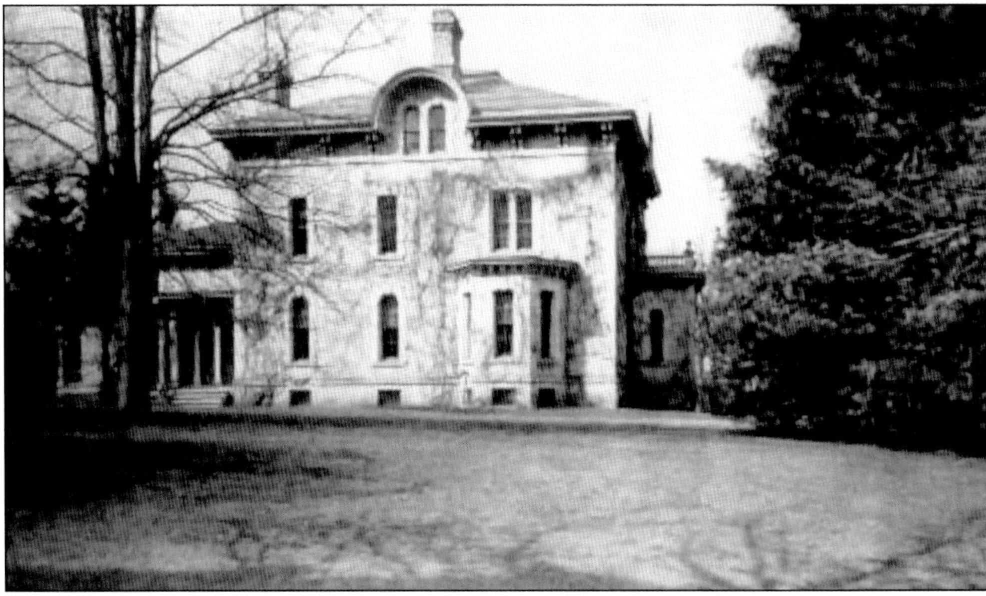

HALSEY HOUSE-NEUN MANSION. This picture taken in 1890 is titled *William L. Halsey's House*, taken at 339 South Avenue. The house was built by George Ellwanger and sold in 1862 to lawyer George H. Mumford. Halsey was Mumford's son-in-law. In 1862, when the Mumfords moved there, they became neighbors of the Frederick Douglass family. This house is an undocumented stop on the Underground Railroad. The Neun family owned it from 1910 until the deteriorated three-story, 17-room mansion was demolished for a modern one-story building. Rochester Children's Nursery moved into its new building at 941 South Avenue in February 1955. (Courtesy Rochester Photo Images.)

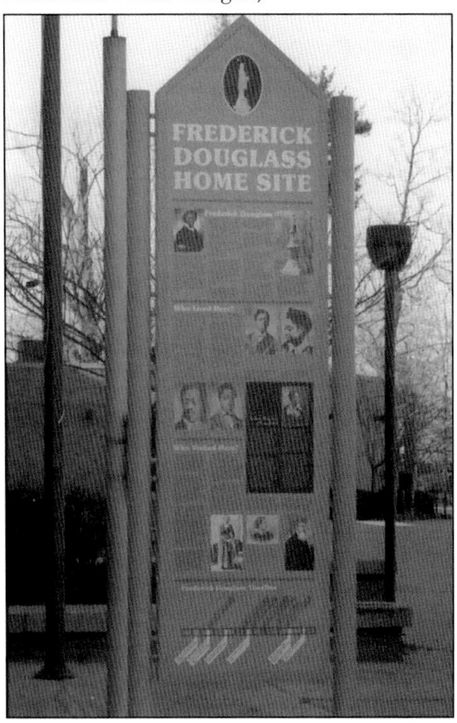

HOME SITE MARKER. In 1855, after eight years on Alexander Street, Frederick Douglass, his wife Anna, and their five children bought a house and barn on a six-acre wooded plot (now 1023 South Avenue). Frederick Douglass stayed so frequently in Washington, D.C., he had moved his paper there. In June 1872, when the house burned to the ground, the Douglass family moved to Washington D.C. This marker was placed next to James P. Duffy No. 12 School, at 999 South Avenue, in February 2005 as a cooperative venture of the Freedom Trail Commission and the Landmark Society. (Courtesy Robert P. Meadows.)

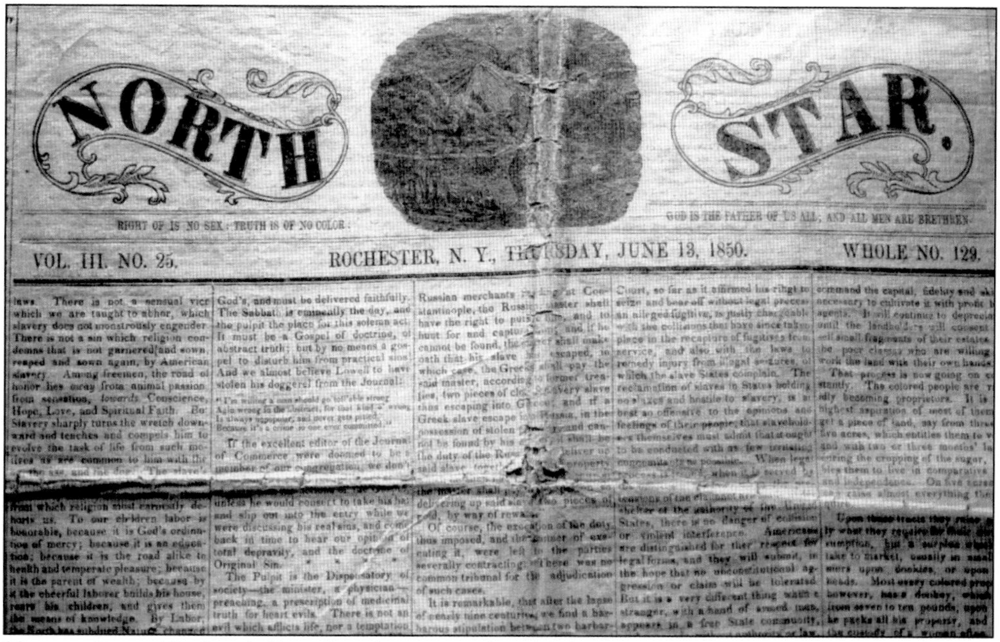

NORTH STAR.

RIGHT IS OF NO SEX: TRUTH IS OF NO COLOR. — GOD IS THE FATHER OF US ALL, AND ALL MEN ARE BRETHREN.

VOL. III. NO. 25. ROCHESTER, N. Y., THURSDAY, JUNE 13, 1850. WHOLE NO. 129.

NORTH STAR. Frederick Douglass (1818–1895) published the first issue of the *North Star* on December 3, 1847, in Rochester. Its motto was: "Right is of no sex. Truth is of no color. God is the Father of us all and we are all Brethren." This issue is from June 13, 1850. (Courtesy City of Rochester Photo Lab.)

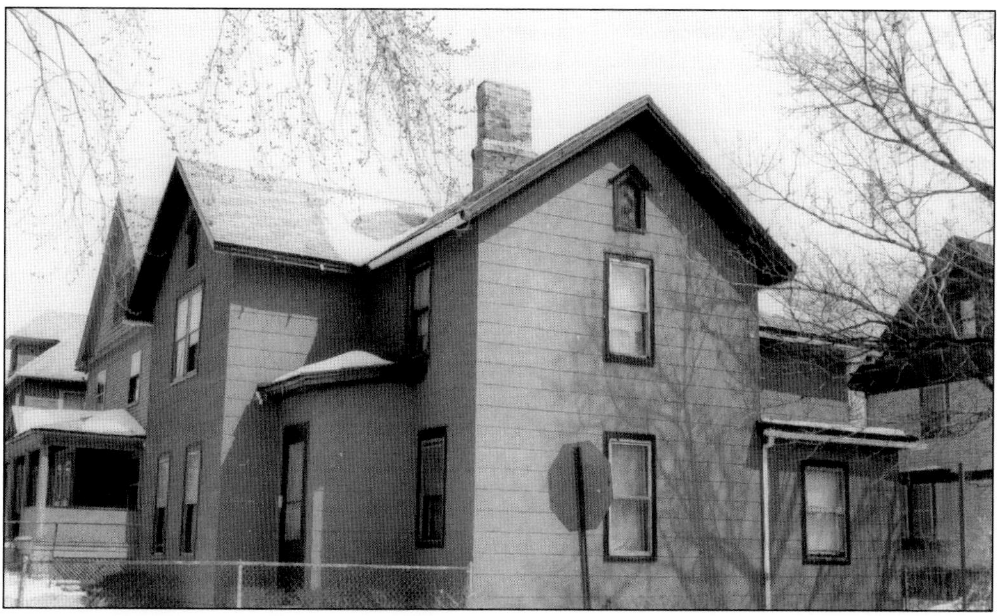

NO. 271 HAMILTON. After the fire that destroyed their South Avenue home, most of the Douglass family moved to Washington, D.C. Rosetta Douglass, who was married to Nathan Sprague and eventually had seven children, stayed in a house her father owned on Hamilton Place. Frederick deeded it to her in 1872 and most likely stayed there whenever he returned to Rochester. The house was sold after Douglass's death in 1895. (Courtesy Landmark Society files, South Wedge Planning Committee.)

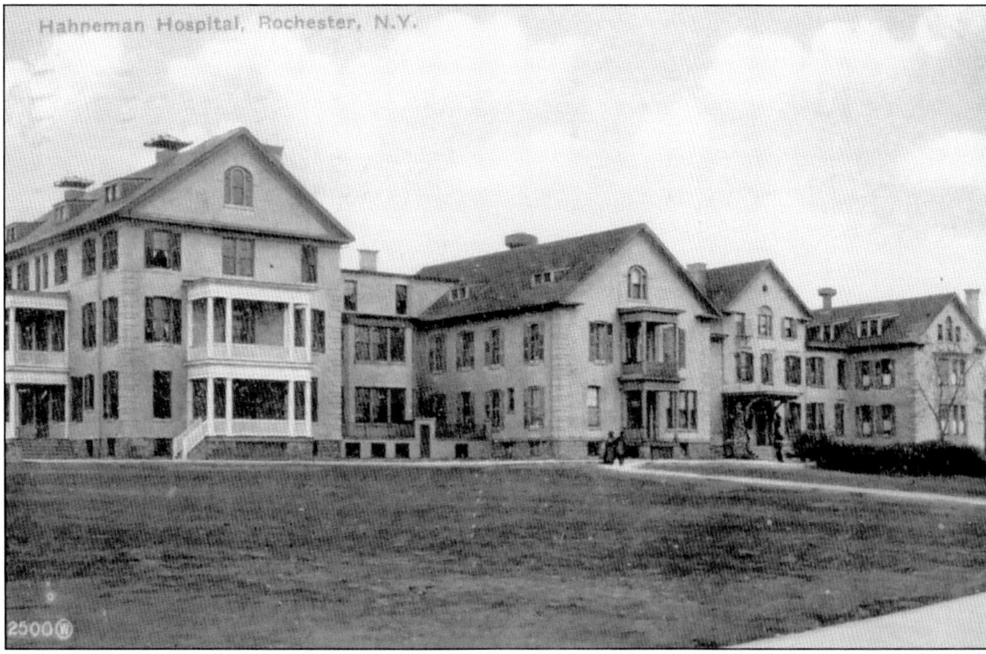

HANNEMAHN HOSPITAL. Hahneman Homeopathic Hospital opened on Oakland Street (now Rockingham Street) in 1889, under the leadership of Dr. Joseph Biegler at a time of strong medical conflicts between homeopathic and allopathic practices. It was in the former home of Judge Henry Selden, in what were called the Pinnacle Highlands. Its first 13 beds were increased to 40 within a decade. After several changes, it became Highland Hospital in 1921. This photograph is from around 1900. (Courtesy City of Rochester Photo Lab.)

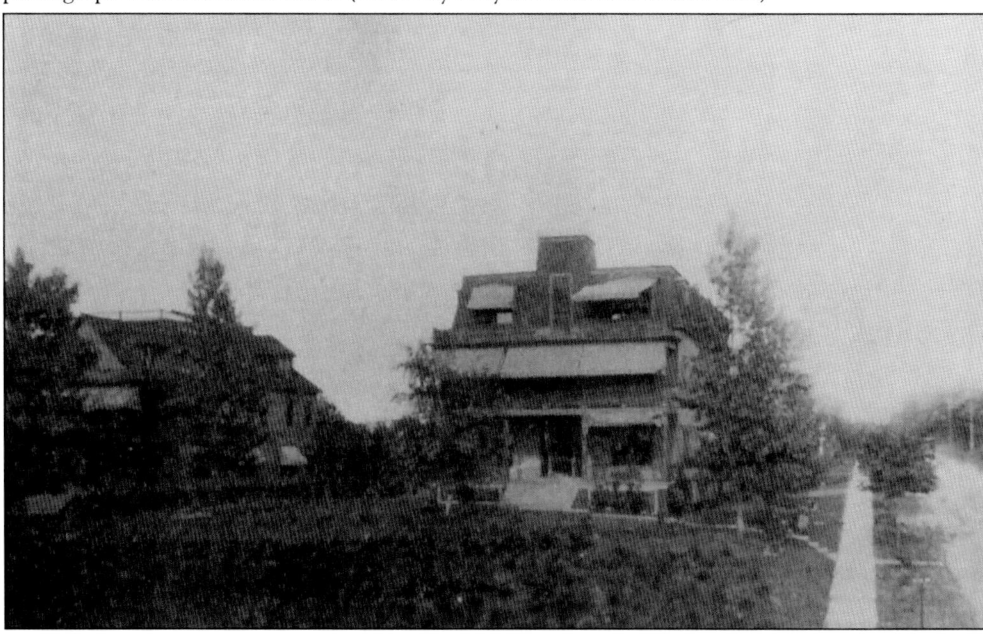

SANATORIUM. Merritt E. Graham opened the Graham Highland Park Sanatorium at 1090–1100 South Avenue in 1899, and the maternity hospital in 1905. This photograph taken in 1911, is looking east from South Avenue toward Alpine Street. (Courtesy Rochester Photo Images.)

SISTER CHRISTINE. In 1903, at the German Homes as a newly-trained religious nurse, Lutheran Deaconess Sr. Christine Schwartz became the first superintendent and matron in a major American city at a time when social work was in its infancy and nursing-home management was not an established profession. She served for 36 years and wisely declined to retire there. (Courtesy St. John's Home.)

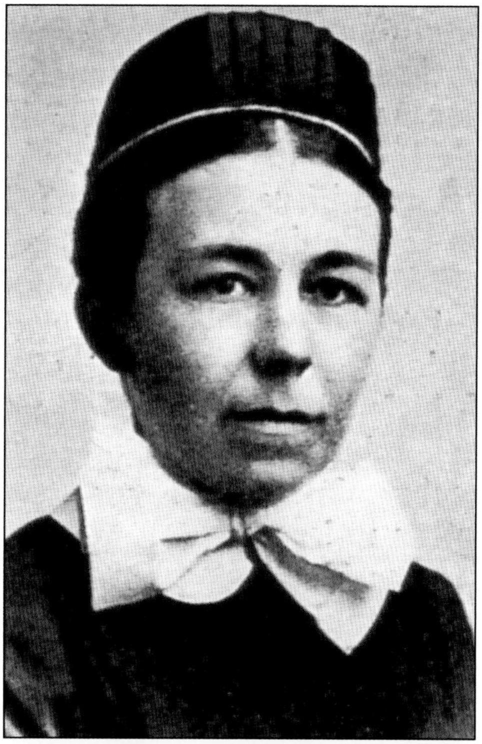

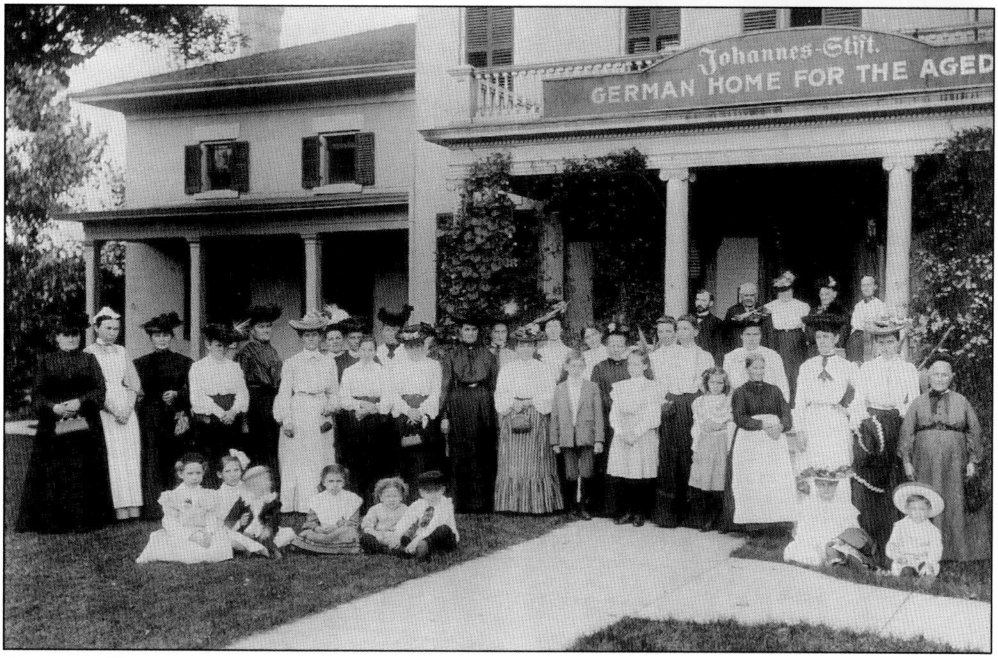

GERMAN HOME FOR THE AGED. St. John's Association was created by several German Protestant churches and community leaders to create housing for the elderly. The first home that opened in November 1888 on Lake Avenue near Flower City Park became too small within a year. George Ellwanger offered a beautiful mansion near Highland Park in the summer of 1890 and the new home was ready in August 1901. (Courtesy St. John's Home.)

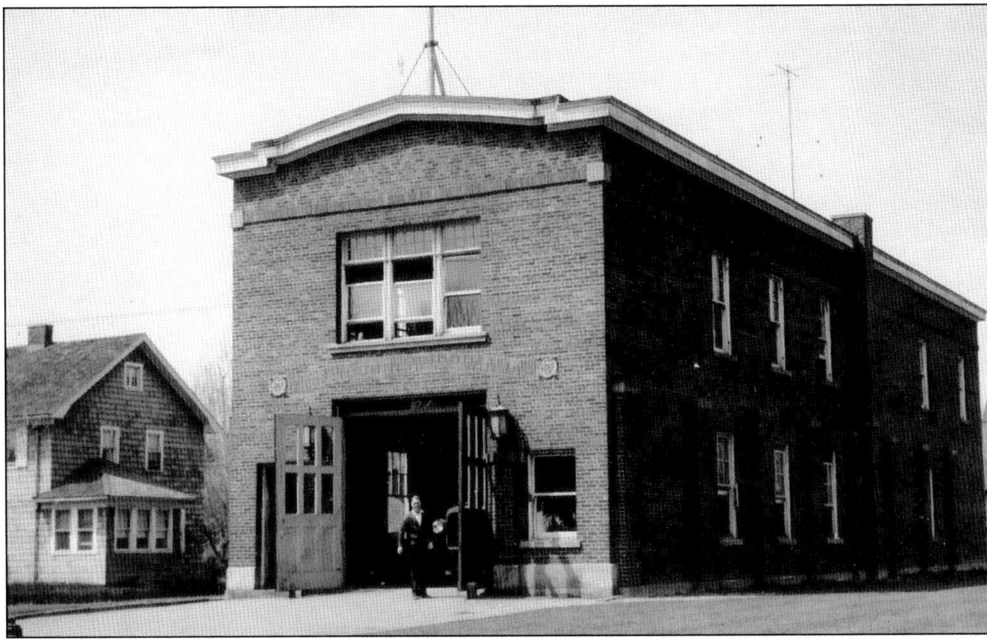

TRUCK HOUSE NO. 7. The first Truck House on South Avenue at Pavilion Street was a single house built in 1910 to hold the trucks that carried the ladders and tools. A bay was added in 1957 when it combined with Engine House No. 8 from Gregory Street that had the pump trucks. A second addition was made in 1984 to accommodate the Quint and Midi 3, two new and larger pieces of equipment that replaced the truck and pumper. This photograph was taken in 1935. (Courtesy City of Rochester Photo Lab.)

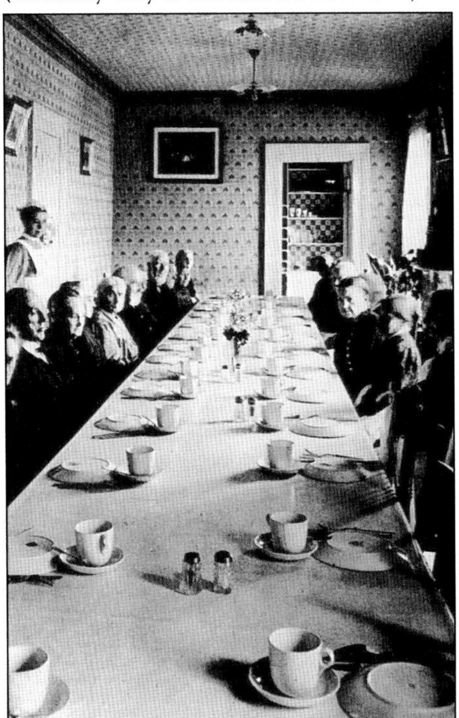

MEALTIME. The German Home for the Aged was such a popular place for elderly German Americans, by 1912 the trustees had to consider an addition for English-speakers. Although the first accommodations at the home were described as "Spartan," first residents enjoyed the peace and quiet of the surrounding Ellwanger and Barry orchards. This dining room has attractive wallpaper and there are flowers on the table. (Courtesy St. John's Home.)

Six

The Highland Park Neighborhood

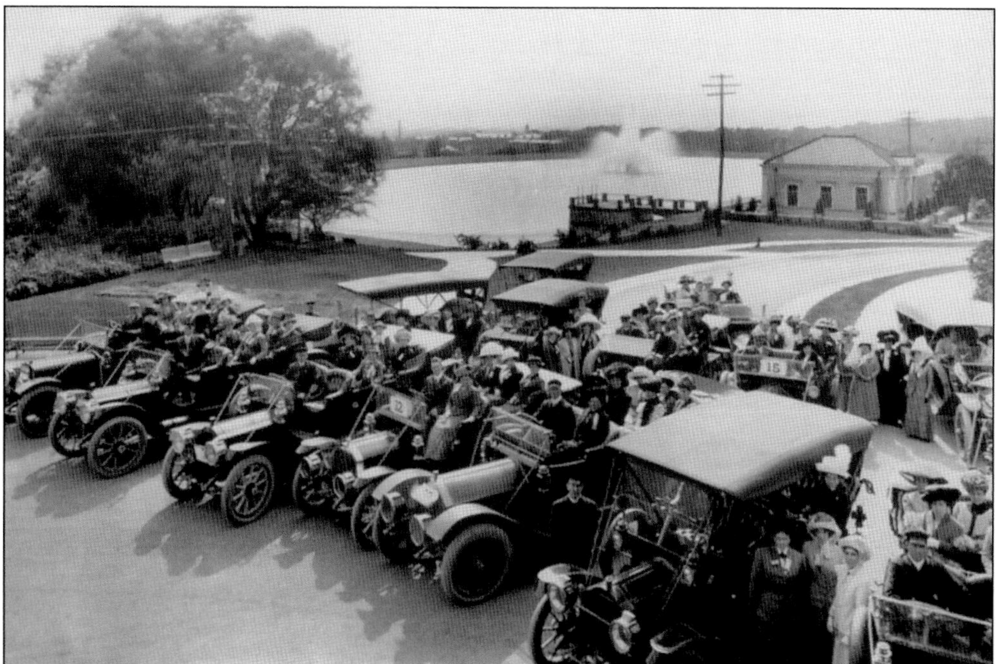

Bank Outing. It looks like the bank had beautiful weather for their convention at Highland Park in 1911. (Courtesy City of Rochester Photo Lab.)

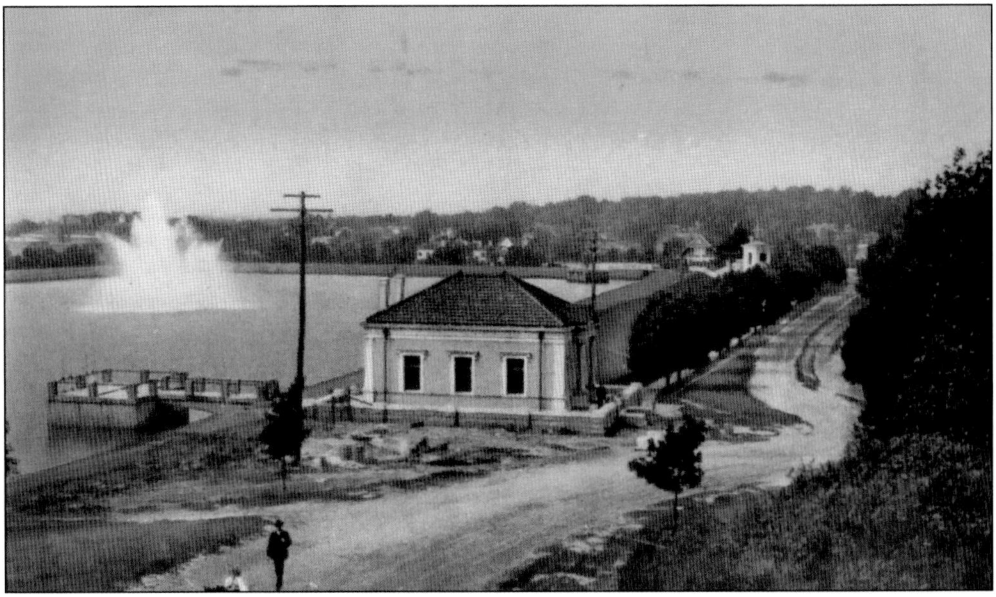

RESERVOIR AND FOUNTAIN. In 1883, George Ellwanger and Patrick Barry offered the city 20 acres for a park as a gift, which was accepted in 1887. The park was designed by the firm of Frederick Law Olmsted (1822–1903), the father of American landscape architecture. In 1891, horticulturist John Dunbar planted over 100 varieties of lilac bushes. The first Lilac Festival was celebrated in May 1905, in the park's 22-acre lilac display area. This postcard of the park in 1900 was started and never sent. The front of the card, dated September 11, 1906 says, "Have been here." There is a name, but no address on the back. The stamp box reads, "United States and Canada, One Cent. Foreign, Two Cents." (Courtesy Josh Canfield.)

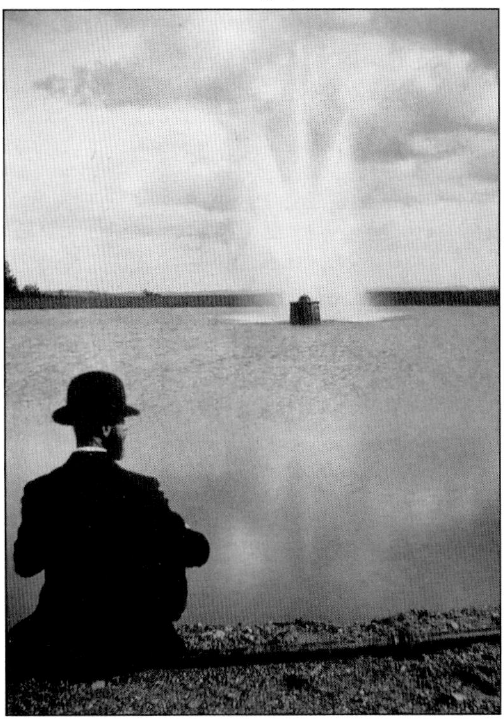

TIME OUT. Generations of visitors have taken a breather by the reservoir at Highland Park. This photograph is from 1878. (Courtesy City of Rochester Photo Lab.)

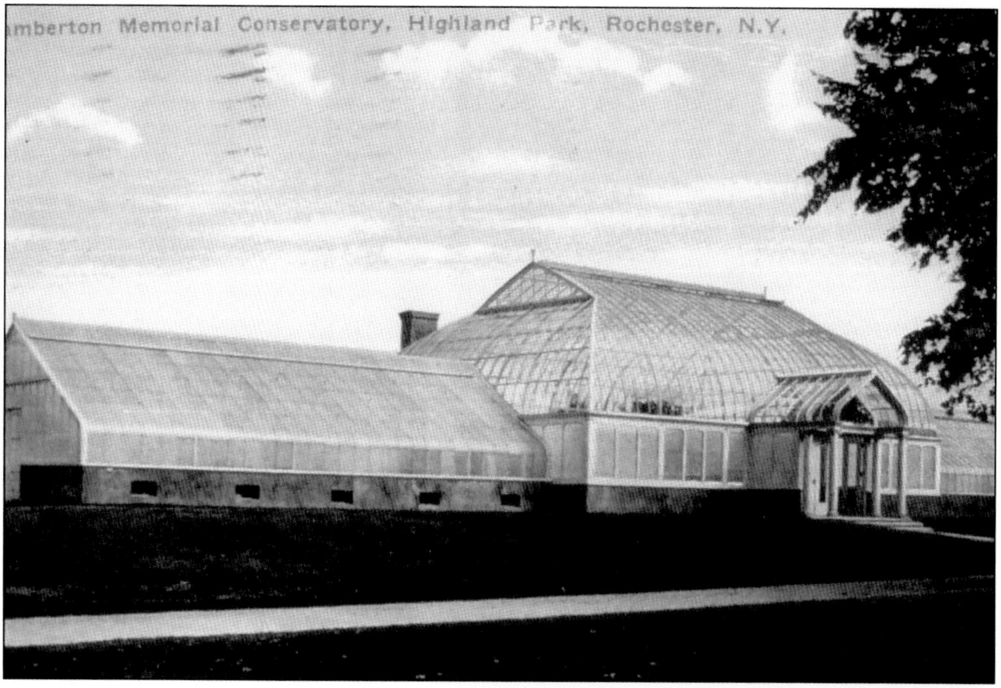

LAMBERTON CONSERVATORY. Alexander B. Lamberton (1839–1919) was a bank vice-president and president of the Public Market. He was an avid outdoorsman, supporter of Rochester's parks, and a commissioner for several years before becoming chairman of the Rochester Parks Commission. The conservatory was built in his honor in 1911. (Courtesy City of Rochester Photo Lab.)

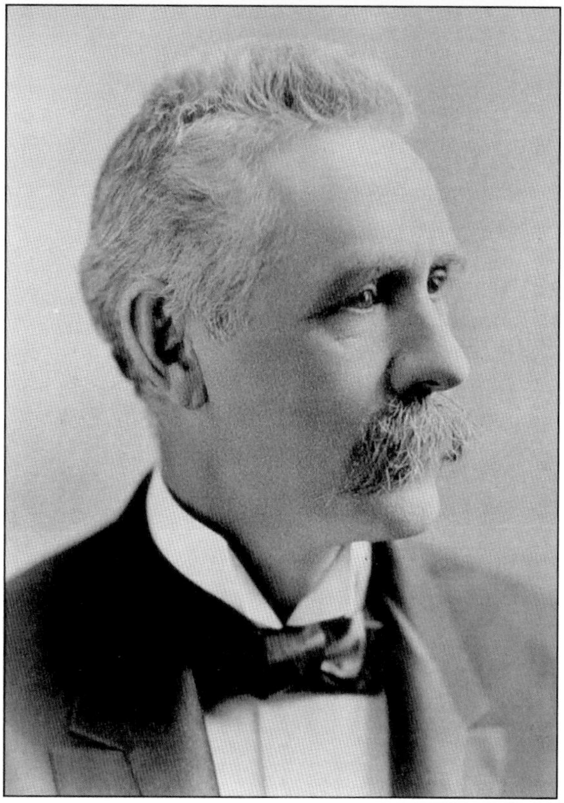

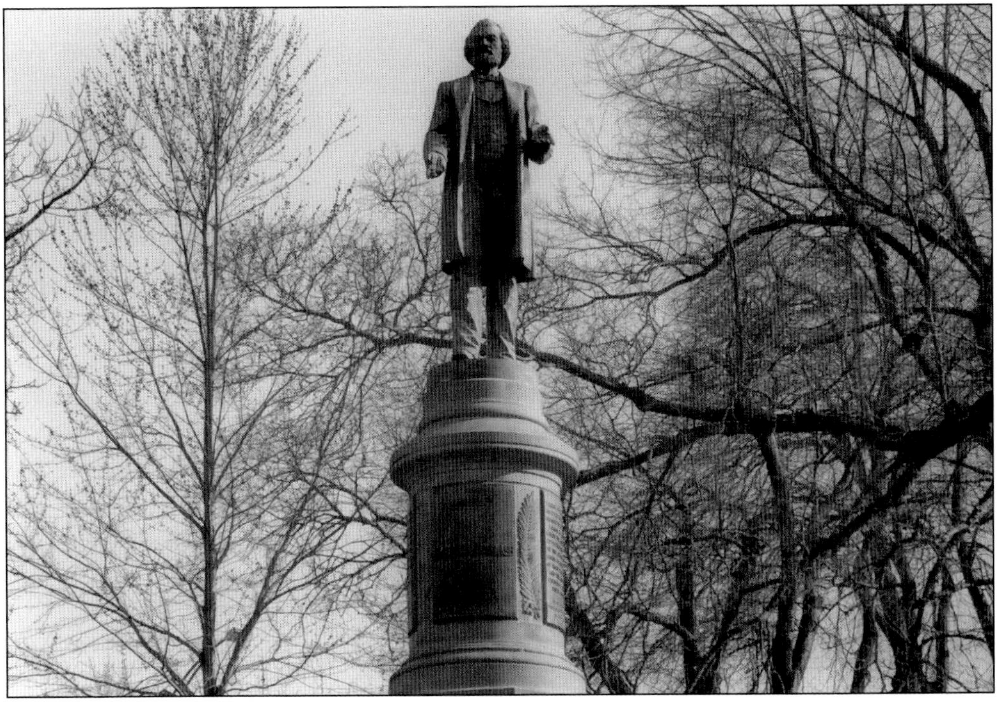

DOUGLASS MONUMENT. The Frederick Douglass monument, made by Sidney W. Edwards, was unveiled in 1899 at Central Avenue and St. Paul Street. It was moved to Highland Park on the southwest corner of South Avenue and Robinson Drive and rededicated on September 4, 1941. (Courtesy Robert P. Meadows.)

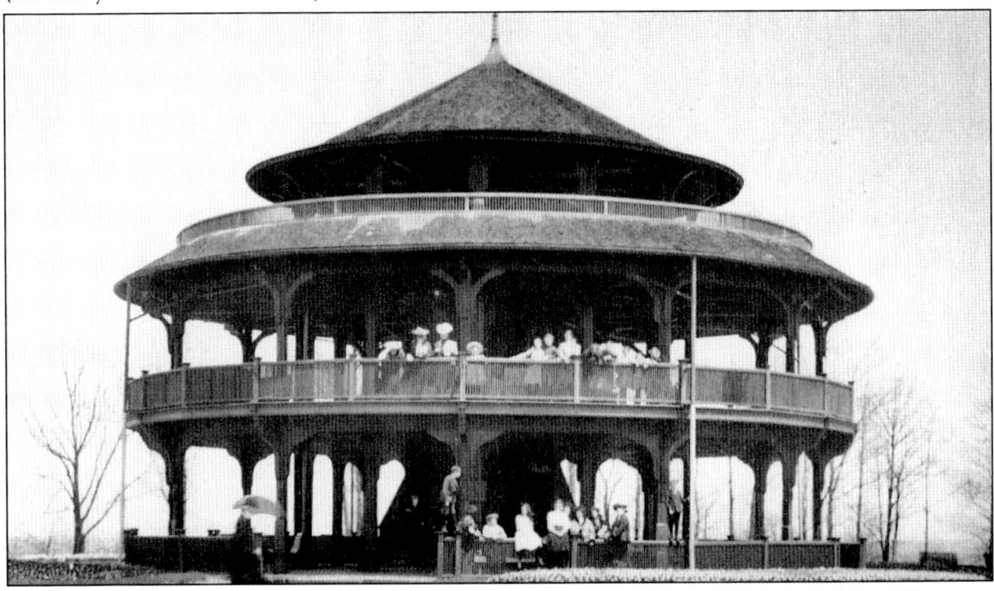

CHILDREN'S PAVILION. This wonderful pavilion was built in 1890, and first called the Ellwanger and Barry Memorial Pavilion, dedicated to all children. It had three floors, with a diameter of 62 feet, and height of 46 feet. In 1962–1963, after the city turned over most of the parks to the county, 60 deteriorated buildings throughout the park system were torn down, including the Children's Pavilion. (Courtesy Ellwanger and Barry Neighborhood Association.)

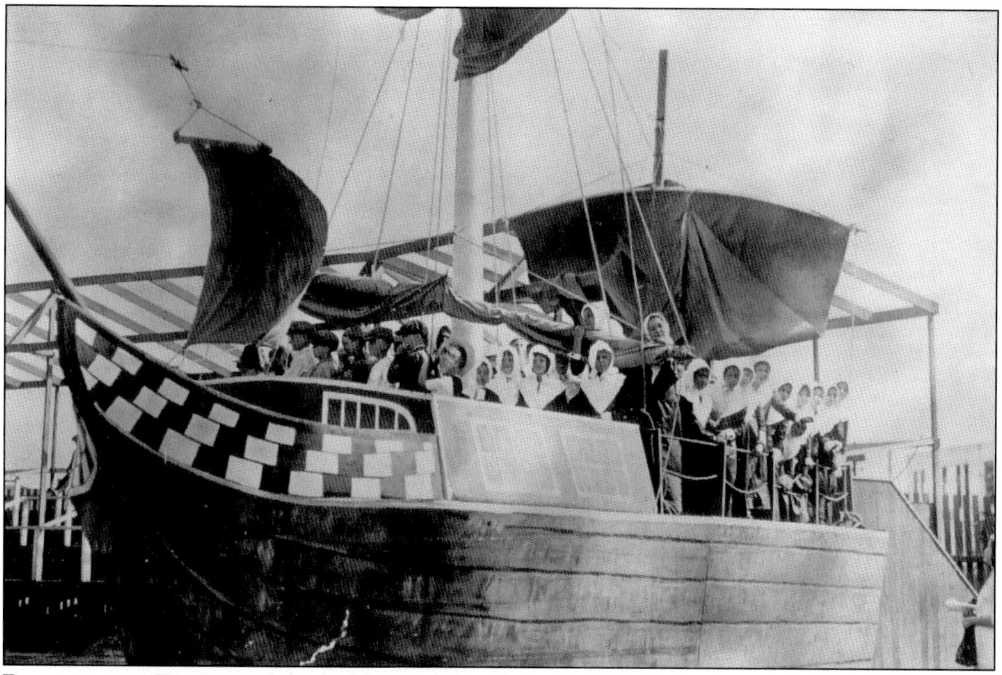

PLAYGROUND PAGEANT. It looks like smooth sailing for this pageant in an ark in the park, dated 1920. (Courtesy City of Rochester Photo Lab.)

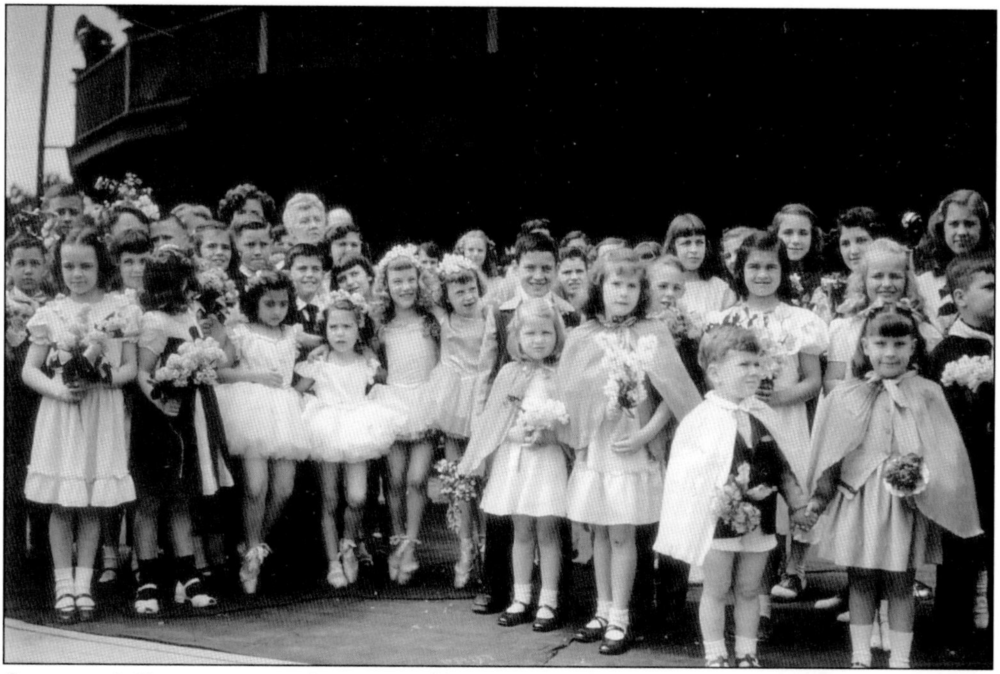

CHILDREN'S PERFORMANCE. It is impossible to estimate how many school children and families had outings to the park that ended in races to the top of the pavilion. It was torn down some time after this group portrait in the 1960s. At least four of the girls in this view are standing on pointed toes. (Courtesy City of Rochester Photo Lab.)

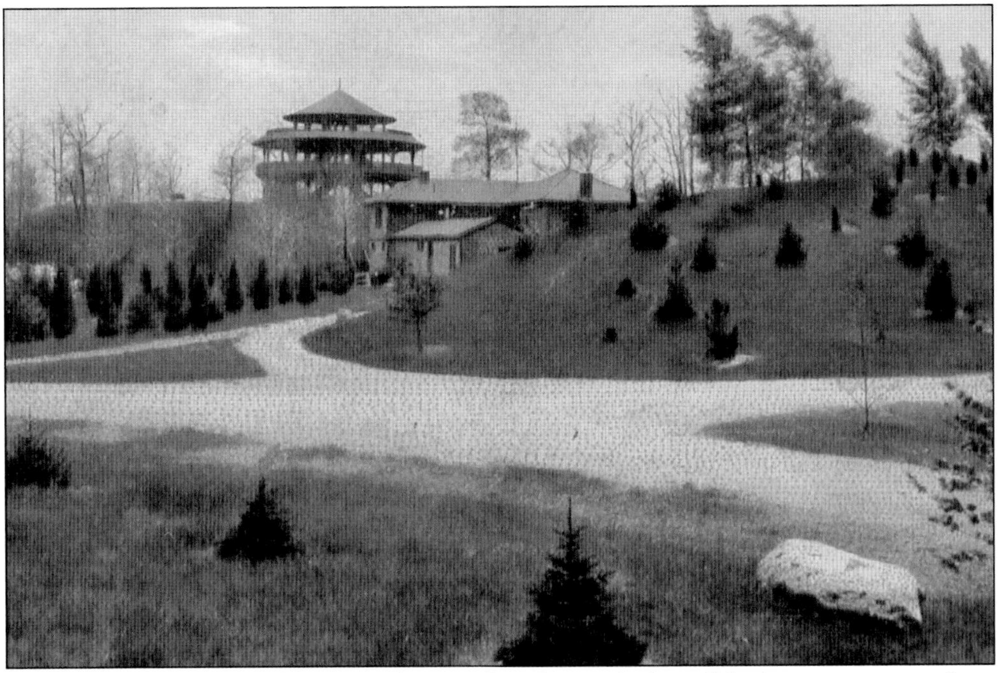

THE REFECTORY. When the city parks were first designed, they all had concession stands so children could have milk and ice cream. All that is left now of the Highland Park Refectory is the concrete platform over the rest rooms, east of where the Children's Pavilion stood. (Courtesy Ellwanger and Barry Neighborhood Association.)

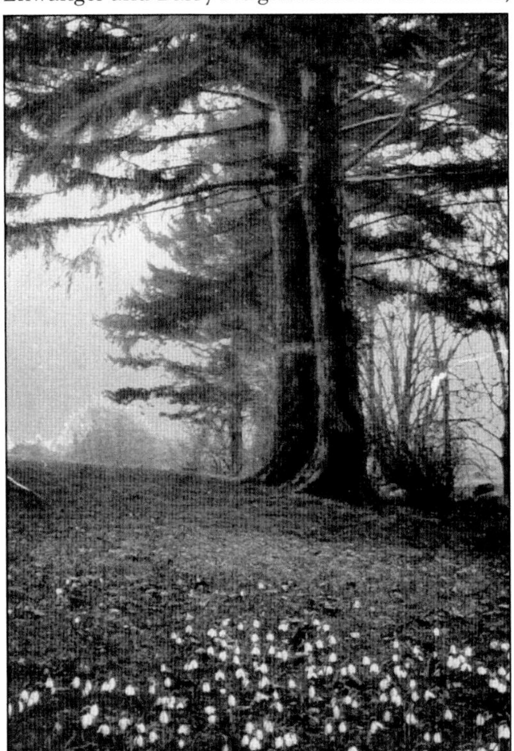

DUNBAR LEGACY. One of the people that can be thanked for such a wonderful park is John Dunbar (1859–1927) who was assistant superintendent of parks and arborculturalist. Dunbar was a noted horticulturalist who created several new lilac varieties. Highland Park was nationally known at the beginning of the 20th century for its exceptional collection of rare Victorian-era trees and shrubs. The park boasts about 4,000 different species and varieties of trees and shrubs. Some of the trees on the current state "big tree" list date from the Frederick Law Olmsted design. This early postcard, *Snow Drops*, was most likely along Pinetum Drive. (Courtesy Ellwanger and Barry Neighborhood Association.)

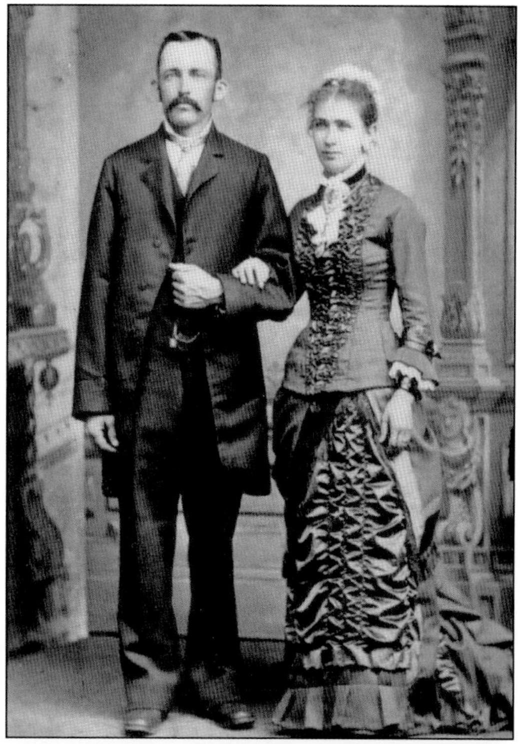

Great-Grandpa 'n Grandma. Henry and Frances Michel Schnacky pose thoughtfully for the camera on their wedding day on May 18, 1880. (Courtesy Bob Schnacky.)

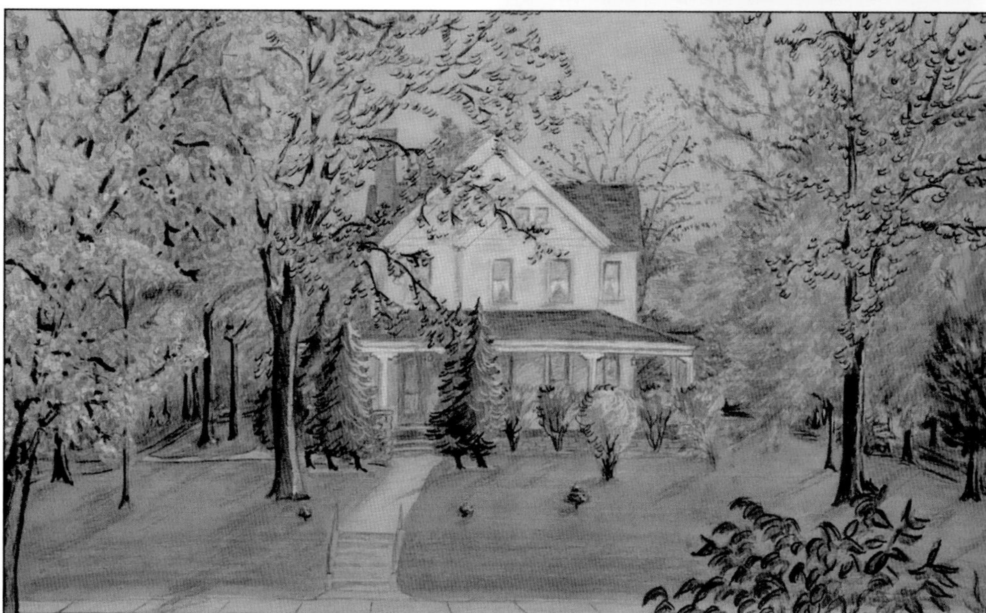

Schnacky Farmhouse. Henry Schnacky bought 30 acres in the town of West Brighton in 1875. He built a farmhouse near the southwest corner of Elmwood and South Avenues and raised corn, potatoes, beans, and hay and kept a few cows. He and his wife Frances had five children. The county and then the state took over the property in 1901 for the expansion of the State Mental Hospital. This painting was done by a patient at the hospital in the 1940s. (Courtesy Al Sigl Center.)

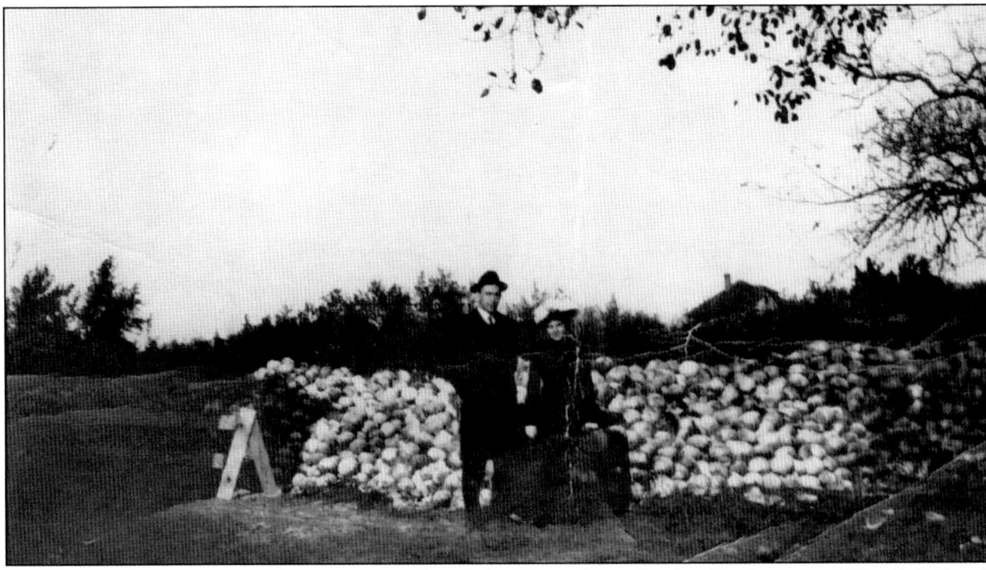

CABBAGE CROP. The family story goes that John B. Le Frois had a dry house at Westfall Road, where cabbage was shredded and dried. When winter came late one year, the annual cabbage crop reeked to high heaven before it could be processed. Grandpa Albert and Grandma Emma Schnacky stand by the harvest around 1922. (Courtesy Bob Schnacky.)

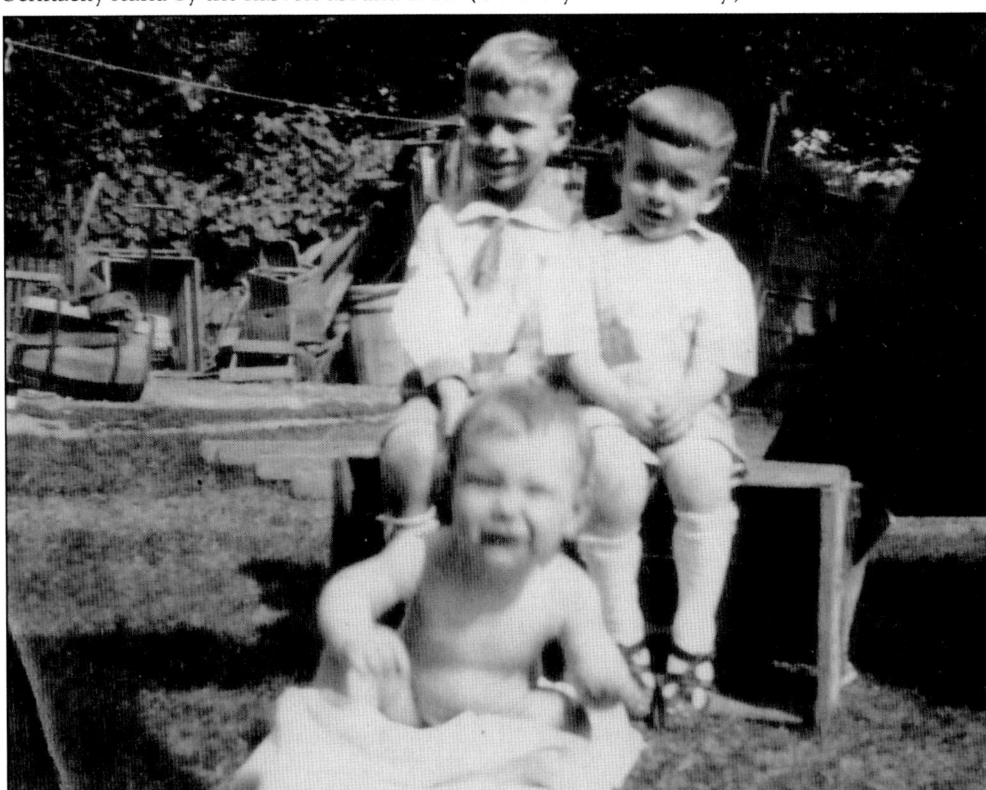

SCHNACKY BROTHERS. New baby brother Bill reaches for the camera around 1920, in front of Charles (left) and Albert (who became monsignor in Mendon). (Courtesy Bob Schnacky.)

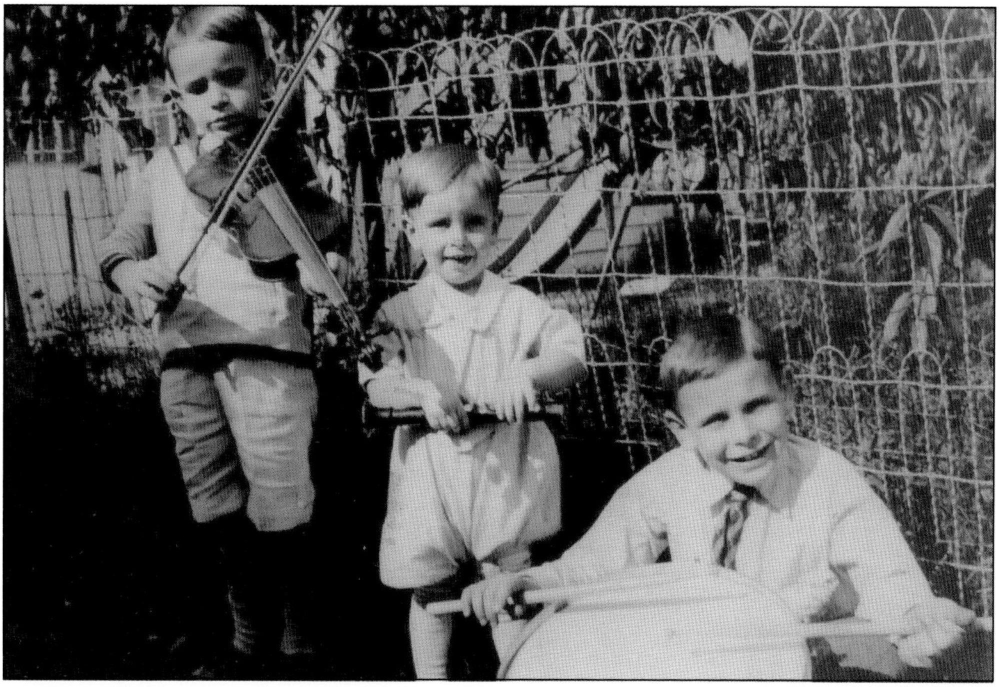

MUSICAL TRIO. The Schnacky boys pose with instruments in 1930: Bob on violin, Paul on recorder, and John on drums. Albert Schnacky Sr. was an employee at Trott Monument Company on Mount Hope Avenue, and bought the business in the early 1930s. In turn, son Bob bought the business in the mid-1960s. It closed around 1997. (Courtesy Bob Schnacky.)

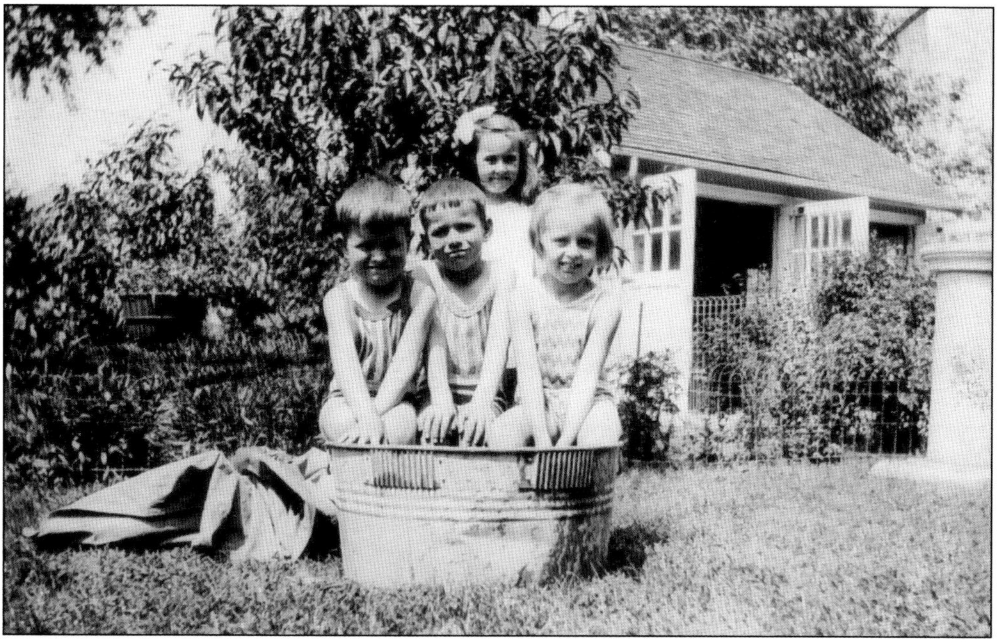

RUB-A-DUB-DUB. Brothers Bernard (left) and Bob Schnacky (center) enjoy the sunshine in their backyard in June 1931 at 36 Highland Parkway. They pose with two neighbor girls, Joanne Wright in the tub and Jane Walton standing in the back. (Courtesy Bob Schnacky.)

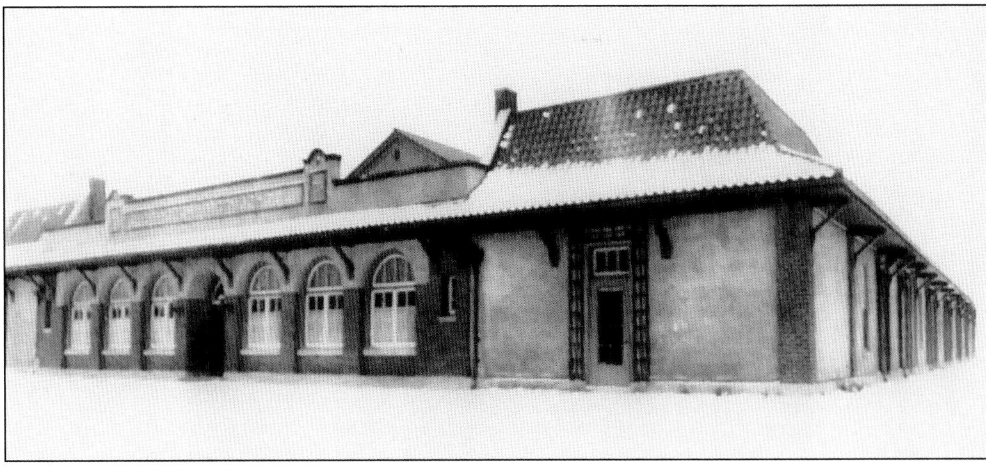

No. 24 School. The Ellwanger and Barry School was first built in 1877 and replaced in 1913. This photograph is from 1935. The newer building closed in 1979 and was turned into condominiums in 1980. (Courtesy Rochester Photo Images.)

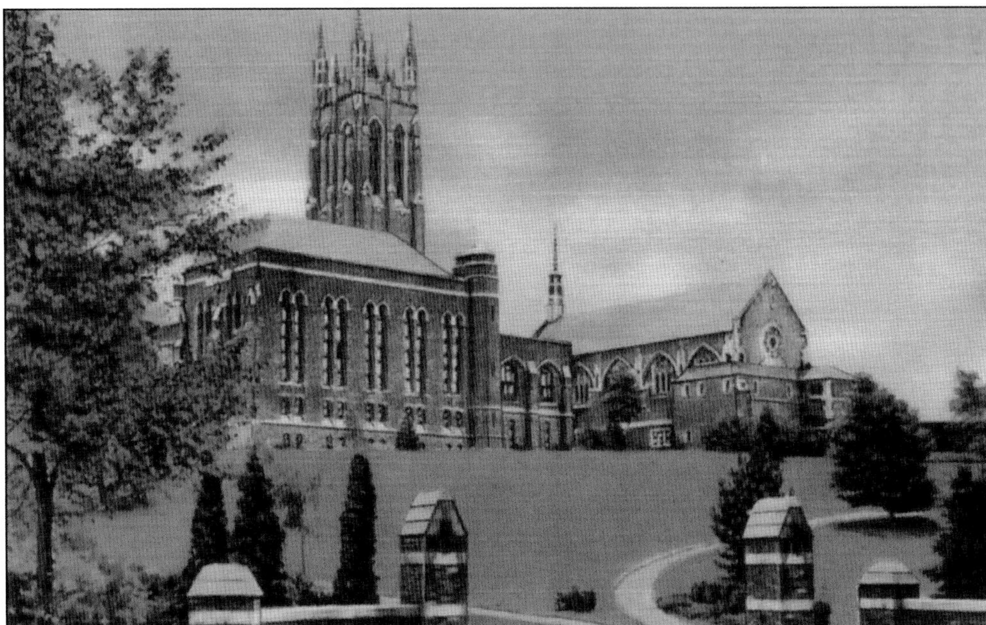

Divinity School. Colgate Divinity School was founded in 1817 in Hamilton, New York, and merged with Rochester Theological Seminary in 1928 at a new campus on the hill at 1100 South Goodman Street. Notables at the school included Helen Barrett Montgomery (1861–1934) who was a leader in the Women's Educational and Industrial Union and, in 1899, the first woman on the Rochester Board of Education. She became the first woman president of any Protestant denomination, then the Northern Baptist Convention. The president's home is named Montgomery House for her. Walter Rauschenbusch (1861–1918) was born in Rochester and went to Rochester Theological Seminary. In 1886, he followed his calling to the Second German Baptist Church in New York City on the edge of Hell's Kitchen, where he lost most of his hearing after an illness. In 1897, Rauschenbusch became a member of the German Baptist Seminary in Rochester. He was a professor of church history at Colgate Rochester Divinity School for 21 years and wrote many books and articles on the "Social Gospel." (Courtesy Rochester Photo Images.)

Seven

From the Park to the Barge Canal

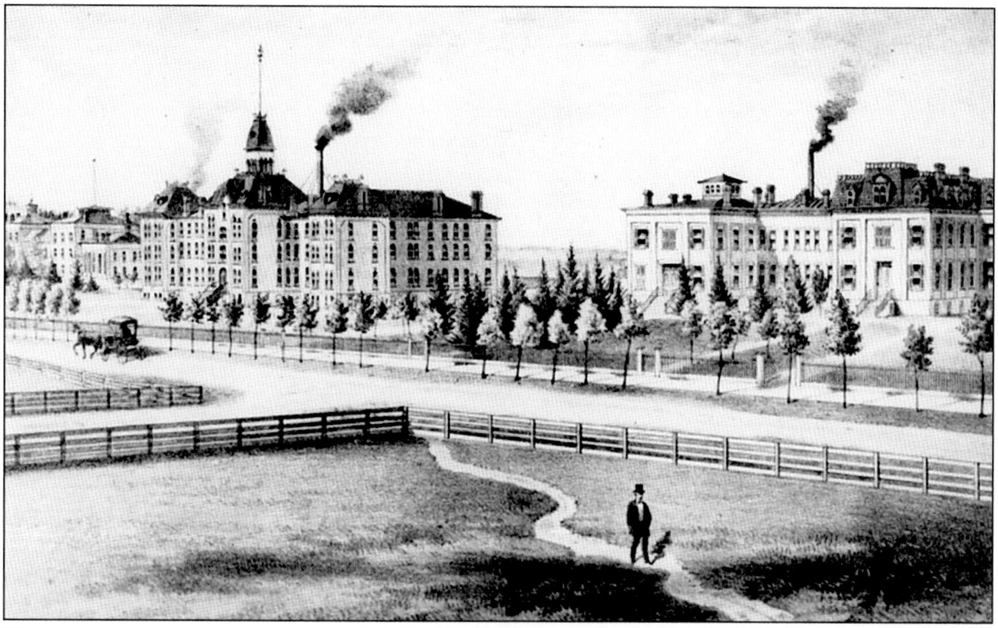

Workhouse, Infirmary, and Insane Asylum. In 1826, a small brick building was built near the corner of South and Highland Avenues, as an almshouse for 75 to 100 people. At the time it was three miles south of the village in West Brighton. Due to the surge in Irish and German paupers, the building was too small by 1859, when nearly two-thirds of the 3,582 residents were given support for poverty caused by alcohol problems. These three buildings were south of the original almshouse. Over 700 people were buried behind the almshouse between 1826 and 1863; 296 remains were reinterred in Mount Hope Cemetery in 1985. This serene postcard view is from the 1870s. (Courtesy Rochester Psychiatric Center.)

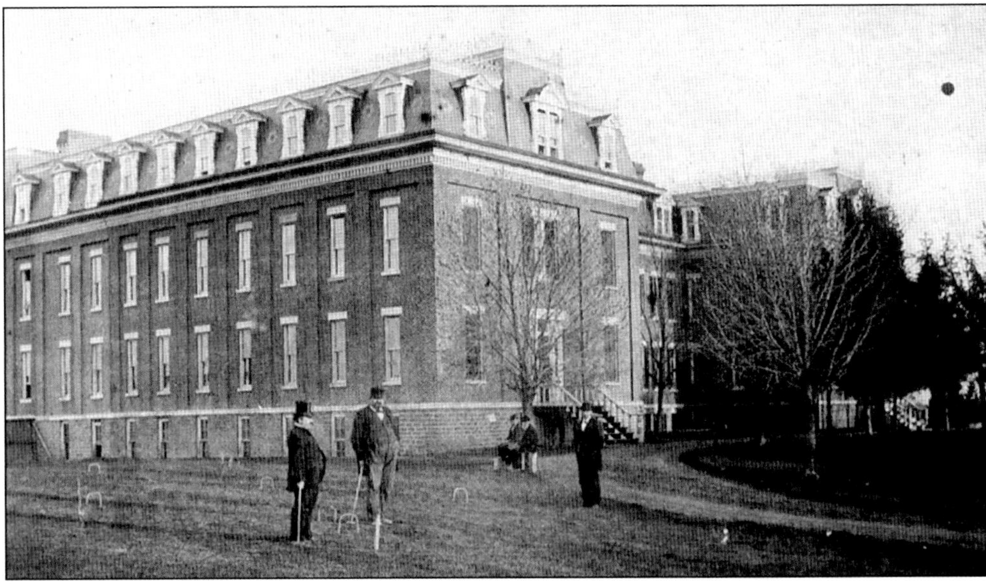

PLAYING CROQUET. This photograph, titled *Men Playing Croquet at Insane Asylum*, was taken sometime between 1872 and 1890 in a building at the southeast corner of South and Highland Avenues. One of them is believed to be the superintendent of the nearby Monroe County Almshouse. Until 1857, the insane were housed in the almshouse. This building was completed in 1872. The Monroe County Insane Asylum was called by that name from 1857 to 1891 when it was renamed Rochester State Hospital. The named changed again to Rochester Psychiatric Center in 1974. (Courtesy Rochester Photo Images.)

OMNIBUSES.

Buffalo Street and West End.

Leaves Arcade at 9 and 10 A. M.; 1:30, 2:30, 4:30 and 6 P. M.

Mount Hope and Penitentiary.

Leaves Arcade at 9 and 10 A. M,; 1:30, 2:30, 4:30 and 6 P. M.

East Avenue and Arcade.

Leaves Arcade at 9 and 11 A. M.; 12:30, 2:30, 4, 5, 6 and 9 P. M

OMNIBUS SCHEDULE. The Monroe County Workhouse opened in 1854 on South Avenue at Highland Avenue. The name changed to the Monroe County Penitentiary in 1858. The Monroe County Penitentiary, Monroe County Poor House, and Monroe County Insane Asylum are all listed in the city directory of 1859. An omnibus ran two times a day earlier in the 1850s, along Mount Hope Avenue to the Monroe County Penitentiary. This schedule was printed in the 1859 city directory. After the penitentiary merged with the county jail and moved downtown to the new civic center in 1971, the building was torn down.

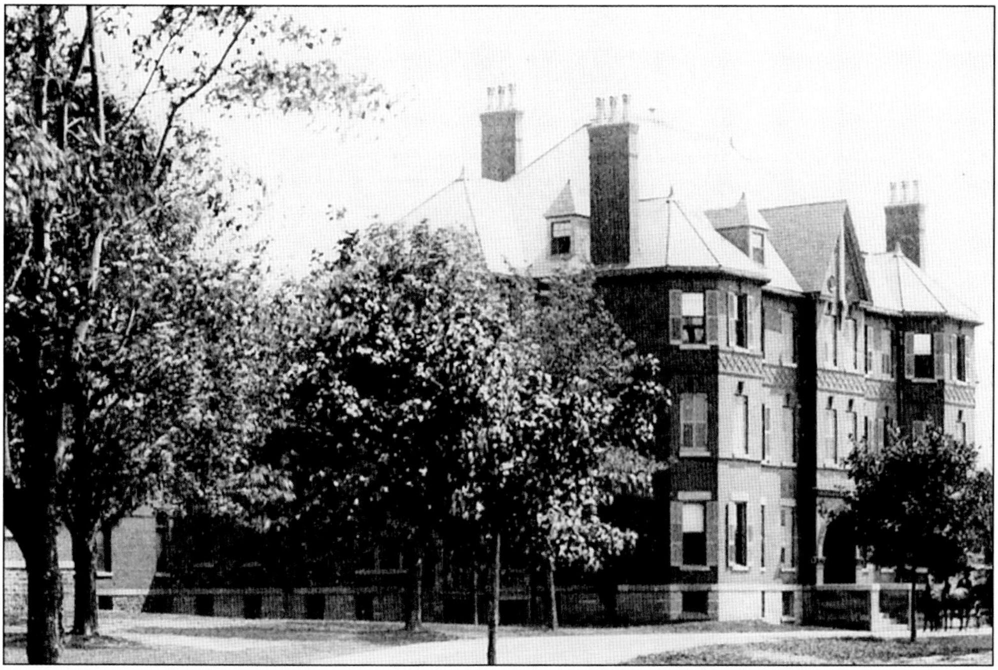

STATE HOSPITAL, 1896. The Monroe County Insane Asylum was founded in 1857 on South Avenue near Elmwood Avenue. It became the Rochester State Hospital in 1891, and it was renamed the Rochester Psychiatric Center in 1974. This photograph was taken by W. H. Parish in 1896. (Courtesy Rochester Photo Images.)

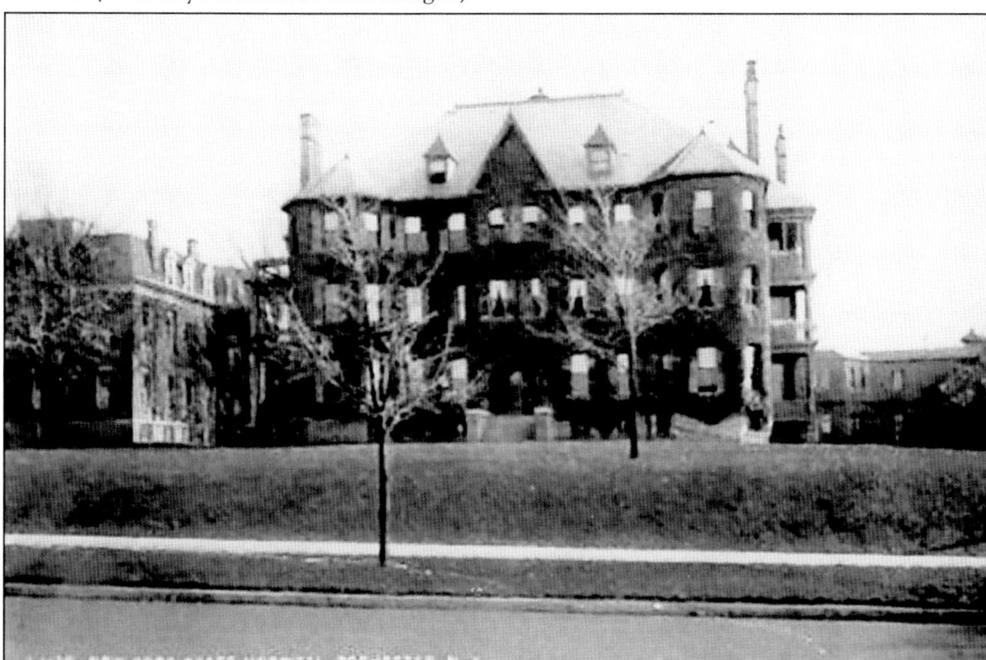

THE MONROE BUILDING. This building, located at the northeast corner of South and Elmwood Avenues, was part of the State Hospital. It is now the location of the Al Sigl Center. (Courtesy Rochester Psychiatric Center.)

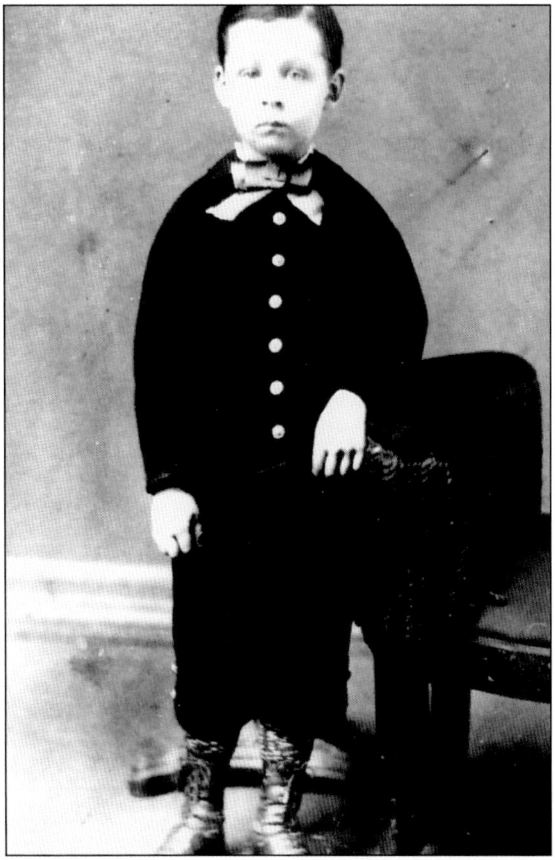

DR. HOWARD. Dr. Eugene H. Howard, (d. 1927) is shown as a boy and later in life, working at his desk in the Monroe Building around 1915 (below). Among his accomplishment during his 42 years at the State Hospital was introducing social services to discharged patients in 1910. (Courtesy Rochester Psychiatric Center.)

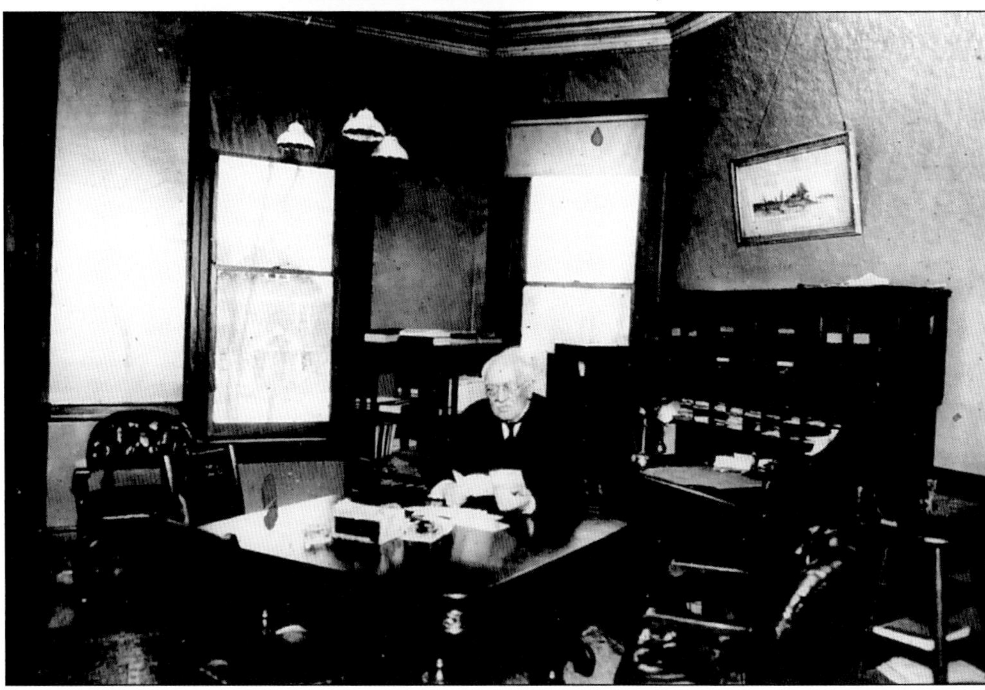

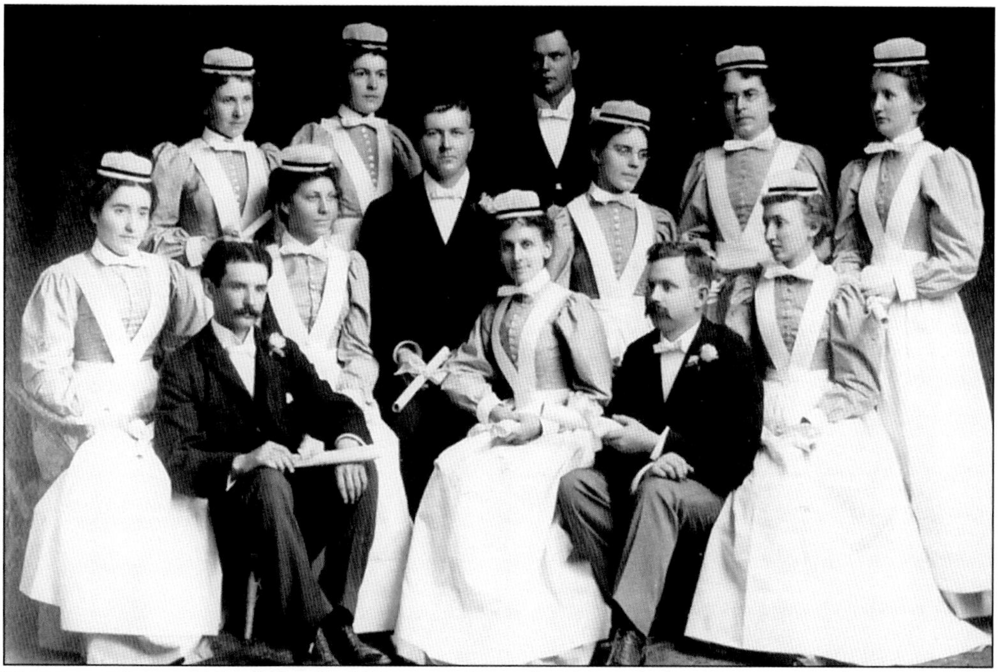

Nursing Class. The School of Nursing class of 1896 includes four men and nine women. (Courtesy Rochester Psychiatric Center.)

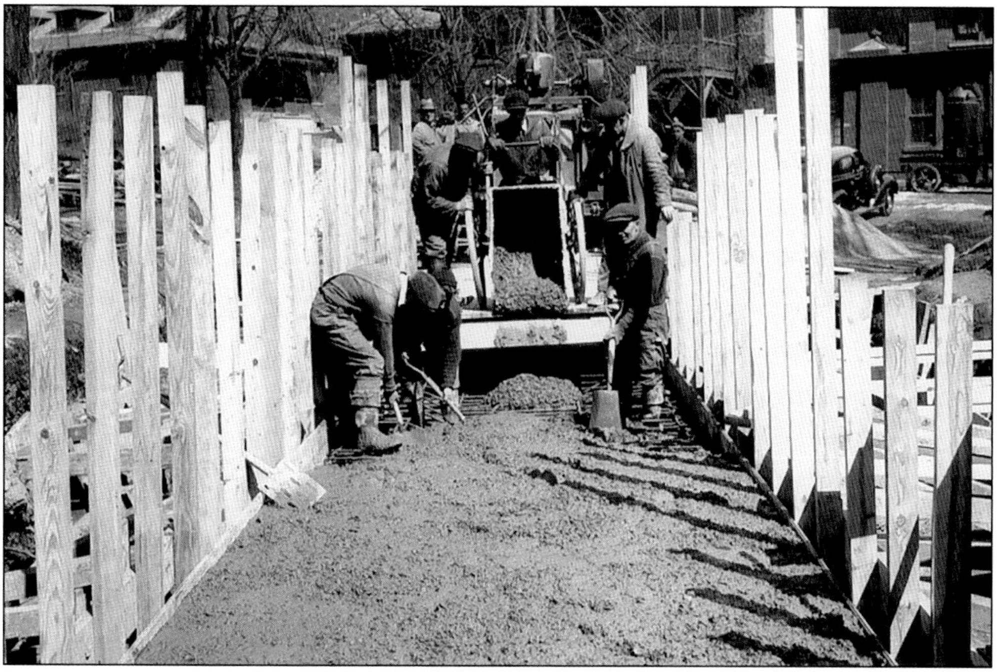

Smoothing the Way. This photographic work record for the city shows men pouring concrete for the Elmwood Avenue underpass April 17, 1938. It may be the underpass that went under Elmwood Avenue from the State Hospital to the Nurses' Dormitory across the street, with State Hospital buildings in the background. (Courtesy City of Rochester Archives.)

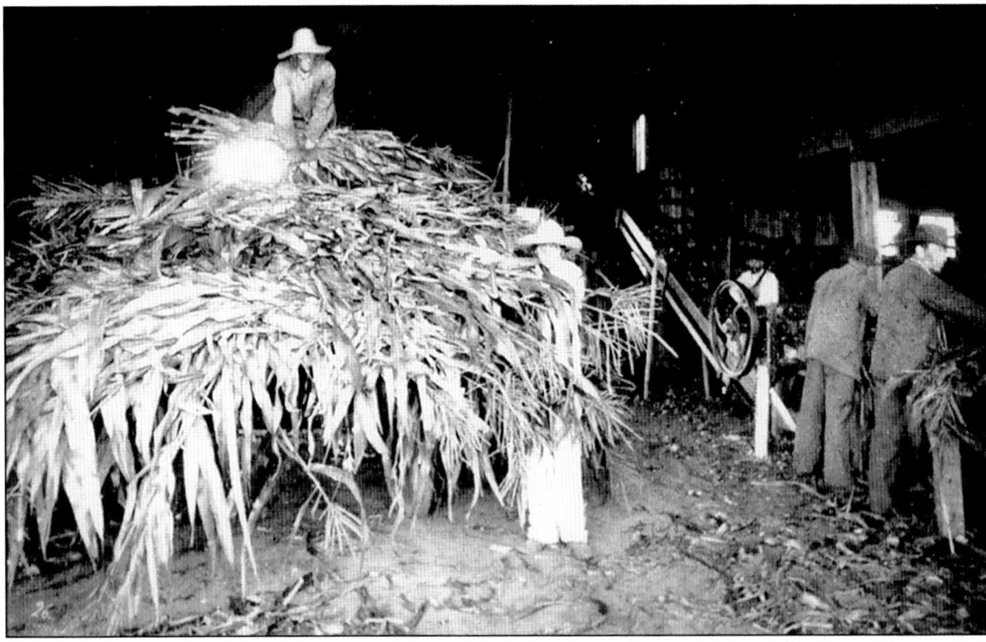

THE BARNS. There were several magnificent brick barns on the grounds of the State Hospital. A group of men work in one of them with "corn for ensilage" in 1898. The second view shows one of the barns today. (Above, courtesy Rochester Psychiatric Center; below, courtesy Al Sigl Center.)

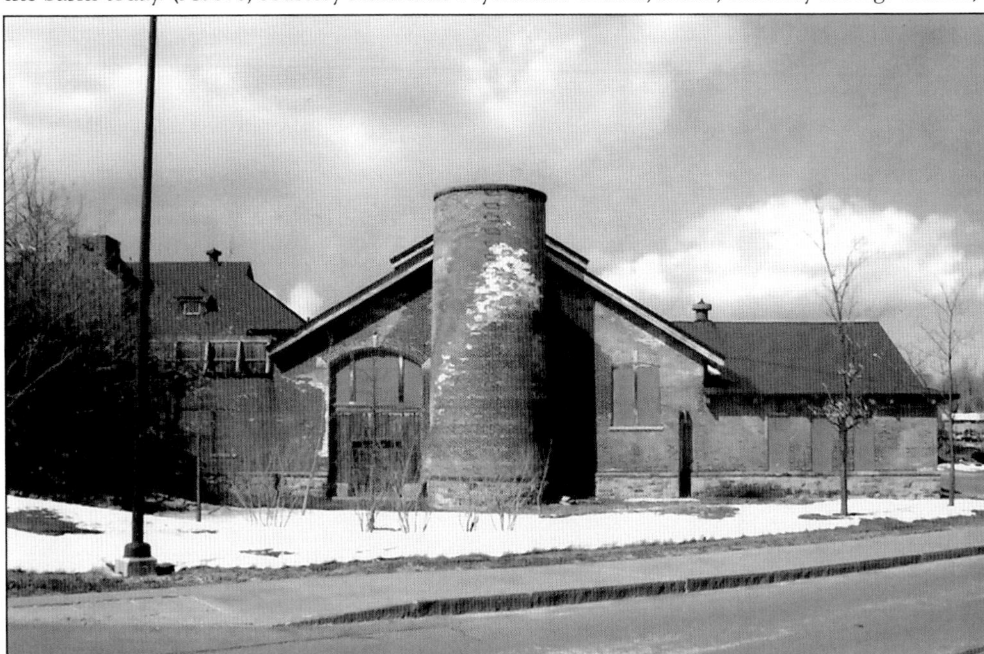

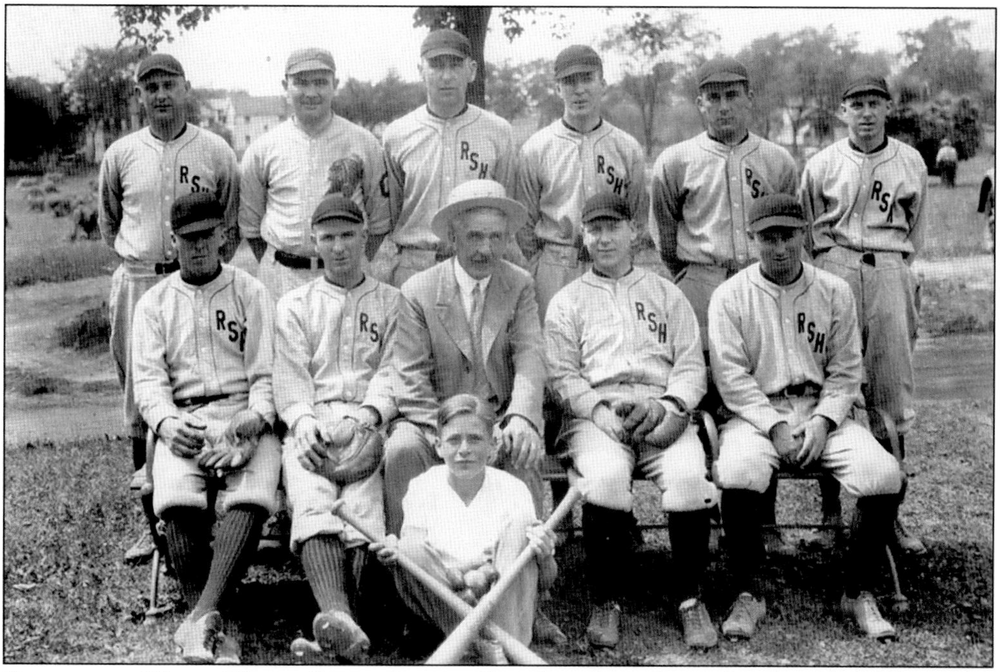

PLAY AFTER WORK. The staff team knows all work and no play makes for a dull fellow. This photograph was taken between 1925 and 1929. Patrick J. McCormack, seated second from the right, later became business director of the State Hospital and lived in the Schnacky Farmhouse near the southeast corner of South and Elmwood Avenues until he retired in 1966. (Courtesy Rochester Psychiatric Center.)

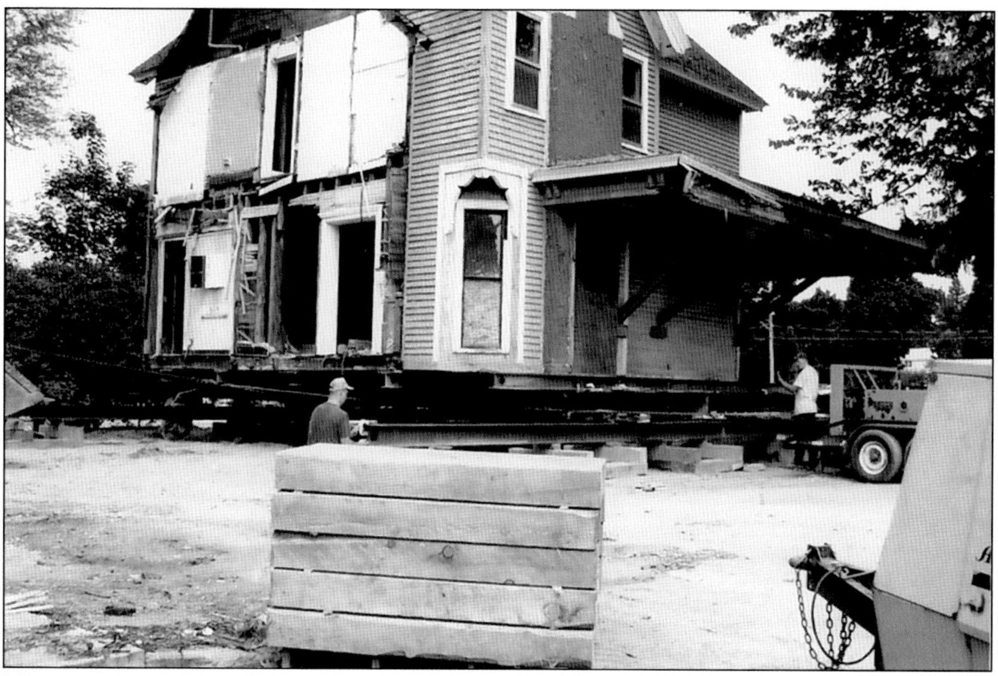

MOVING DAY. The Lathan House, as the Schnacky Farmhouse was later called, was carefully relocated on the property in October 2005. (Courtesy Al Sigl Center.)

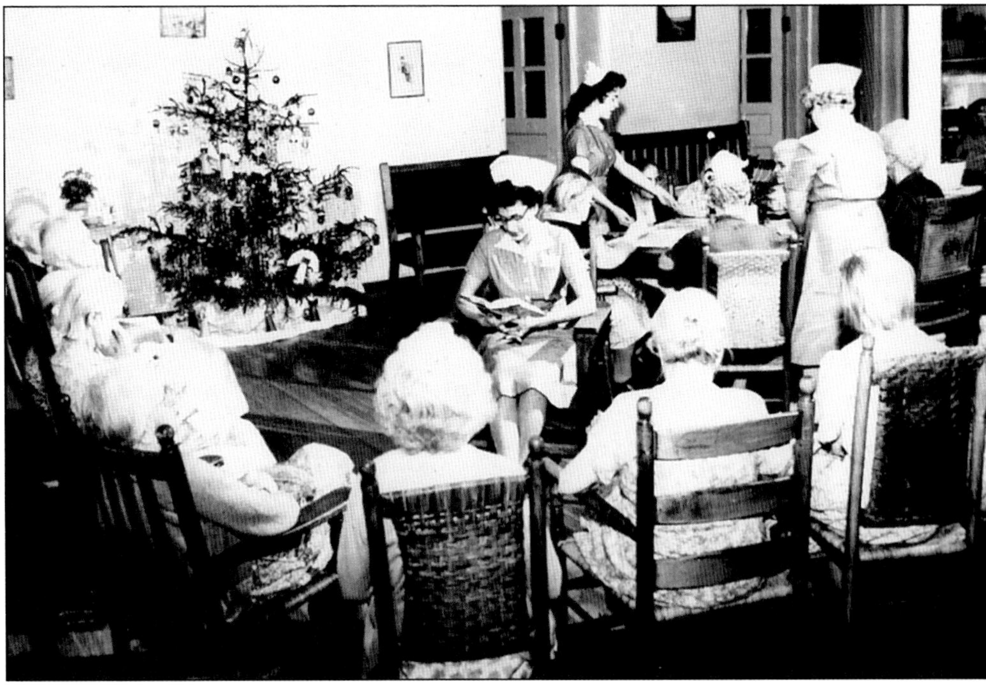

GRAY LADIES. Red Cross volunteers were called Gray Ladies. One reads to elderly women in the women's lounge, gathered near a modest Christmas tree, around 1950. (Courtesy Rochester Psychiatric Center.)

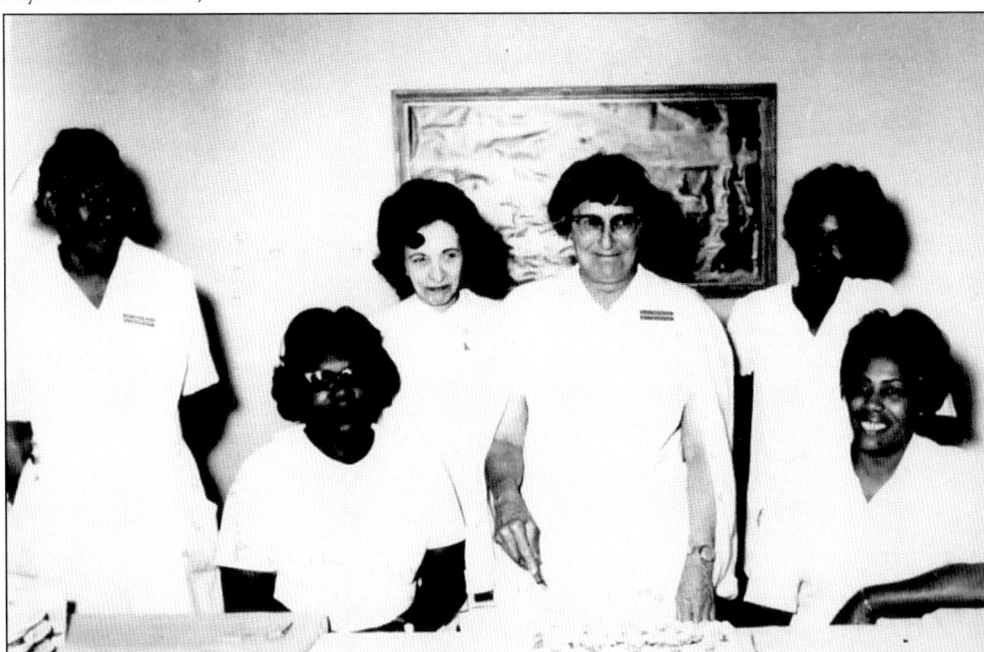

DEDICATED STAFF. This group of female attendants includes the first African American women hired at the State Hospital in the early 1960s. The woman cutting the cake was a popular supervisor in her day. (Courtesy Rochester Psychiatric Center.)

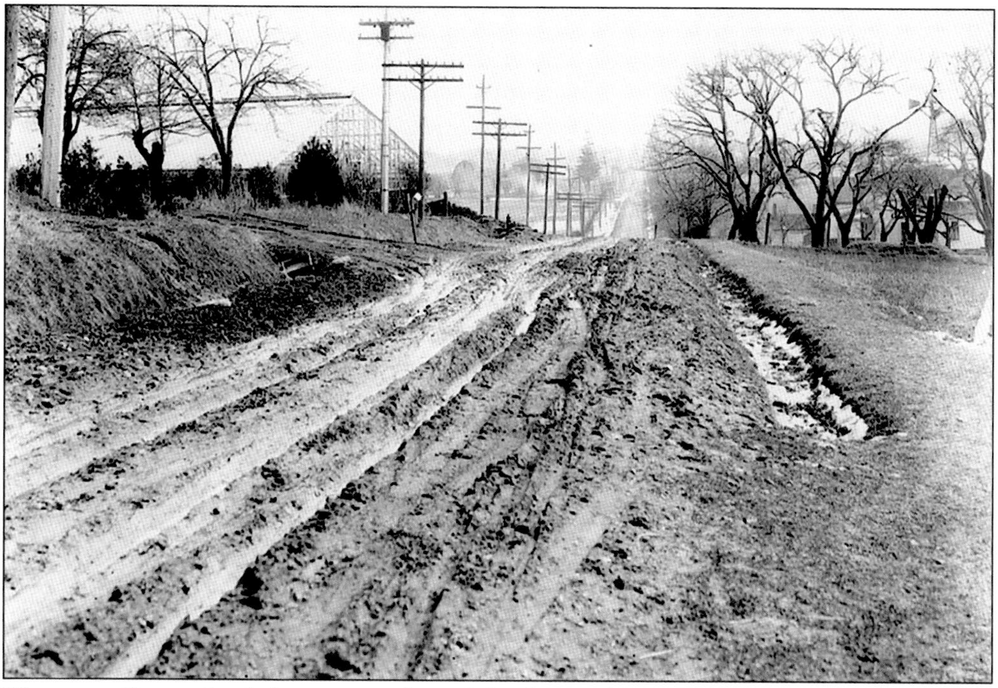

WESTFALL ROAD. April showers may bring May flowers, but in the top Department of Public Works photograph labeled, "Westfall Rd. looking E. of South Ave., April 4, 1924," they brought a ribbon of mud. The greenhouse belonged to Hugo Teute. It may be hard to believe that the bottom photograph, of the same date, is of East Henrietta Road looking north from Westfall Road, but it matches up with early maps from that time. After 1929, the farms on the south side of Westfall Road were owned by the Ganzenhauers. (Courtesy City of Rochester Archives.)

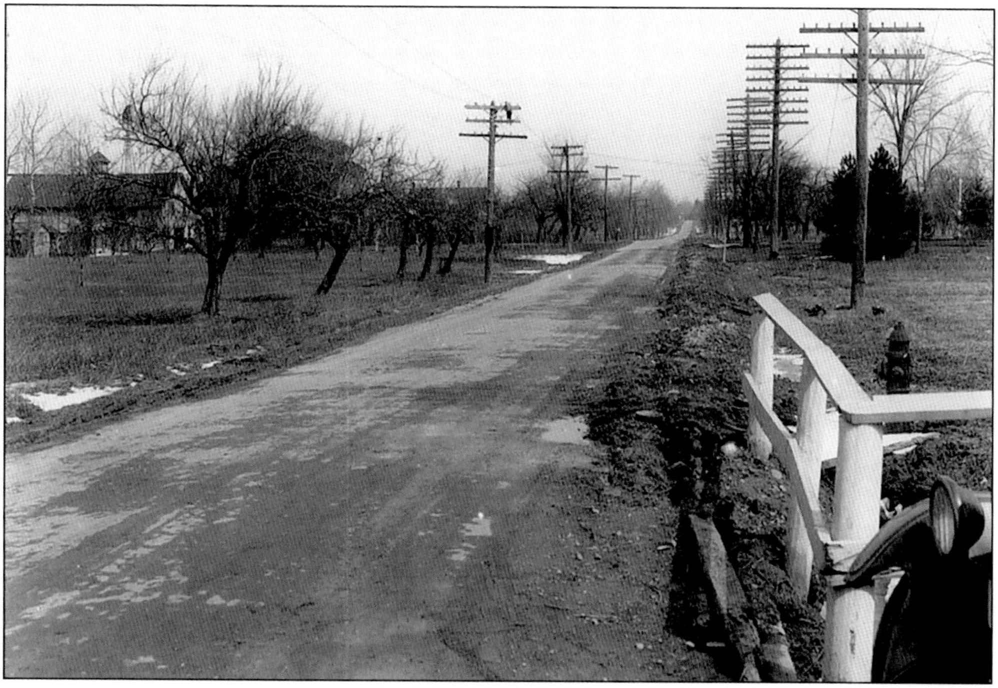

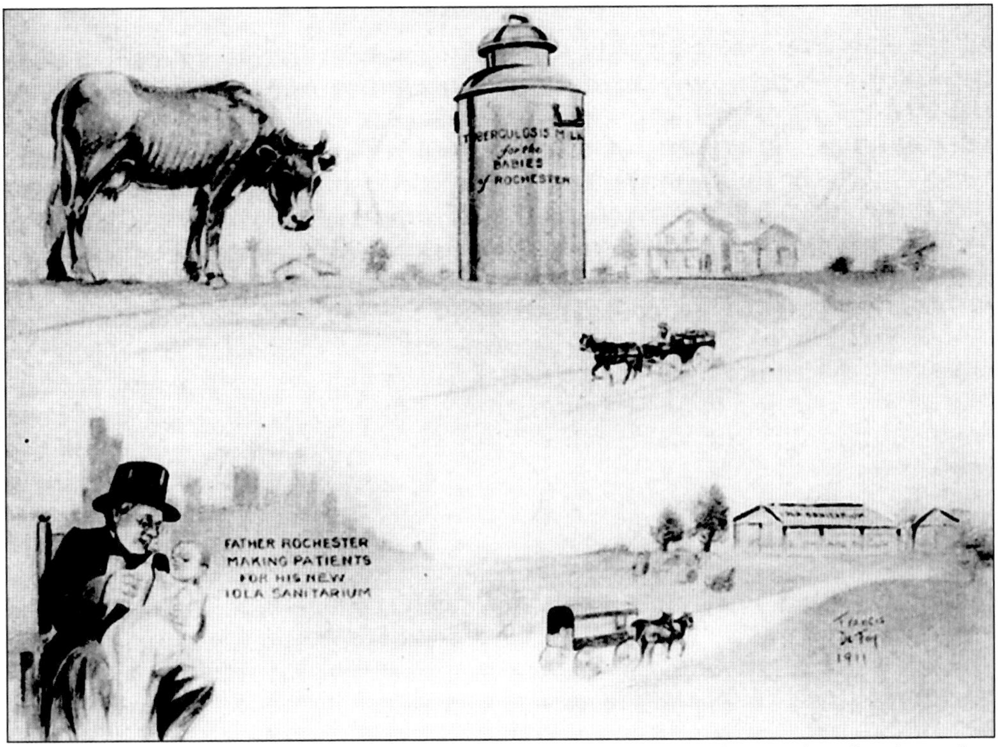

MILK CAMPAIGN. When Father Rochester fed the baby improperly-stored milk, the infant mortality rates were disastrous. This poster came out at the time Iola was built. George Goler (1864–1940) became a Board of Health inspector in 1892 and chief health officer in 1896. His supporters formed the Public Health Association in 1896 to combat the "white plague" of tuberculosis. City and county combined their efforts to open the first locally-run TB sanitarium in 1910. Iola Sanitarium was named using an American Indian name meaning "never discouraged." (Courtesy City of Rochester Photo Lab.)

NIGHT PHONE	NIGHT PHONE	DAIRY PHONE
Genesee 6271	Culver 2365J	Genesee 531

Tomorrow NOV 24 1928 will be our last early morning delivery. Beginning NOV 25 1928 our delivery will be in the fore-noon instead of early morning.

We would appreciate you paying your Bills to our drivers. Thanking you for your patronage.

BOWKER DAIRY

TRY OUR FRESH CHURNED BUTTERMILK

BOWKER BUTTERMILK. This delivery card dated tomorrow as November 24, 1928, and notified customers at 191 Crittenden Boulevard of a change in the delivery time from early morning to forenoon. It came to light in 2003, during renovations in the house that was built about 1920, when the new owners found it behind wainscoting in the kitchen. (Courtesy Robert Good and Susan Schickler.)

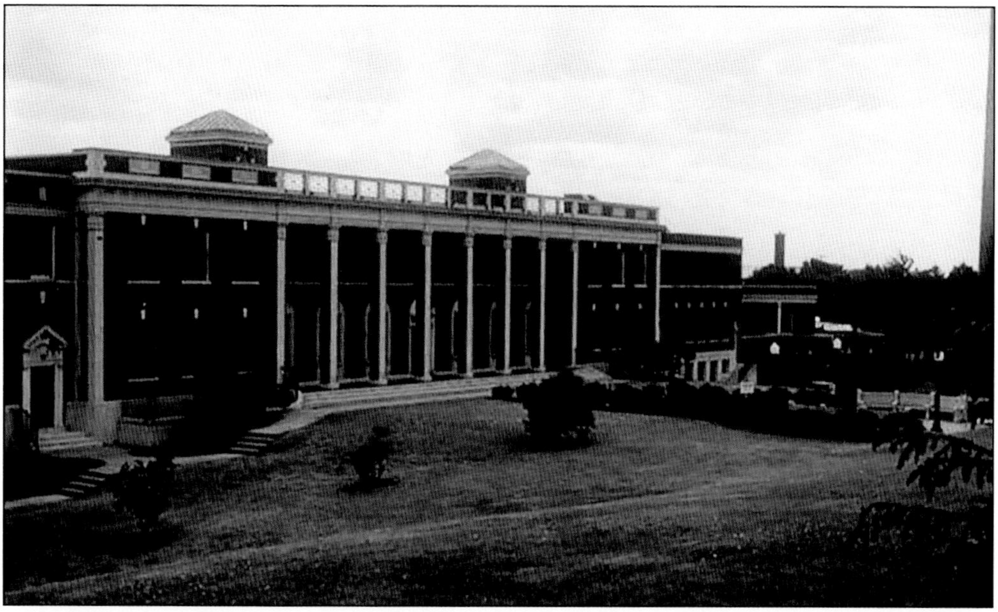

IOLA CHILDREN'S BUILDING. The Infirmary at Iola was built in 1915 and was part of the Iola complex on East Henrietta and Westfall Roads. The sanatorium closed in 1964 and was torn down in 1985. When the Children's Building, shown in 1966, was built in 1927, it was the largest sanatorium in New York. The building closed in 1963. (Courtesy Rochester Photo Images.)

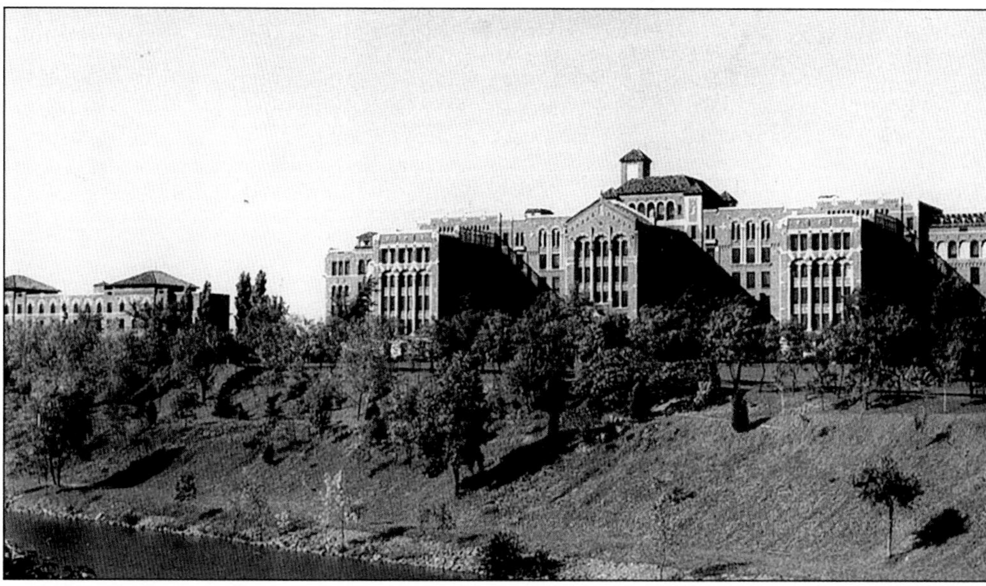

COUNTY HOSPITAL. The first county hospital was built on South Avenue in 1903, near the Monroe County Almshouse, to continue the work of the almshouse with the indigent sick. The county commissioned Siegmund Firestone to design and oversee the construction of a new facility on East Henrietta Road at Westfall Road. Construction began in 1931, hiring all local contractors whose workers used to cool off in the nearby Barge Canal. One of Firestone's assistants was Thomas Boyde Jr. (1907–1981), an architectural student and draftsman who became the first African American architect in this community. This photograph was made into a postcard. (Courtesy Josh Canfield.)

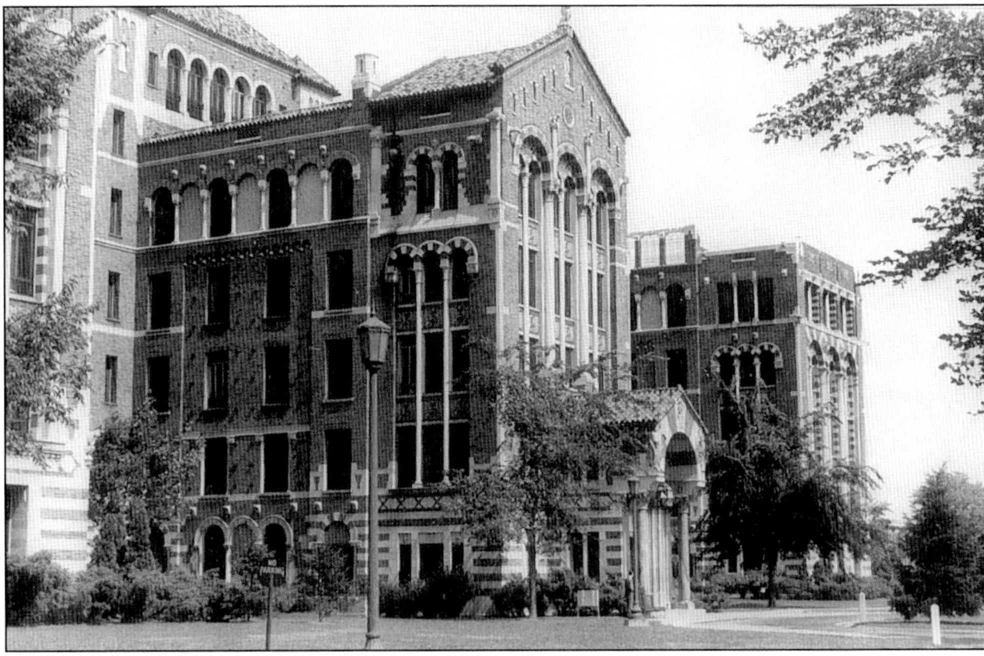

DETAILS, DETAILS. Monroe Community Hospital is famous for the amazing architectural details throughout the building. Over the years, it has shaken off its poorhouse heritage and gained a national reputation as one of the top 10 long-term care facilities for quality of resident and patient care. (Courtesy Josh Canfield.)

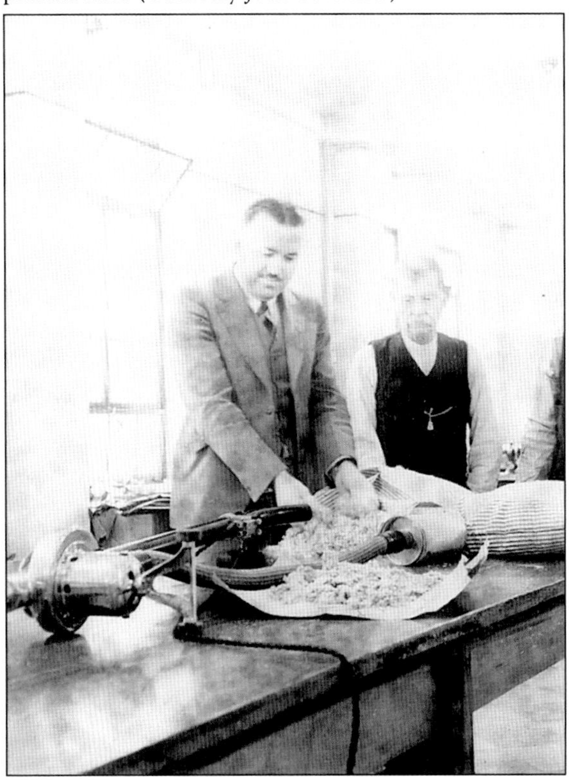

AIR-WAY RENOVATOR. This photograph, taken at the Monroe County Infirmary in March 1934, shows two men using the new Air-Way Renovator to extract dirt from pillows. It was made into a postcard. (Courtesy Josh Canfield.)

Eight

Around South Clinton Avenue

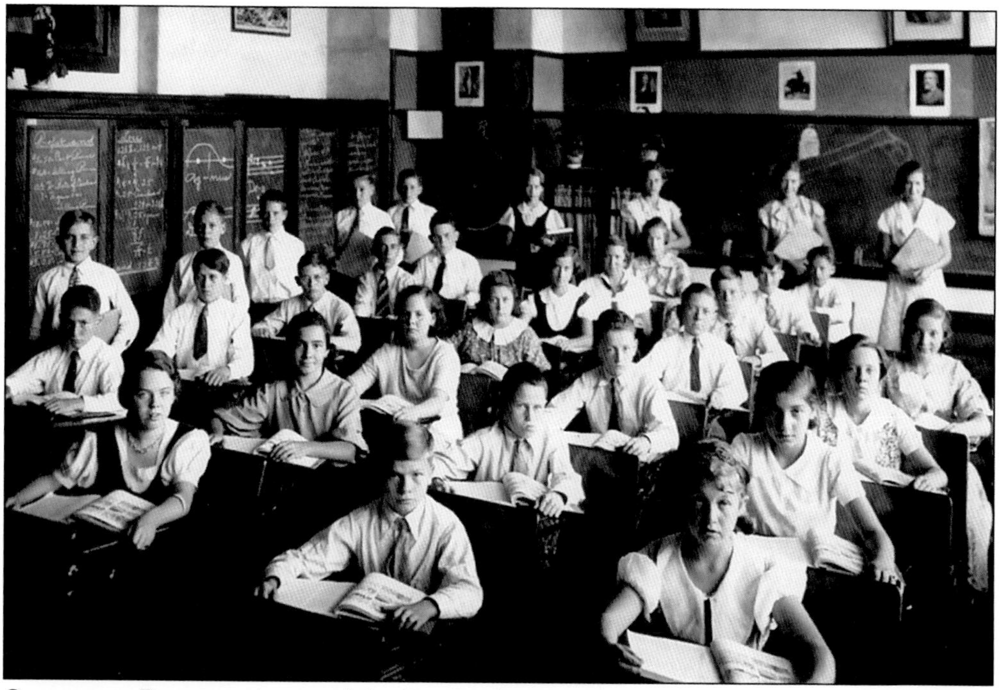

Classroom Picture. A young John Reinhardt is seated second on the left by the blackboard at St. Boniface School, around 1930. (Courtesy Bernice Reinhardt.)

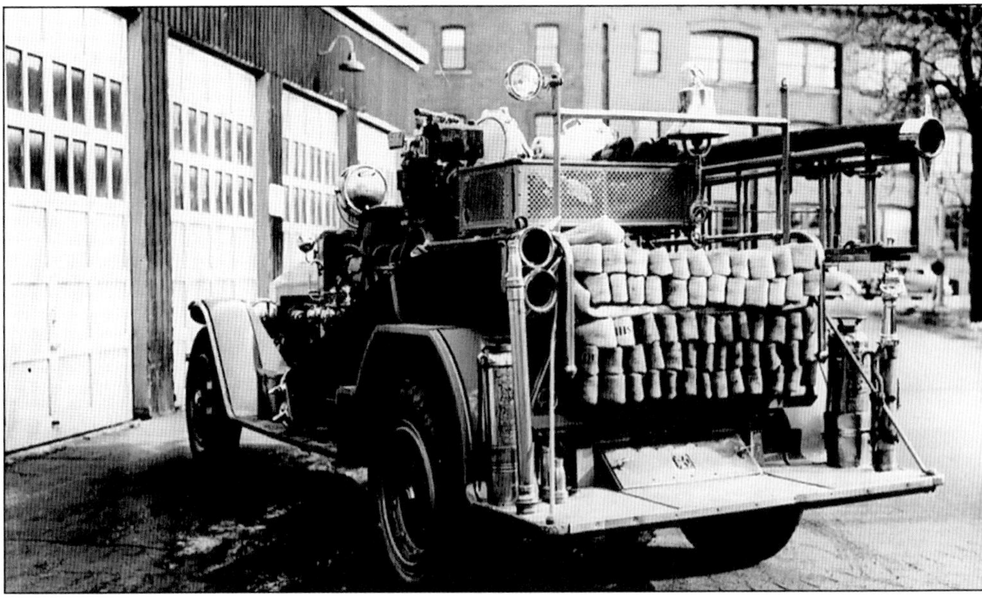

HOSE CAR. This fire department hose car is shown, from the rear of a garage on Byron Street, in 1938. The Max Lowenthal building is in the background. Pinnacle Street was changed to South Clinton Avenue when the trolley lines were electrified and extended to the city line in 1893. Gregory Street, which ends in South Clinton Avenue, was most likely named for James H. Gregory, a farmer with a home listed at Spring Farm, Fourth Ward, in the 1844 city directory, and at Nelson near Cayuga Street (Meigs Street and South Clinton Avenue) in 1845 and 1847. (Courtesy Rochester Photo Images.)

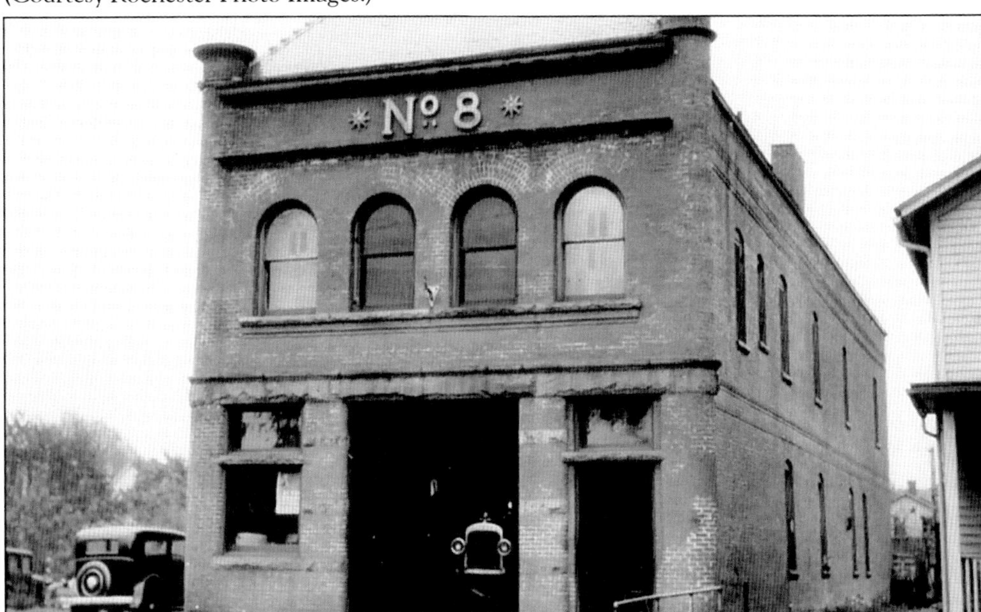

ENGINE NO. 8. Engine House No. 8 is first listed in the 1861 city directory at West Alexander Street. The fire station is listed at 357 Gregory Street in the 1902 directory and remained there until 1957 when it merged with Truck House No. 8 on South Avenue at Pavilion Street. This photograph was taken in 1935. (Courtesy City of Rochester Photo Lab.)

SOLEMN VOWS. Florence Servatius, who lived on Cayuga Street and Mount Vernon Avenue, married Anthony Scheible on February 4, 1919, at St. Boniface Church. (Courtesy Bernice Reinhardt.)

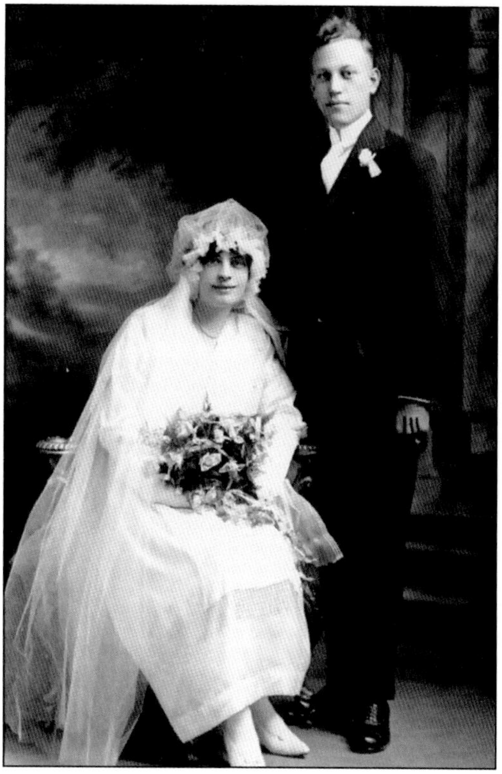

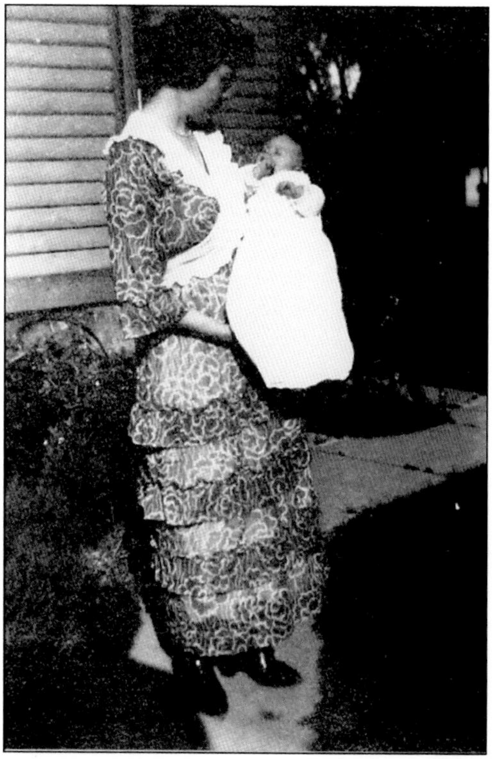

NEW BABY. Florence Scheible holds her new daughter Bernice, age two months, in August 1920. (Courtesy Bernice Reinhardt.)

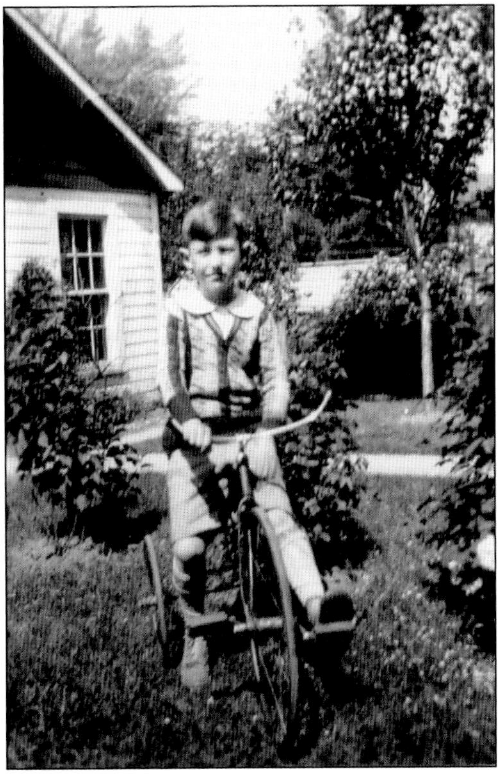

Out in the Sun. John Reinhardt looks ready to roll on a large tricyle in the backyard on Mulberry Street. (Courtesy Bernice Reinhardt.)

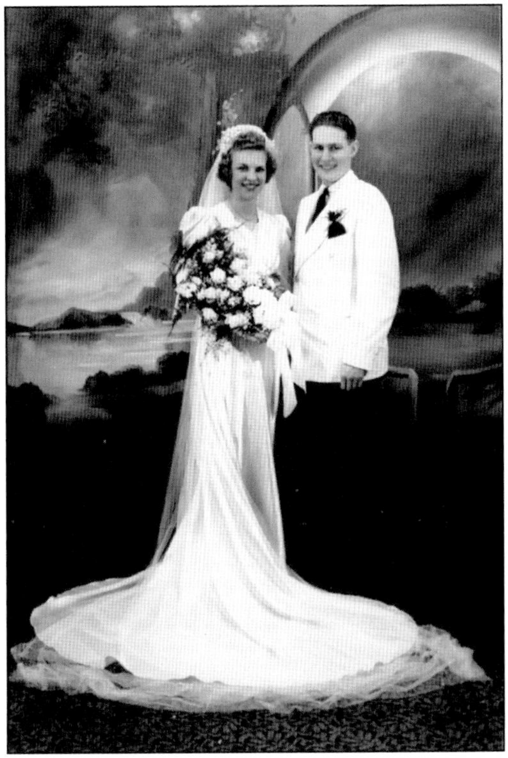

Orange Blossoms. Bernice Scheible married John Reinhardt at St. Boniface Church on June 14, 1942. She used her mother's head band of wax orange blossoms with a new veil. Bernice and John lived at 7 Mount Vernon Avenue for four years, and eventually had seven children; six went to St. Boniface School. (Courtesy Bernice Reinhardt.)

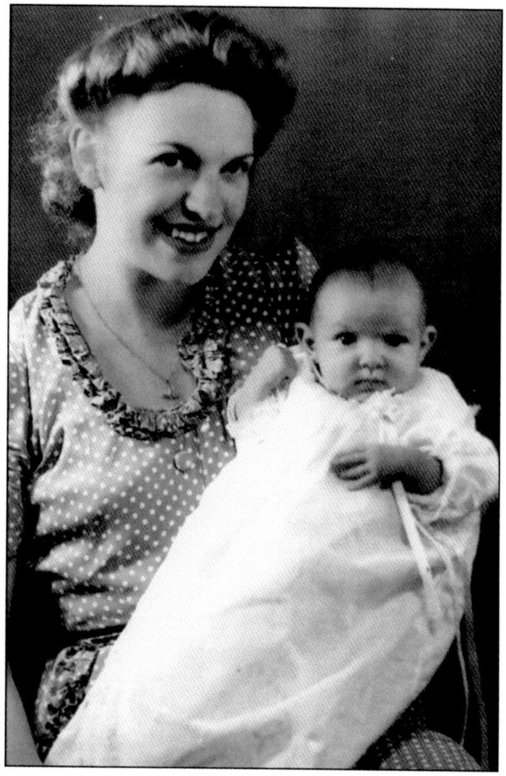

PRECIOUS DAUGHTER. Bernice Reinhardt holds her new daughter Maryann, in a christening gown, in 1944. (Courtesy Bernice Reinhardt.)

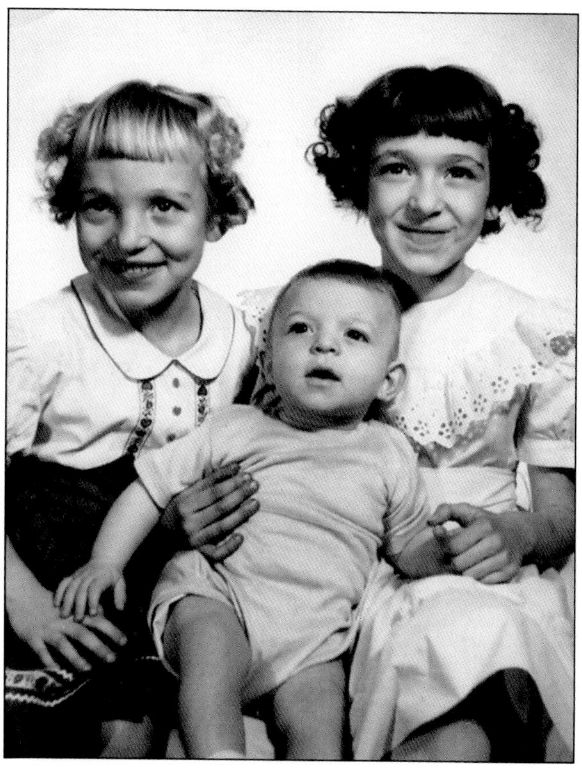

NEW BROTHER. Jeanne and Maryann Reinhardt smile sweetly for the camera, while their new brother John is captivated by the photographer. The caption on the back says, "Childhood Studios, 'Art in Children's Portraits' 430 East Main St. Rochester 4, N.Y." (Courtesy Bernice Reinhardt.)

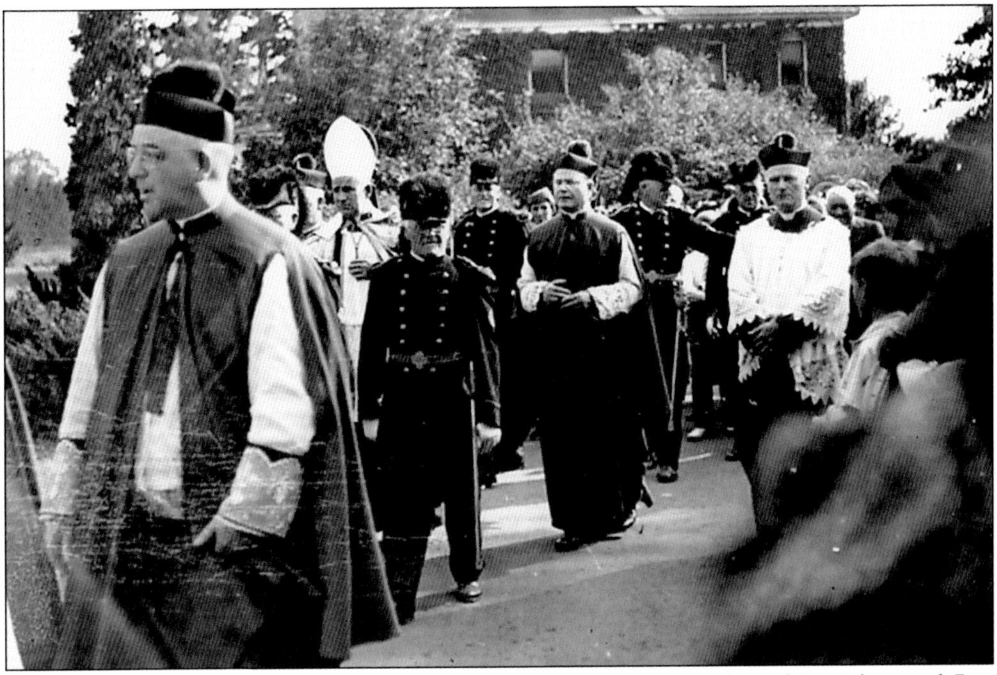

OLD COUNTRY TRADITION. The St. Boniface parish priests, Knights of St. John, and Boy Scouts marched to the home of a newly-ordained priest to walk him back to his first mass at his home parish on the first Sunday in June, closest to the feast of St. Boniface. These views from around 1950 are near Mulberry Street. The little girl below is Maryann Reinhardt with her grandmother, Clara Reinhardt. (Courtesy Bernice Reinhardt.)

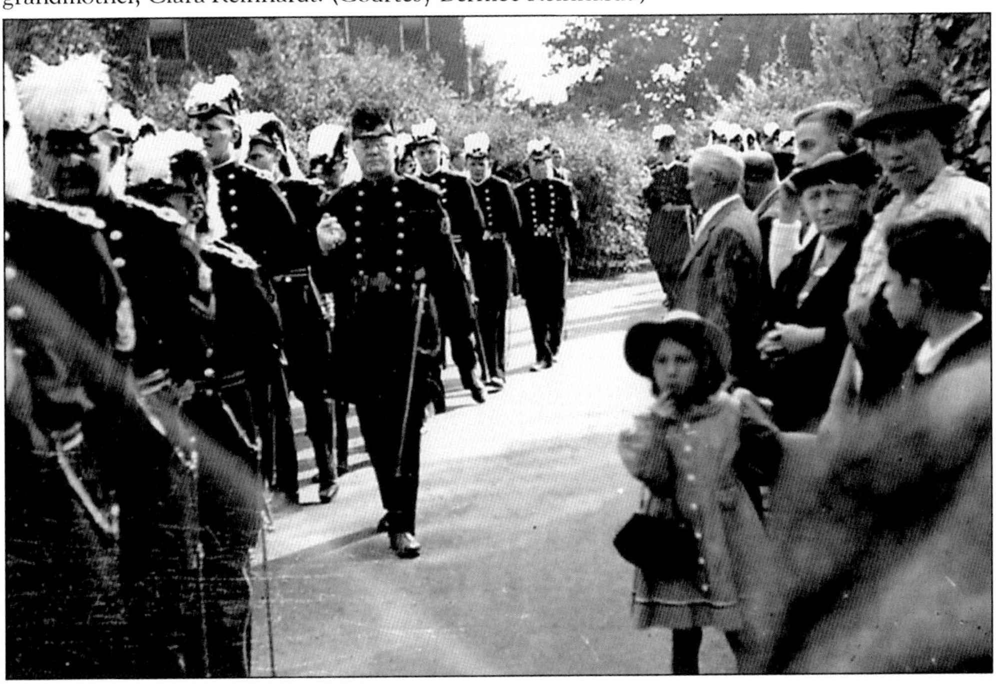

THE PATRIARCH. Joseph Langenbacher Sr. (1825–1911) poses by a fruit tree in the backyard of the family homestead on Caroline and Seager Streets. He came over from Alsace Lorraine and worked as a stone mason on the building of St. Boniface Church. His 83rd birthday celebration was written up in the paper in 1908. (Courtesy Agnes Coon.)

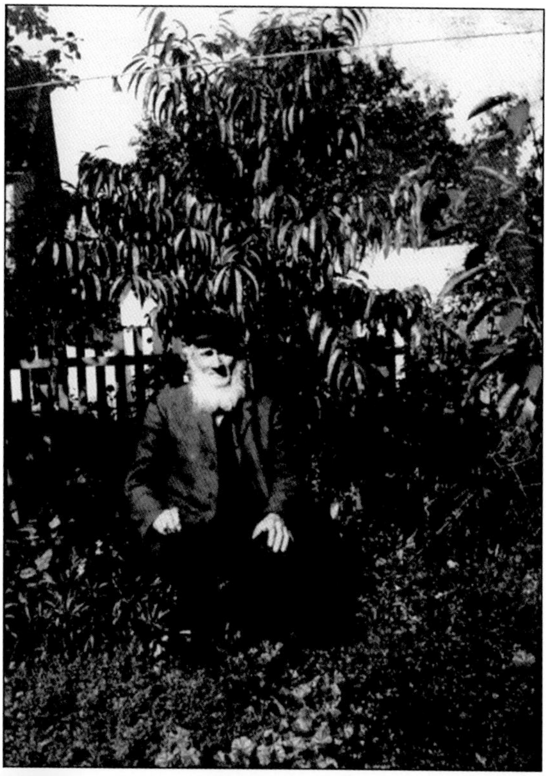

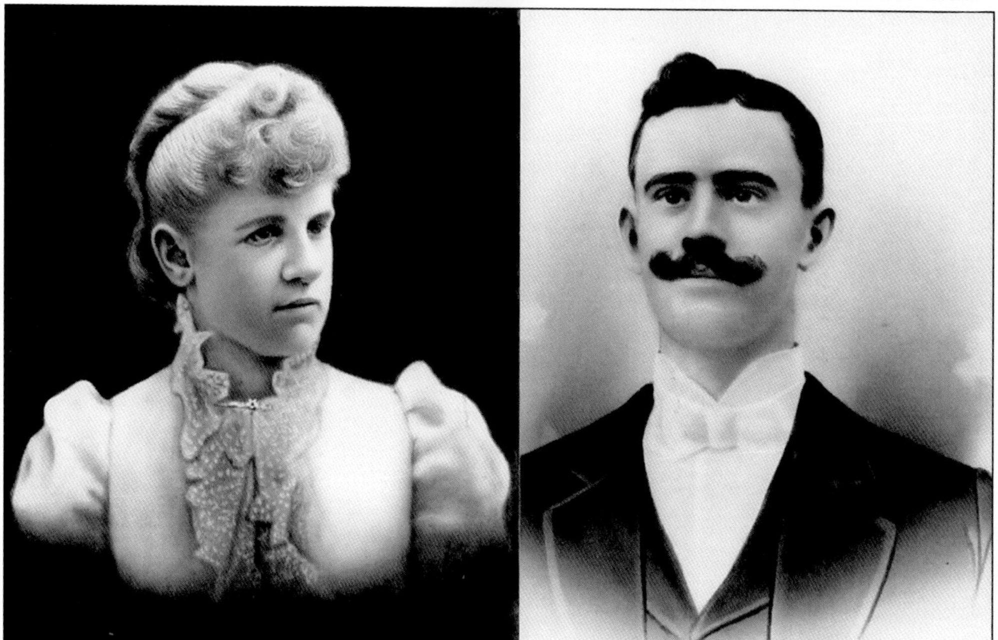

WEDDING DAY. Catherine "Kate" Garney and Joseph Langenbacher were married on June 21, 1894. They first lived on Henrietta Street, then Mount Vernon Avenue and Cayuga Street. Her father, Christian Garney, owned a blacksmith and tailor shop on South Clinton Avenue next to the building at the southwest corner of Meigs Street. (Courtesy Agnes Coon.)

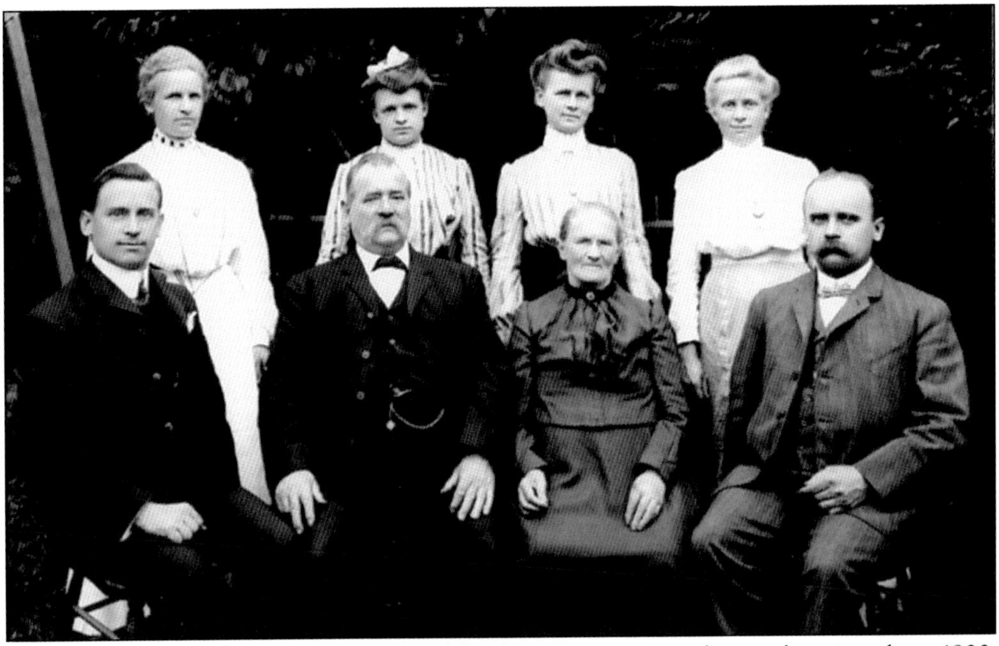

THE GARNEY FAMILY. The family gathered for this picture at an unknown location about 1900. From left to right are (first row) Andrew, Grandpa Christian, Grandma Anna, and George Garney; (second row) Catherine "Kate," Rose, Abby, and Mary. (Courtesy Agnes Coon.)

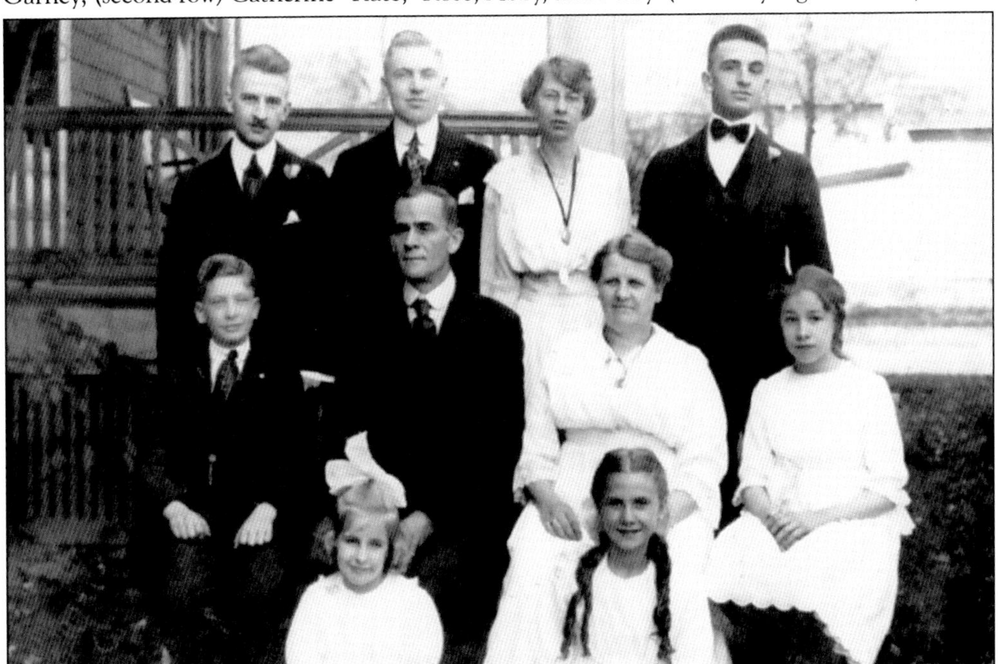

NO. 7 CAYUGA. After their rent on Mount Vernon Avenue rose from $1 to $5 a month, the Langenbachers decided to buy their own home. The family poses outside 7 Cayuga Street around 1915. From left to right are (first row) Lillian and Zita; (second row) Earl, Joseph Jr., Catherine, and Beatrice; (third row) George, Walter, Margaret (Agnes's mother), and Charles (a drummer in vaudeville). (Courtesy Agnes Coon.)

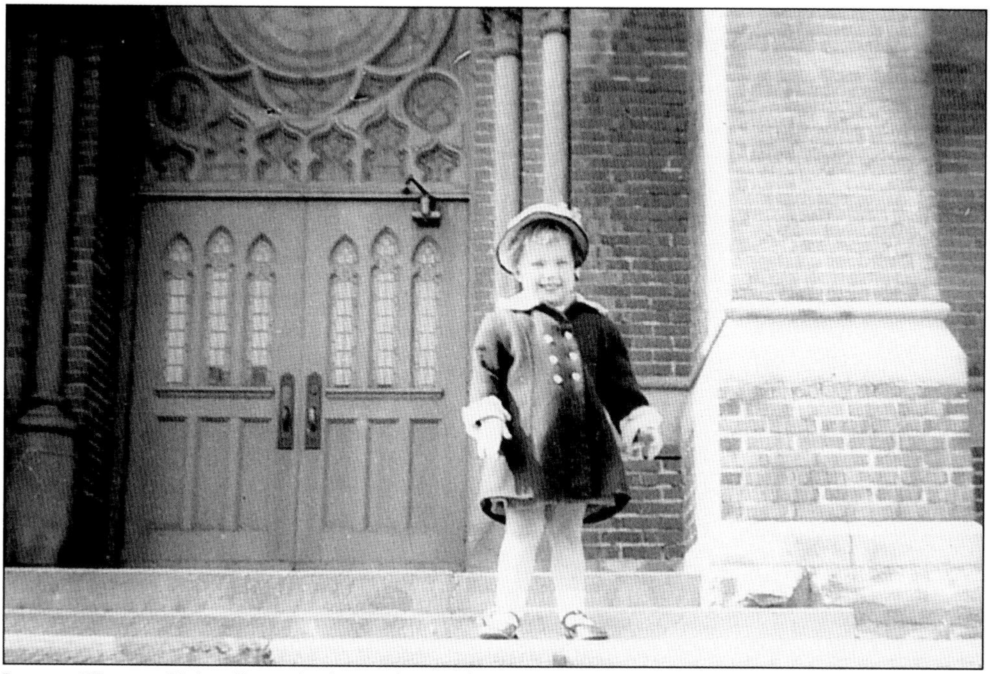

Little Helen. Helen Bayer looks ready to take on the world with a smile, from the steps of the old St. Boniface Church, at age 3 around 1953. The Bayer family homestead was on the corner of Oakland and Linden Streets. In 2005, Helen Bayer Hogan became executive director of the South East Area Coalition, which her parents helped found in 1981. (Courtesy Martha and Billy Yatteau.)

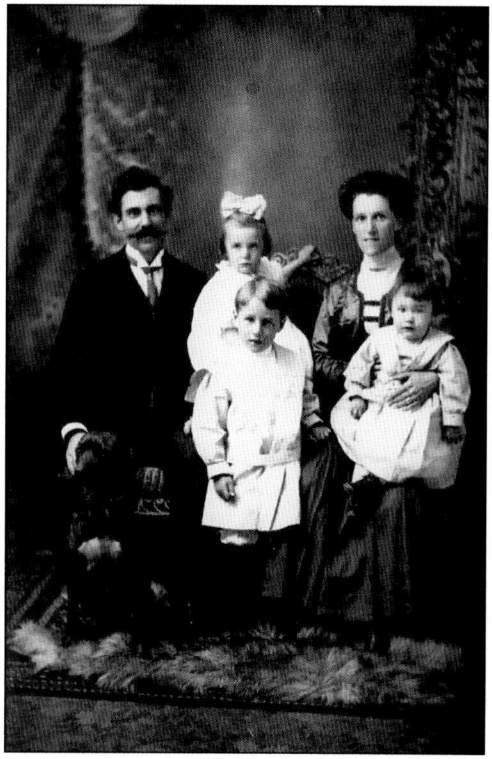

The Epple Family. How did Tom Leavitt's great-grandfather Alois Epple keep the dog still for this family portrait? Next to the dog from left to right are (front row) great-uncle Richard and great-uncle Henry on his mother's lap; (second row) Alois, young Grandma Rose, and Caroline Aman Epple. Alois was a stone cutter who carved the altar at St. Boniface Church. He is listed as a machinist in the 1915 city directory at 410 Linden Street. According to the family, Caroline, who died in 1982 at age 93, was the last of eight sets of twins out of 17 children in the extended family. (Courtesy Tom Leavitt.)

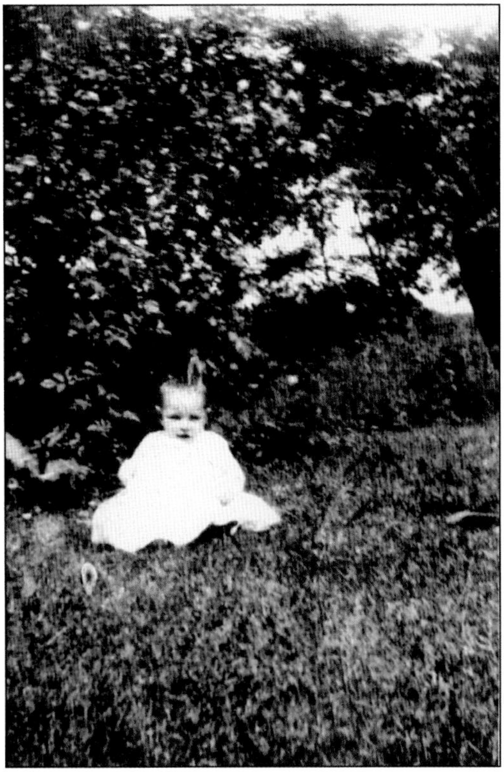

BABY WALT. The back of the top photograph reads, "Walter Leavitt, Slater Freich Farms, Rochester, NY, Latta Road and Dewey Ave." The bottom was made into a postcard. (Courtesy Tom Leavitt.)

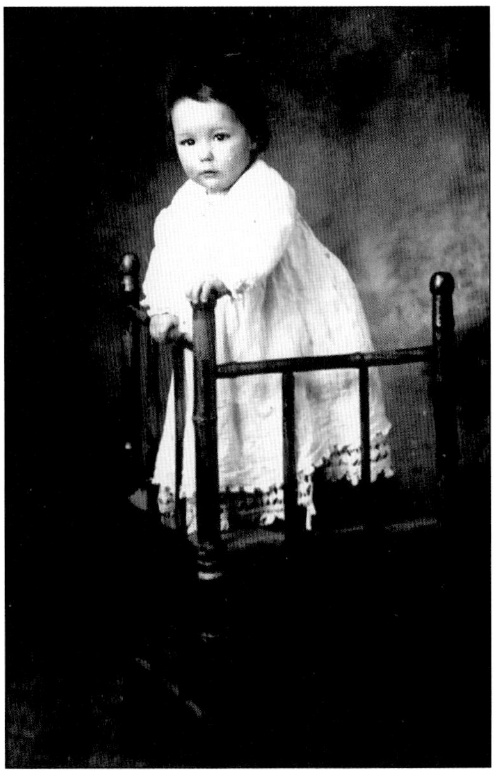

GRANDMA ROSE AND HER DAUGHTER. Maryanne Epple, the only child of Grandma Rose Epple, went to St. Boniface School. (Courtesy Tom Leavitt.)

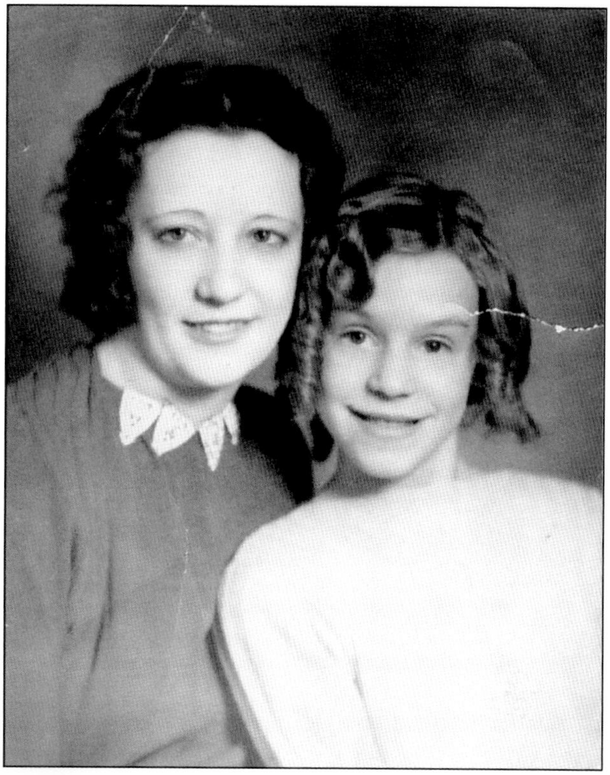

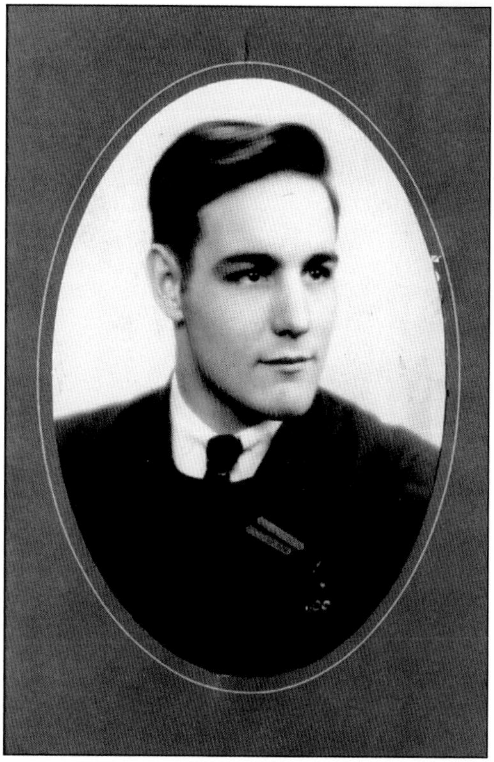

GRADUATION PICTURE. Walt Leavitt was a Seneca-Mohawk-Ojibwe who graduated from Charlotte High School in the 1930s. He married Maryanne Epple. They had two children, Tom and Katherine, who grew up with their Grandma Rose on Linden Street. (Courtesy Tom Leavitt.)

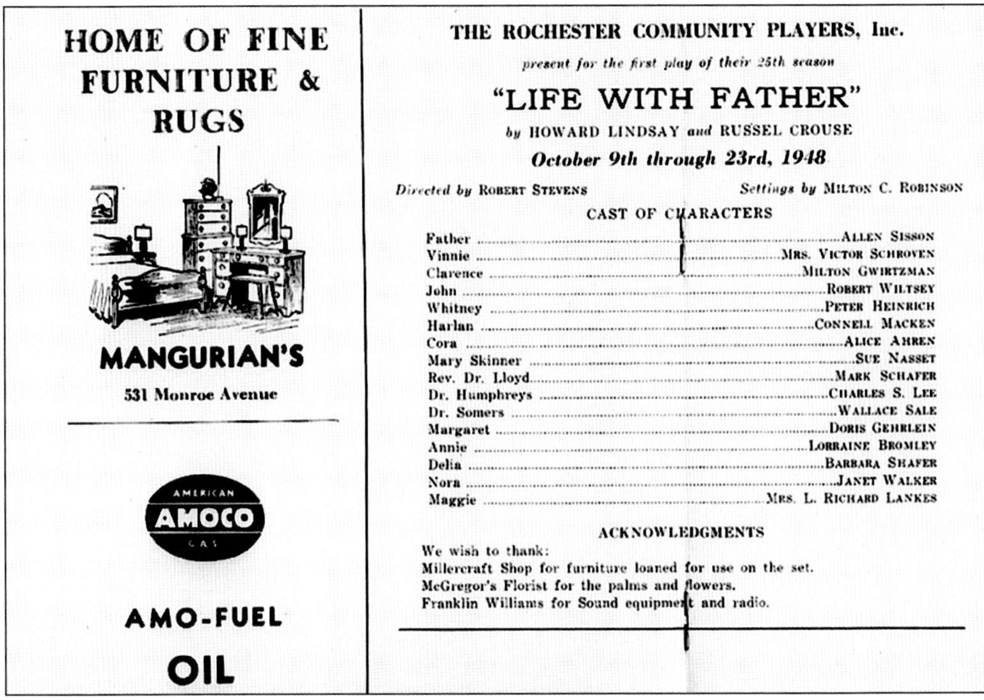

HOME OF FINE FURNITURE & RUGS

MANGURIAN'S

531 Monroe Avenue

AMERICAN AMOCO GAS

AMO-FUEL OIL

THE ROCHESTER COMMUNITY PLAYERS, Inc.

present for the first play of their 25th season

"LIFE WITH FATHER"

by HOWARD LINDSAY *and* RUSSEL CROUSE

October 9th through 23rd, 1948

Directed by Robert Stevens — *Settings by* Milton C. Robinson

CAST OF CHARACTERS

Father	Allen Sisson
Vinnie	Mrs. Victor Schroven
Clarence	Milton Gwirtzman
John	Robert Wiltsey
Whitney	Peter Heinrich
Harlan	Connell Macken
Cora	Alice Ahren
Mary Skinner	Sue Nasset
Rev. Dr. Lloyd	Mark Schafer
Dr. Humphreys	Charles S. Lee
Dr. Somers	Wallace Sale
Margaret	Doris Gehrlein
Annie	Lorraine Bromley
Delia	Barbara Shafer
Nora	Janet Walker
Maggie	Mrs. L. Richard Lankes

ACKNOWLEDGMENTS

We wish to thank:
Millercraft Shop for furniture loaned for use on the set.
McGregor's Florist for the palms and flowers.
Franklin Williams for Sound equipment and radio.

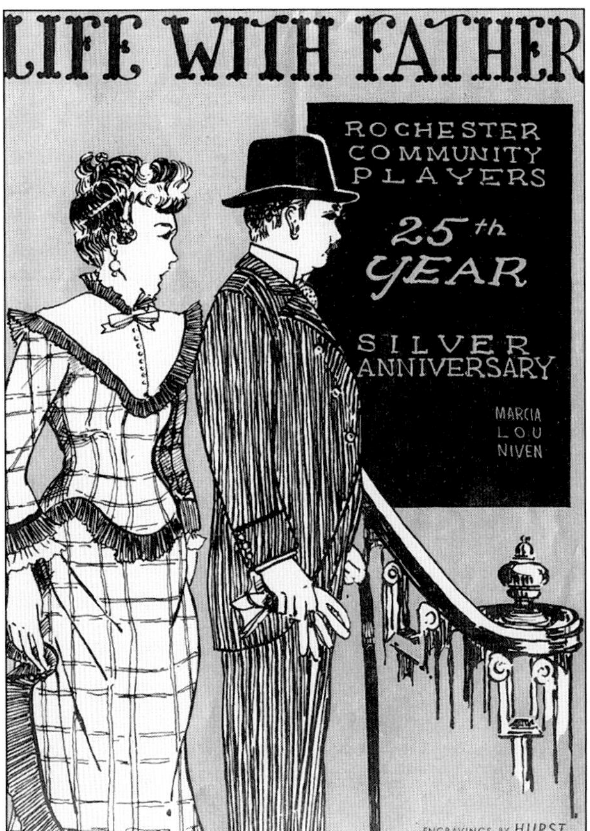

COMMUNITY PLAYERS. After two Baptist students developed a mission station and Sunday School on Sanford Street, the Second German Baptist Church was built on (then) Pinnacle Street at Meigs Street in 1890. The non-profit Rochester Community Players bought the building on South Clinton Avenue around 1924, used it until 1974, and moved back for a time in 1980. This play bill for *Life with Father* was from October 1948. (Courtesy Donovan A. Shilling.)

ST. PATRICK CEMETERY. This picture of the Bradley family monument was taken in 1935, just before the St. Patrick Cemetery was closed. The photographer was Bunnell Commercial Photo of 21 Bly Street. The most notable burial is that of Civil War hero Col. Patrick Henry O'Rorke who died at the Battle of Gettysburg in July 1863. His widow buried him at the Pinnacle Hill Catholic Cemetery. St. Patrick Catholic Church moved the first graves from behind their church to Pinnacle Hill in 1838. Remaining burials were moved to Holy Sepulchre in 1935. (Courtesy Diocese of Rochester.)

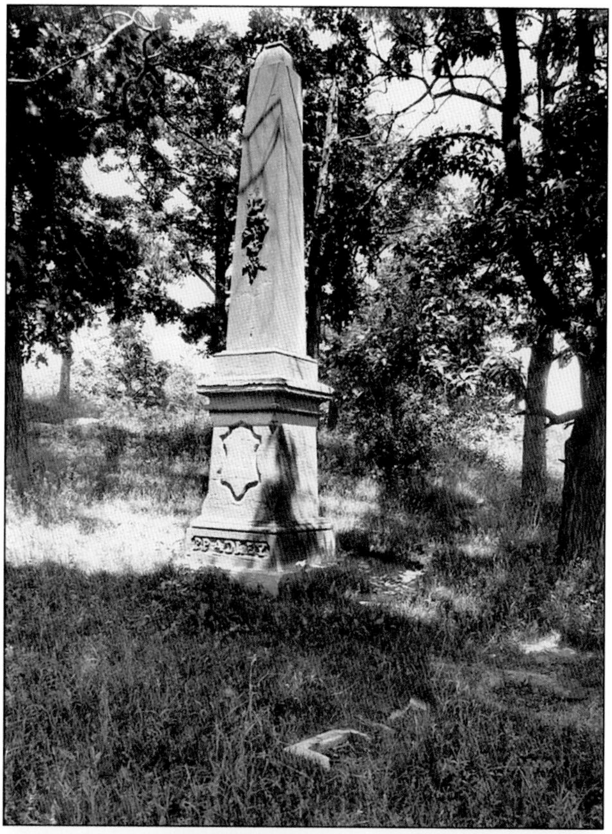

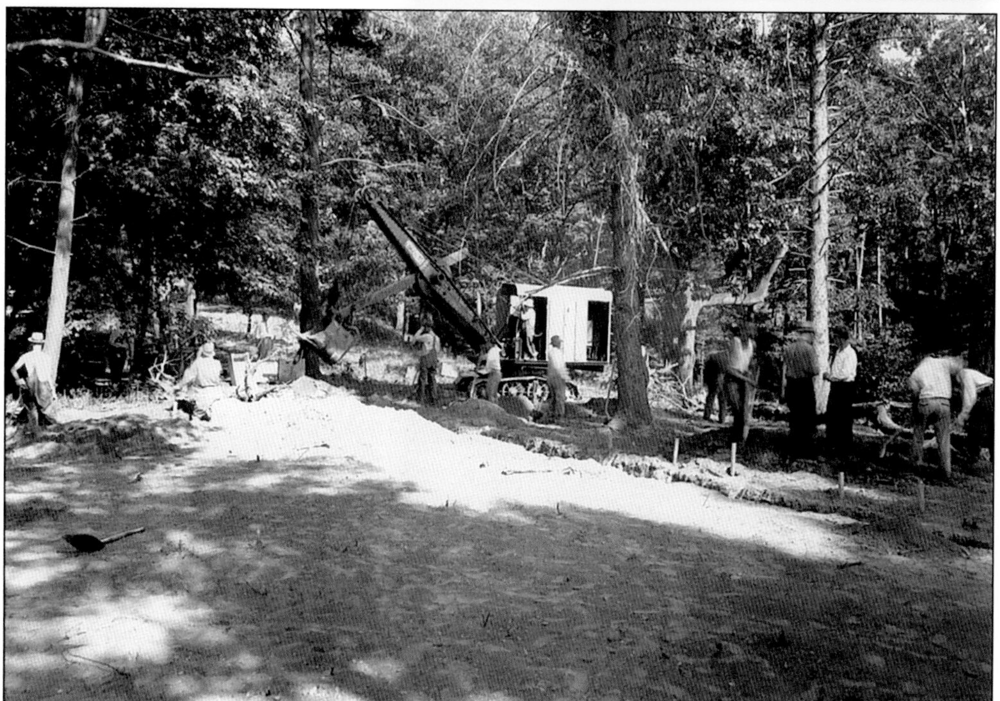

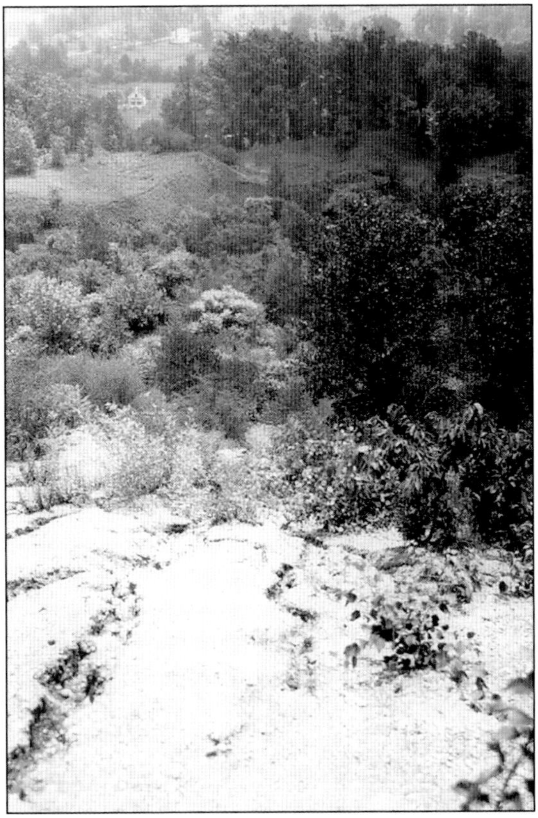

ON A CLEAR DAY. On a clear day, one can see the Bristol Hills from Pinnacle Hill. This photograph, looking south over Brighton, is labeled St. Patrick Cemetery, 1935–1936. The photographer was Bunnell Commercial Photo of 21 Bly Street. By the late 1880s, there were no trees on Pinnacle Hill because they had all been cut down for lumber. (Courtesy Diocese of Rochester.)

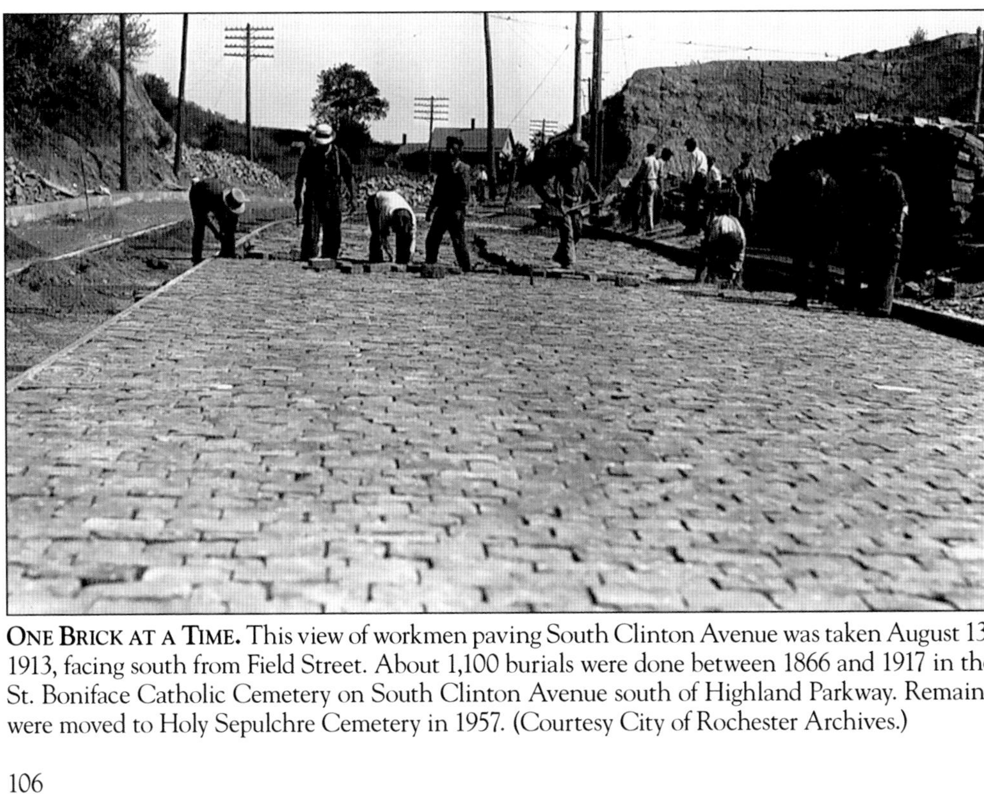

ONE BRICK AT A TIME. This view of workmen paving South Clinton Avenue was taken August 13, 1913, facing south from Field Street. About 1,100 burials were done between 1866 and 1917 in the St. Boniface Catholic Cemetery on South Clinton Avenue south of Highland Parkway. Remains were moved to Holy Sepulchre Cemetery in 1957. (Courtesy City of Rochester Archives.)

Nine

Around South Goodman Street and Monroe Avenue

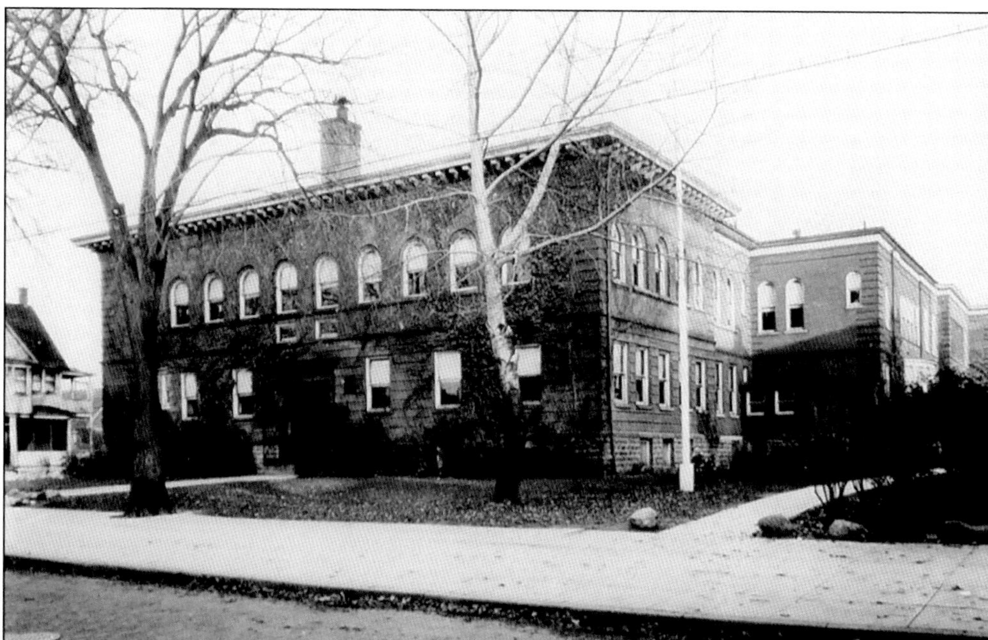

No. 35 School. School No. 35 was built in 1895 on Field Street and renamed Pinnacle School in 1911. This building was torn down in 1963 and a new school was built on a lot next to it. (Courtesy Josh Canfield.)

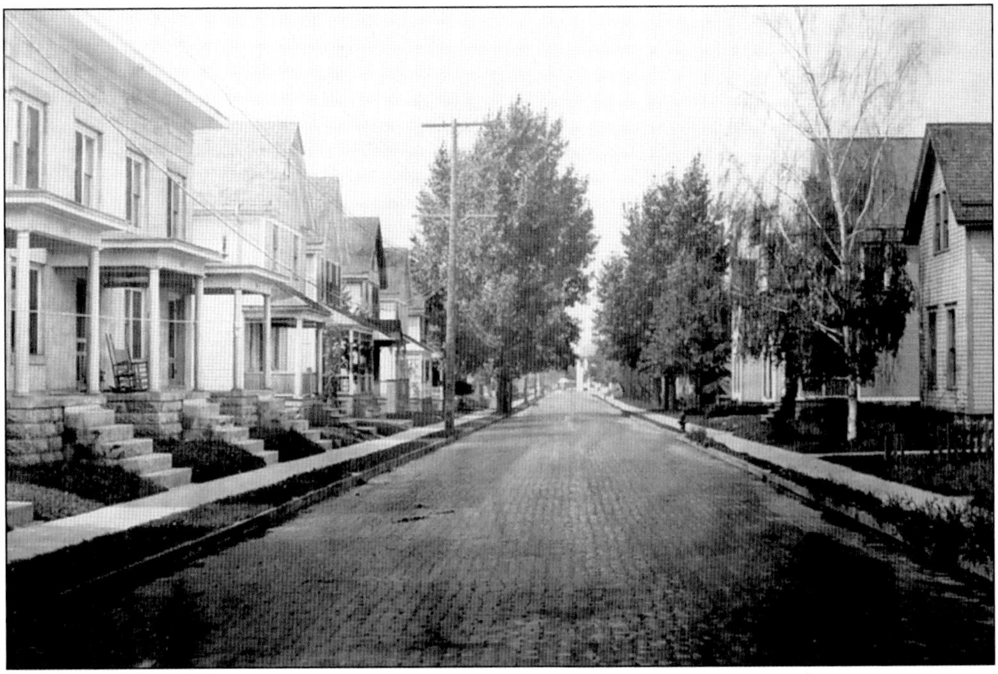

HENRIETTA STREET. All is clean as can be in this undated view of a bricked Henrietta Street, west of Field Street. (Courtesy City of Rochester Photo Lab.)

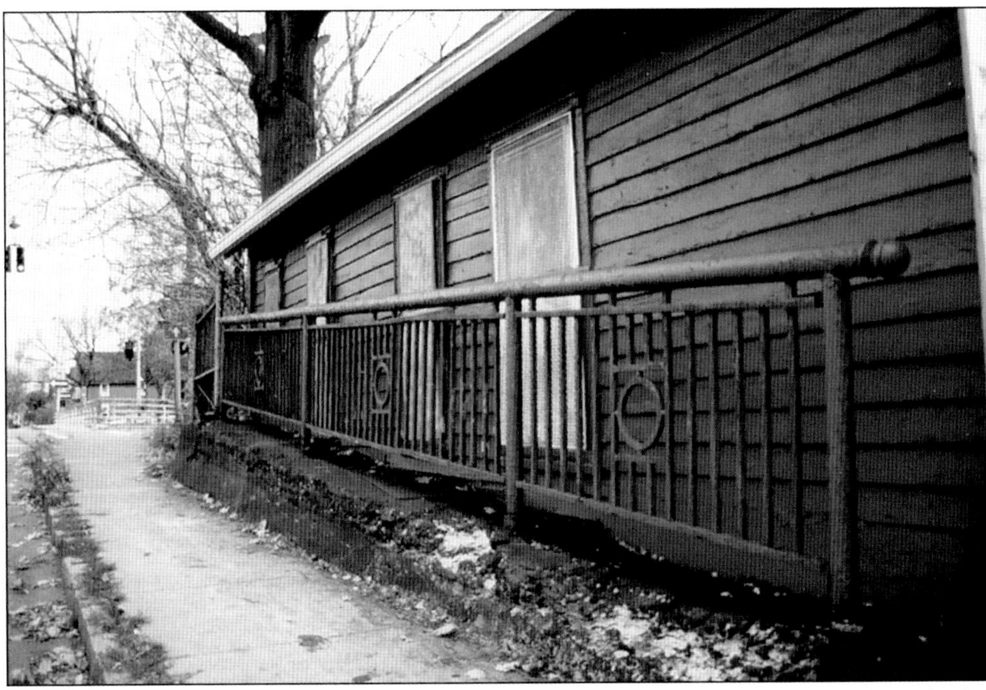

OLD RAILING. This section of railing is the remainder of the bridge across the subway bed at South Goodman Street. The Sherwood Shoe Factory had a massive building along the canal at 625 South Goodman Street, by Uhlen Place. The building burned down in the late 1950s. (Courtesy Robert P. Meadows.)

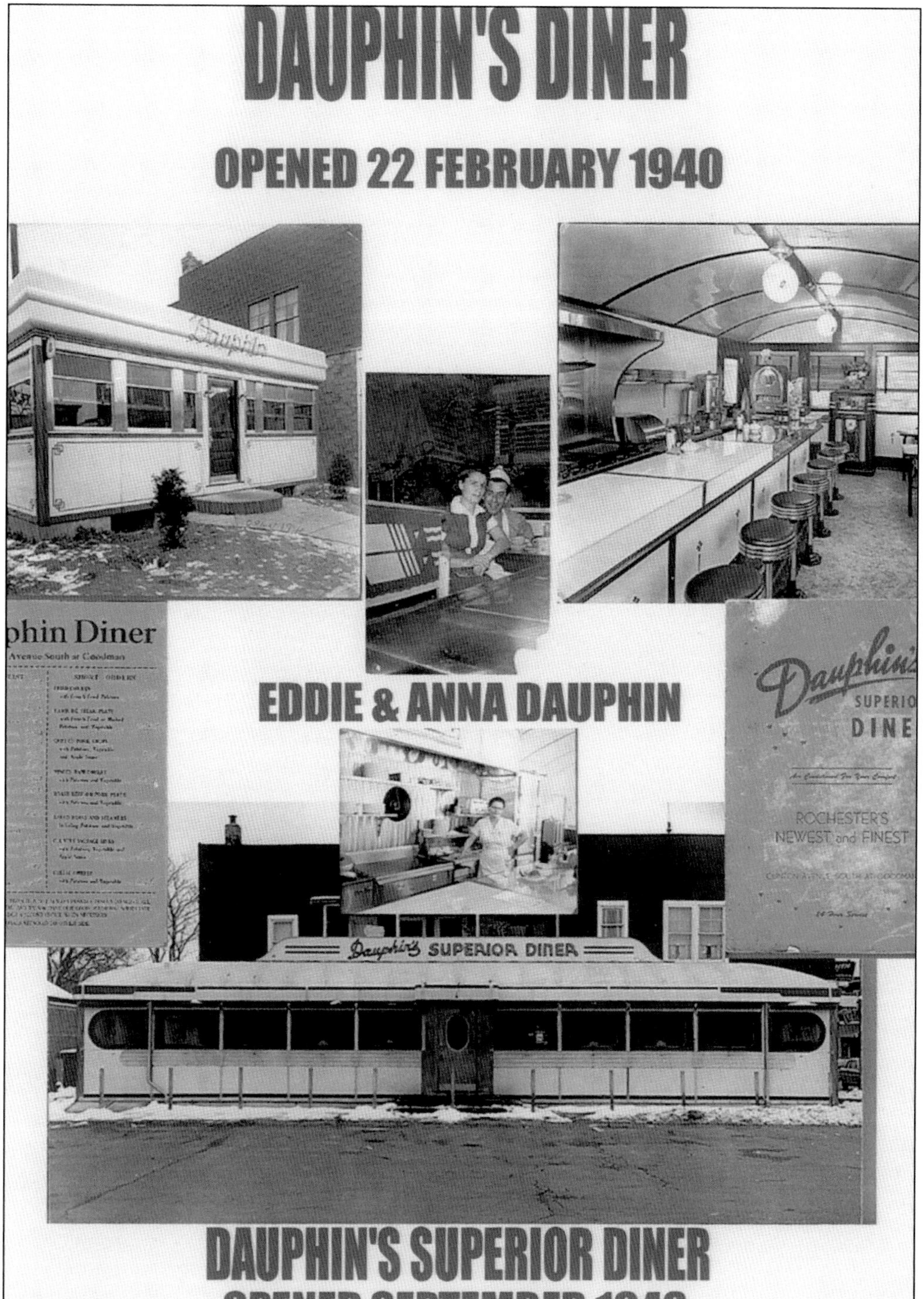

DAUPHIN'S DINER. The first small prefabricated diner opened in 1940. It quickly became too small and was moved to Ridge Road. The second opened in 1948. Both were built by the Orleans Diner Car Company in Albion. After a time as an off-track betting parlor, it was extensively renovated in the 1980s. (Courtesy Jim Malley.)

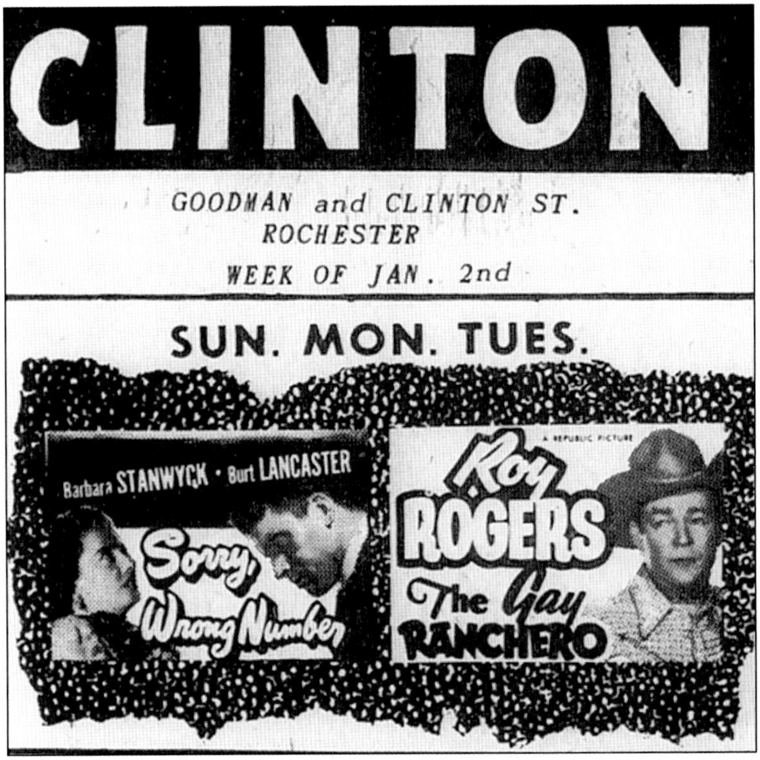

THE CLINTON. The Clinton Theater started as a playhouse at 953 South Goodman Street in 1916. This is a portion of a postcard mailing announcing six movies for the week of January 2, 1948. Stars that week included Barbara Stanwyck and Burt Lancasater; Roy Rogers; Louis Hayward and Joan Leslie; and John Garfield and Lilli Palmer. It is now the Cinema Theater. (Courtesy Donovan A. Shilling.)

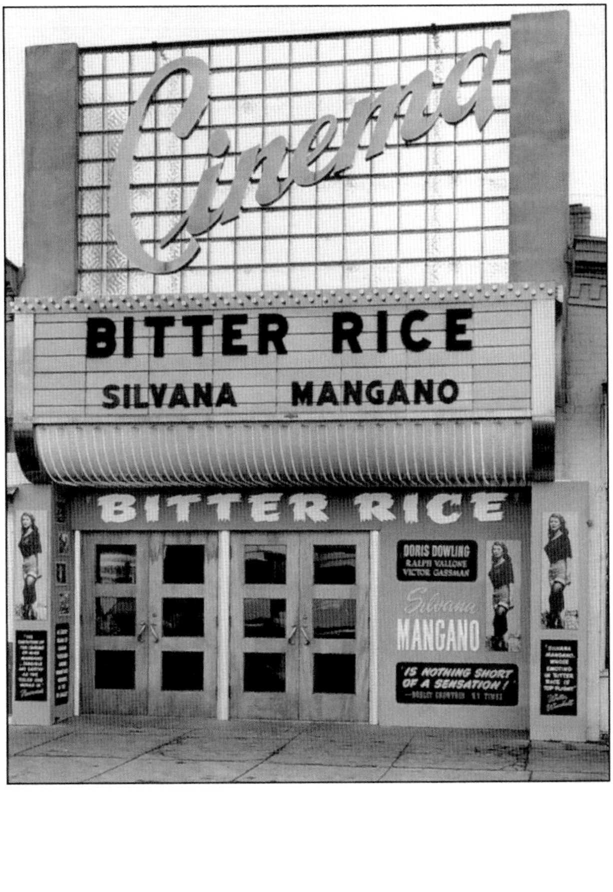

BITTER RICE. This movie starring the sensational Silvana Mangano came out in 1949. This is one of only a few photographs currently in the Cinema's collection. (Courtesy Cinema Theater.)

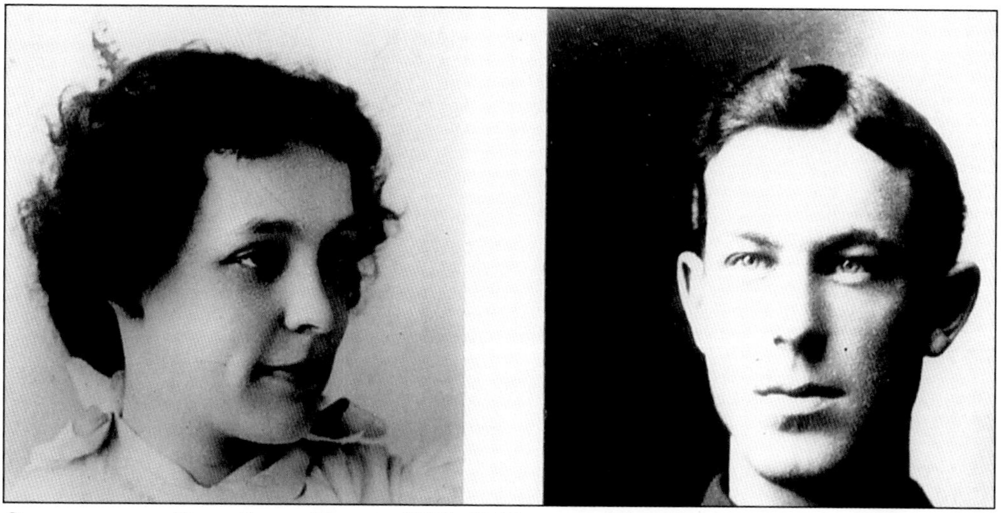

GRANDMA AND POPS. Emma Gagnier (1875–1942) married Frank A. "Pops" Yatteau (1871–1956). Together they had 11 children, 10 who made it to an adult age. Pops, who worked for Rochester Gas and Electric Corporation, was the man who had the homestead built at 70 Sycamore Street. (Courtesy Martha and Billy Yatteau.)

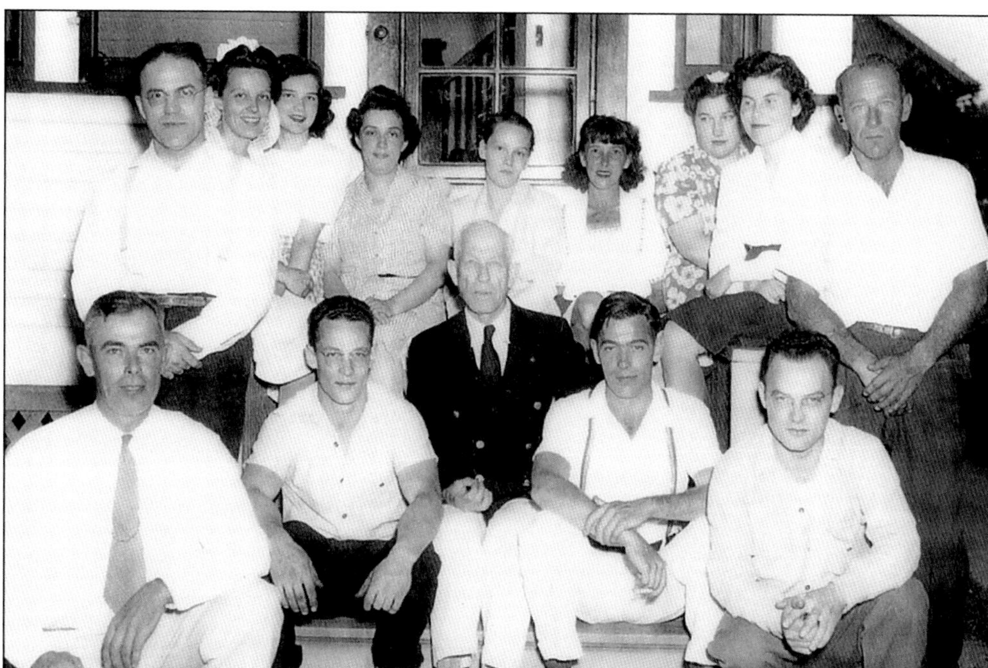

THE YATTEAUS. The Yatteau family gathered around Pops at 70 Sycamore Street, around 1945. From left to right, they are (first row) Al, Frank, Pops, Tom, and Bob; (second row) Jean, Ruth, Beeba, Lauretta, Florence "Bub," Celia, Rita, Pearl, and Walt Young. (Courtesy Martha and Billy Yatteau.)

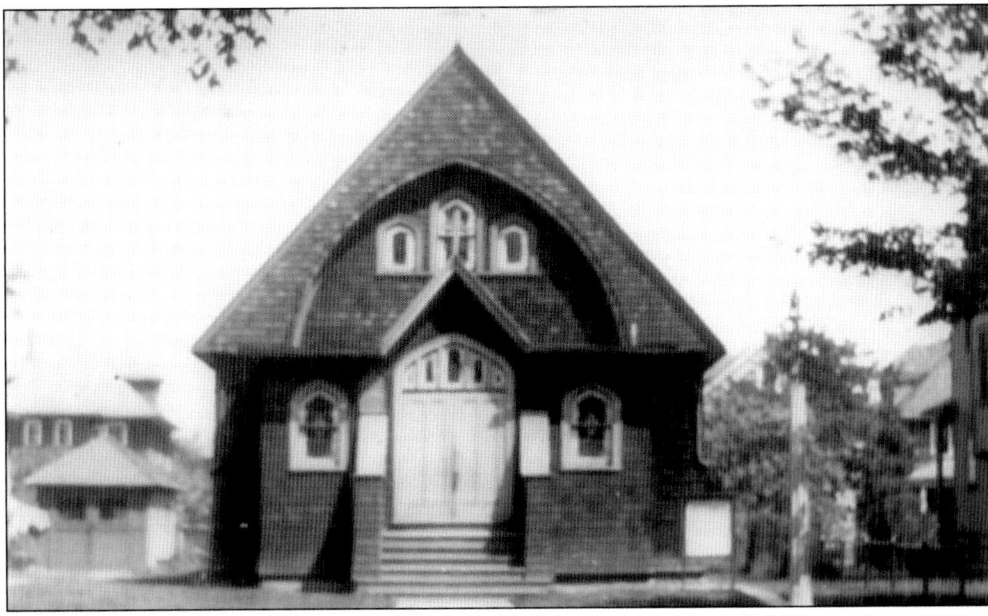

ST. THOMAS CHURCH. St. Thomas Episcopal Church was located on Field Street from 1902 to 1929. There were no street numbers when it was listed in the 1926–1927 city directory at Field Street and Monroe Avenue; the address was numbered 30 Field Street in the 1928 directory. After the building was sold to Congregation Beth Sholom in 1929, the church moved to a new building on the corner of South Winton Road and Highland Avenue. (Courtesy St. Thomas Episcopal Church Archives.)

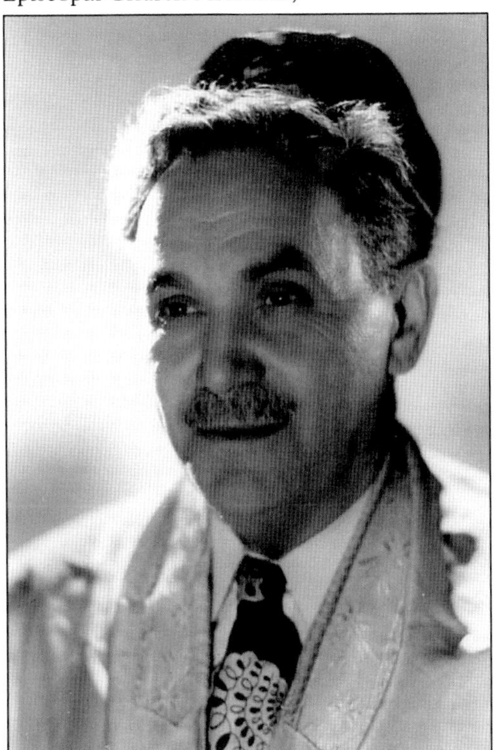

RABBI GORDON. Congregation Tipherath Israel is listed at 326 Meigs Street in the 1930 city directory. Max L. Gordon is listed in 1930s directories at 36 Laburnum Crescent. Rabbi Gordon, who died in 1948, is pictured here in an undated photograph. Rabbi Max N. Schreier is listed at Congregation Beth Sholom at 30 Field Street in the 1955 city directory. The Field Street Shul was located there until the congregation moved to upper Monroe Avenue during the 1950s. The congregation celebrated its 75th anniversary in 2005. (Courtesy Florence Gordon and Bessy Bloom.)

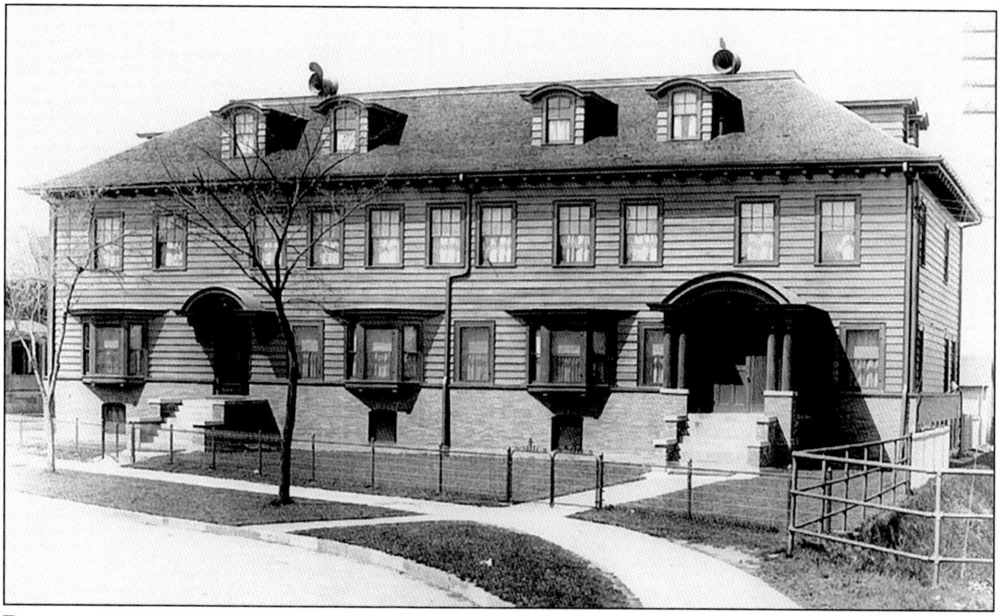

BOARDINGHOUSE. This undated photograph shows St. Elizabeth Guild House, a Catholic boardinghouse for working girls and students established with a $20,000 contribution from J. Adam Kreag in 1915. The building, at 1 Field Street in the former Pinnacle Club, was torn down in 1958 to make way for the new expressway. The Guild House then moved to the Walter Todd residence at 1475 East Avenue and remained there until that building became Becket Hall for seminarians in 1965. (Courtesy University of Rochester Rare Books and Prints.)

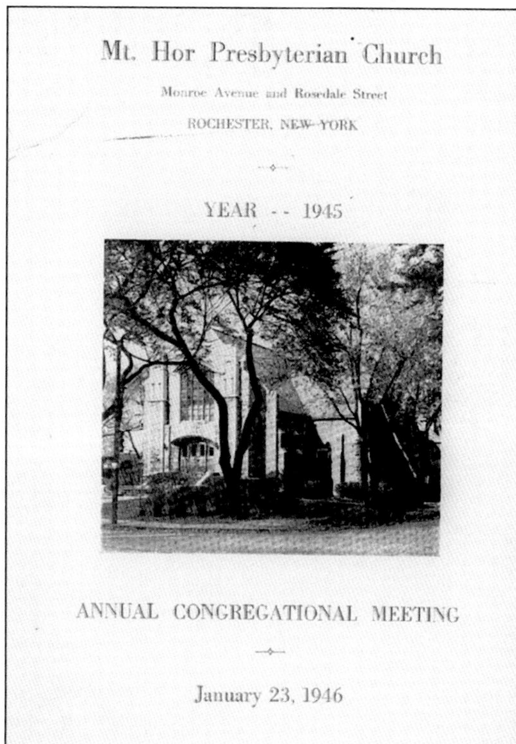

Mt. Hor Presbyterian Church

Monroe Avenue and Rosedale Street

ROCHESTER, NEW YORK

YEAR -- 1945

ANNUAL CONGREGATIONAL MEETING

January 23, 1946

ROSEDALE CHURCH. Mount Hor Presbyterian Church, which was organized in 1893, dedicated their new building at 243 Rosedale Street in 1901. It was expanded in 1924 and renamed New Life Community Church in 1974. (Courtesy Donovan A. Shilling.)

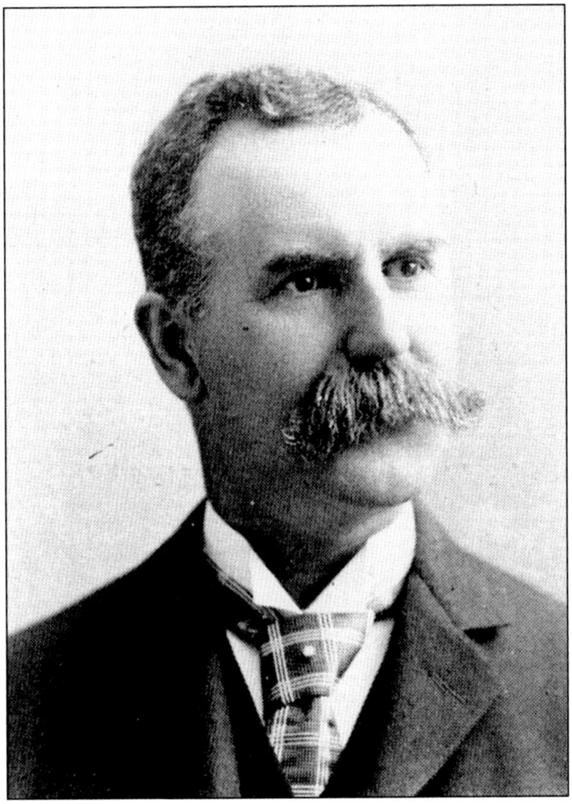

Charles W. Crosman. Charles Crosman had been a seed peddler for a Shaker community, the earliest American seed company, near Albany before coming to Rochester around 1838. He declined a partnership with George Ellwanger and started a seed garden where Crosman Terrace is today. Despite being ranked as an amateur seedsman when Ellwanger and Barry were winning awards for their exceptional fruits, by 1880, Crosman Seeds was one of the largest seed houses in the world. (Courtesy City of Rochester Photo Lab.)

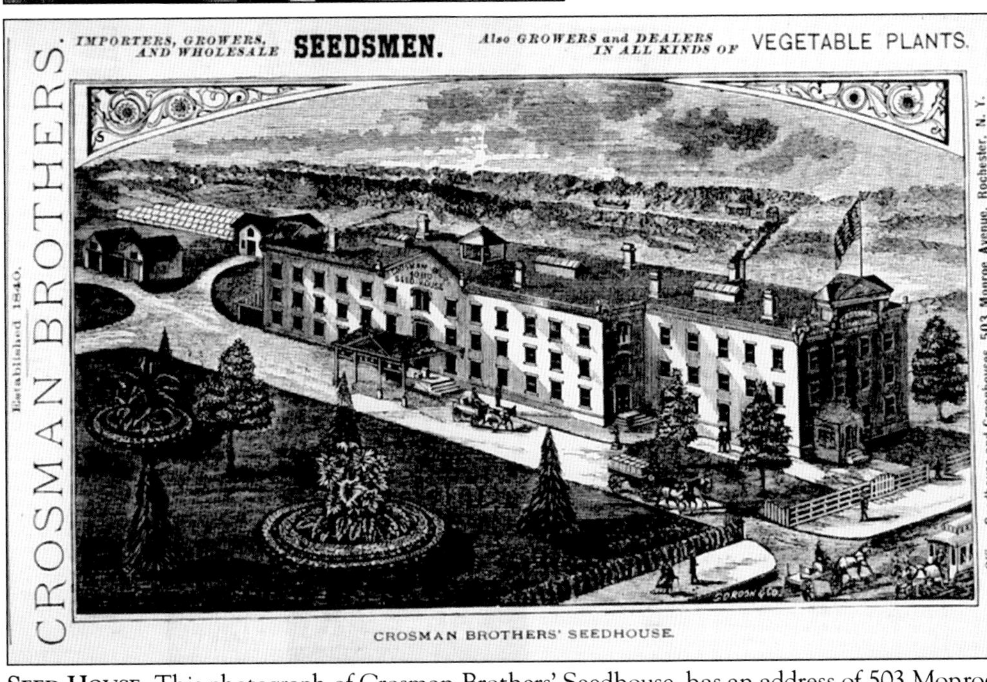

Seed House. This photograph of Crosman Brothers' Seedhouse, has an address of 503 Monroe Avenue. It was the wholesale location, on Monroe Avenue south of the canal. Most of the building still remains. (Courtesy City of Rochester Photo Lab.)

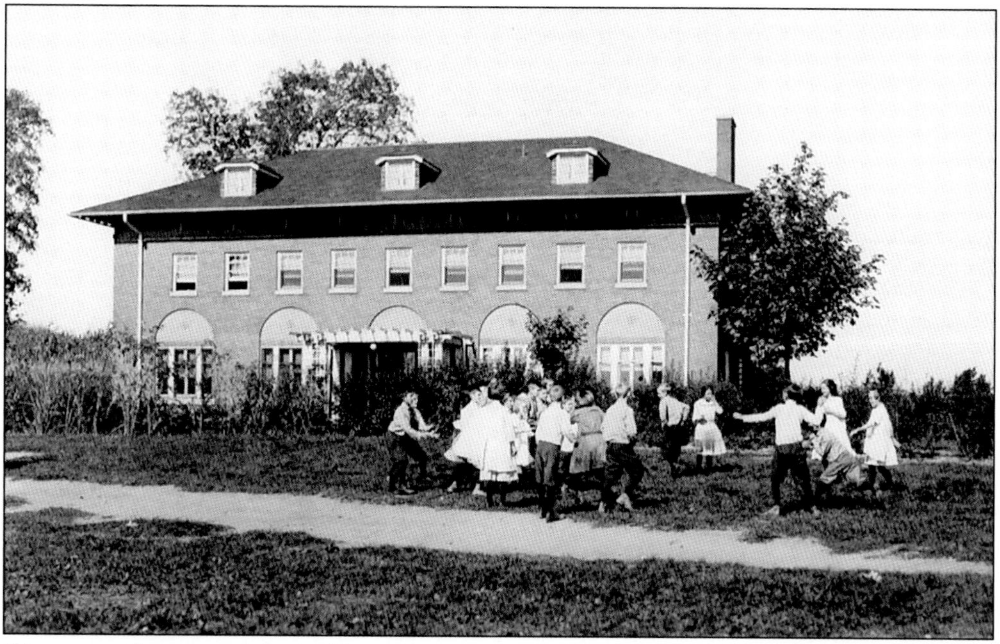

Woodside Cottage. It looks like a sunny day as children play near the Woodside Cottage for Girls, around 1921. The cottage was built in 1912, when the Rochester Orphan's Asylum moved to a larger space and changed its name to Rochester Hillside Home for Children. (Courtesy Rochester Photo Images.)

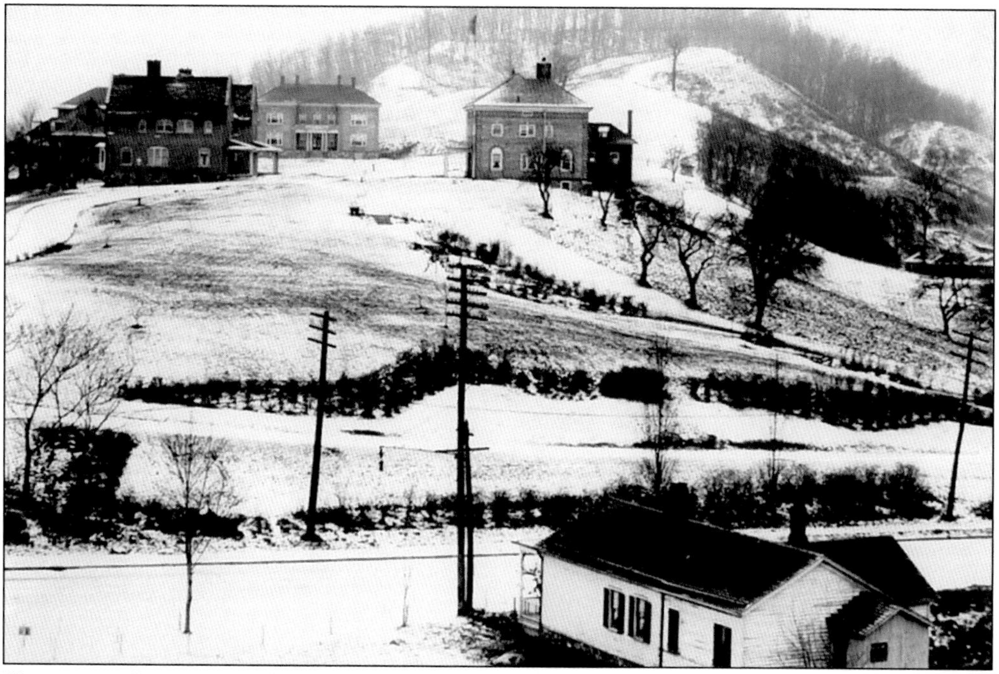

Home for Orphans. The Rochester Orphan Asylum had its beginnings downtown in 1836 and was incorporated in 1838 between Greig and Exchange Streets. The photograph of the home in winter also shows a white house across the street near the northeast corner of Monroe and Highland Avenues. (Courtesy City of Rochester Photo Lab.)

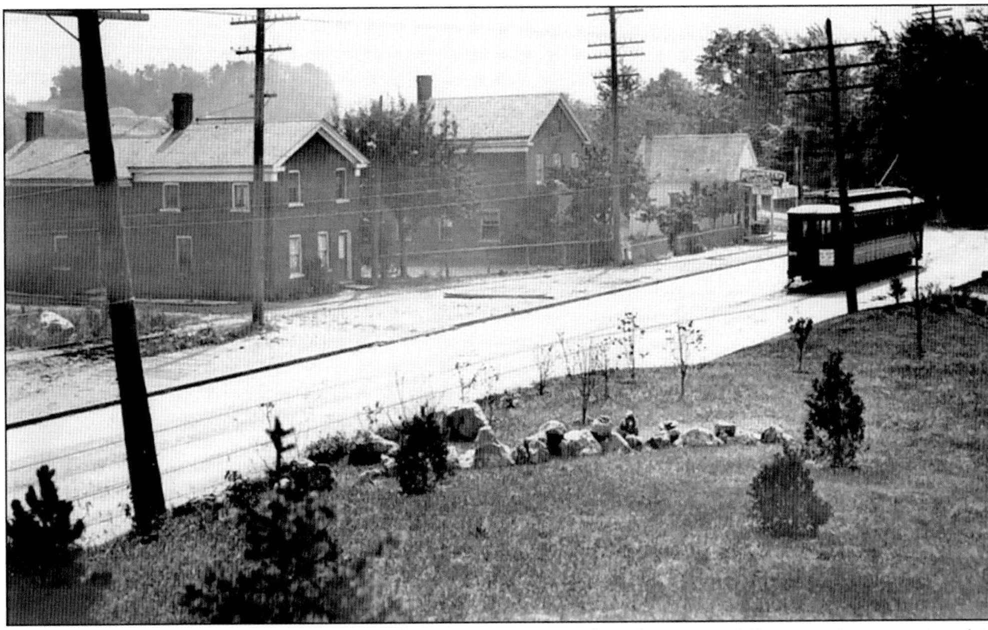

MONROE AND HIGHLAND. The trolley is moving right along on Monroe Avenue in this photograph from July 1, 1909. (Courtesy City of Rochester Photo Lab.)

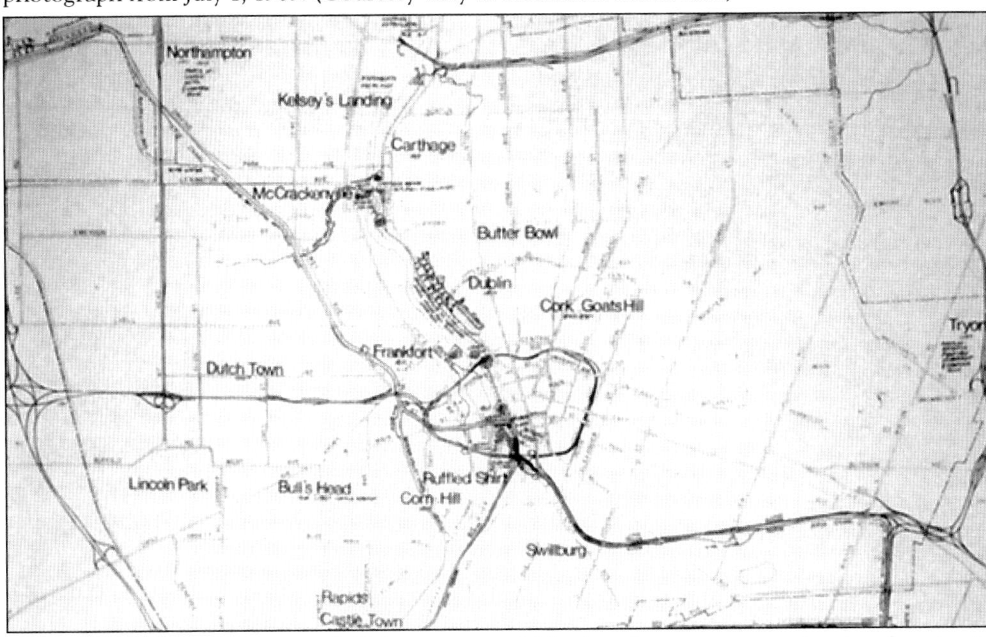

NEIGHBORHOODS. This map of 19th-century neighborhoods was put together by the city in observance of Rochester's sesquicentennial in 1984. It shows Swillburg, south of the Erie Canal near South Goodman Street, which was named for a pioneer family who farmed a tract around East Avenue, North Goodman Street, and Main Street. That area was settled around 1818 by Titus Goodman. The 1853 city directory lists George W. Goodman as "farmer, h. Goodman n. R.R." According to a 1995 interview with Clem Bayer, a founder of the Southeast Area Coalition, the Swillburg neighborhood got its name by 1890 when the area became known for local farmers' pigs eating garbage off of the canal banks. (Courtesy City of Rochester Photo Lab.)

Ten

CULVER ROAD AND COBBS HILL

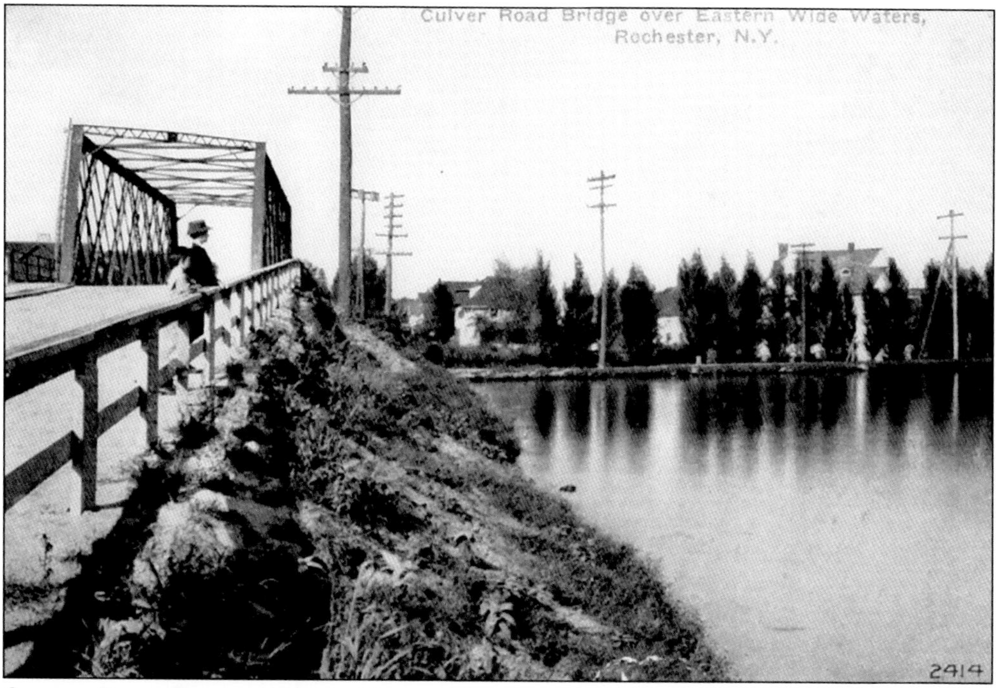

CULVER ROAD BRIDGE. It looks like a perfect day for fishing off the bridge over the Eastern Wide Waters. This postcard is from 1900. (Courtesy City of Rochester Photo Lab.)

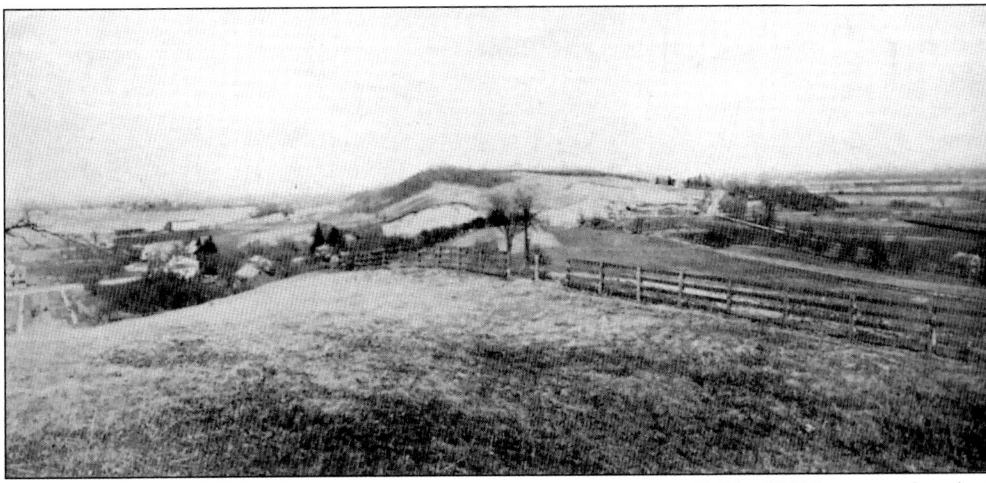

KLINCK KNOLL, 1895. By the late 1880s, there were no trees on Cobbs Hill because they had all been cut down for lumber. After the Civil War, a large house at 1145 Monroe Avenue was owned by Col. John Graham Klink. The house, with two-story Greek columns, was originally built in 1830, and was close to the Hillside Home for Children. This photograph from Cobbs Hill, looking east from Klinck Knoll was taken in 1895. The Klinck Estate is drawn on the 1900 city map from Monroe Avenue to Hinsdale Street along Culver Road with a Klinck Street (now Belmont) between Avondale and Werner Parks. The city line then was at Culver Road. (Courtesy Rochester Photo Images.)

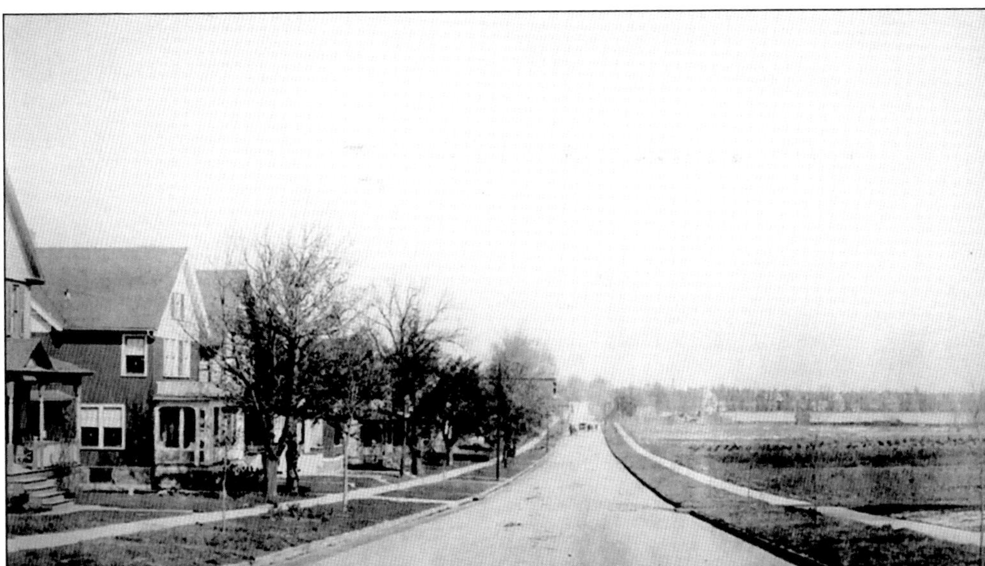

CULVER ROAD. There is no date on this picture of a quiet Culver Road, looking north from Monroe Avenue, but there seems to be only one street light and no telephone poles. The shapes farther down the road may be horses and wagons. (Courtesy City of Rochester Photo Lab.)

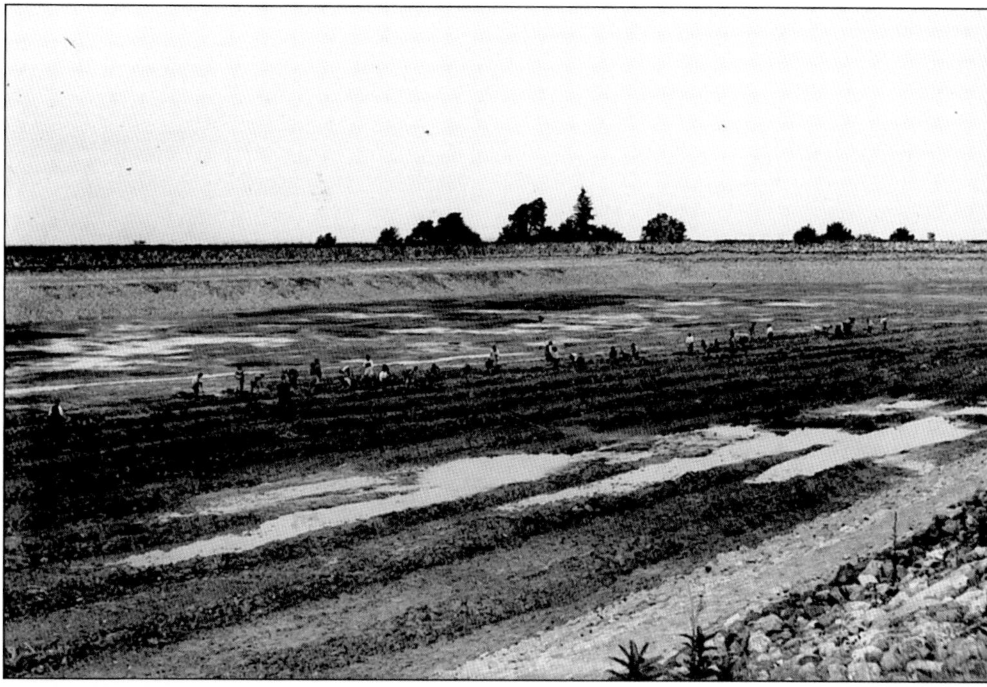

SIMPLE BEGINNINGS. These straightforward pictures show the beginnings of a major construction project from 1905 to 1908, to build Cobbs Hill Reservoir. (Courtesy City of Rochester Photo Lab.)

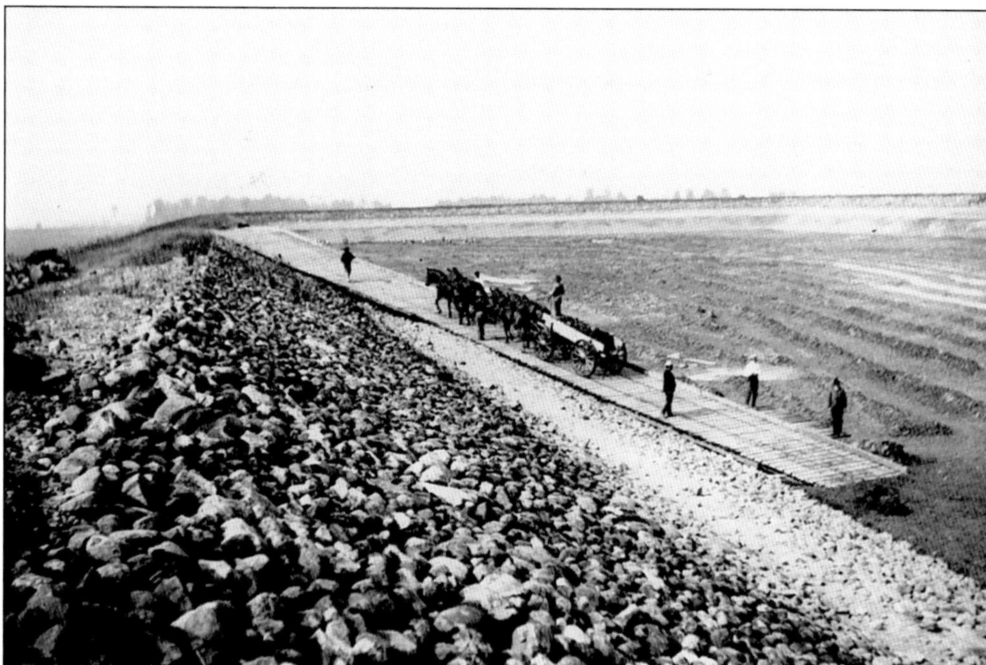

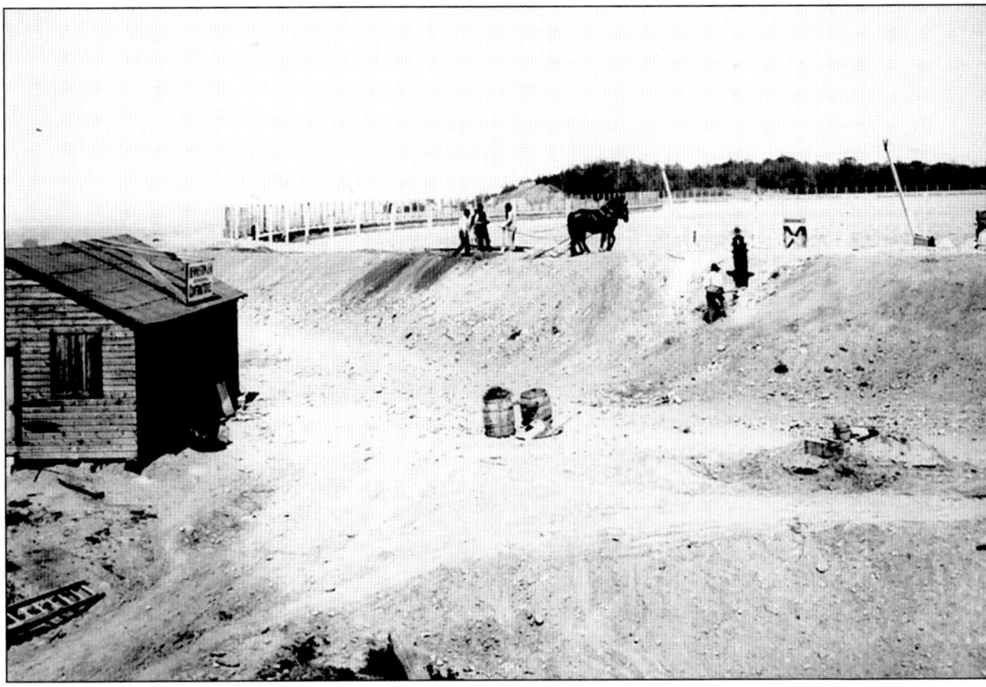

EARLY PHASES. It may be hard to imagine that such a large project as the construction of the Cobbs Hill Reservoir was undertaken with picks, shovels, and horse and carts. (Courtesy City of Rochester Photo Lab.)

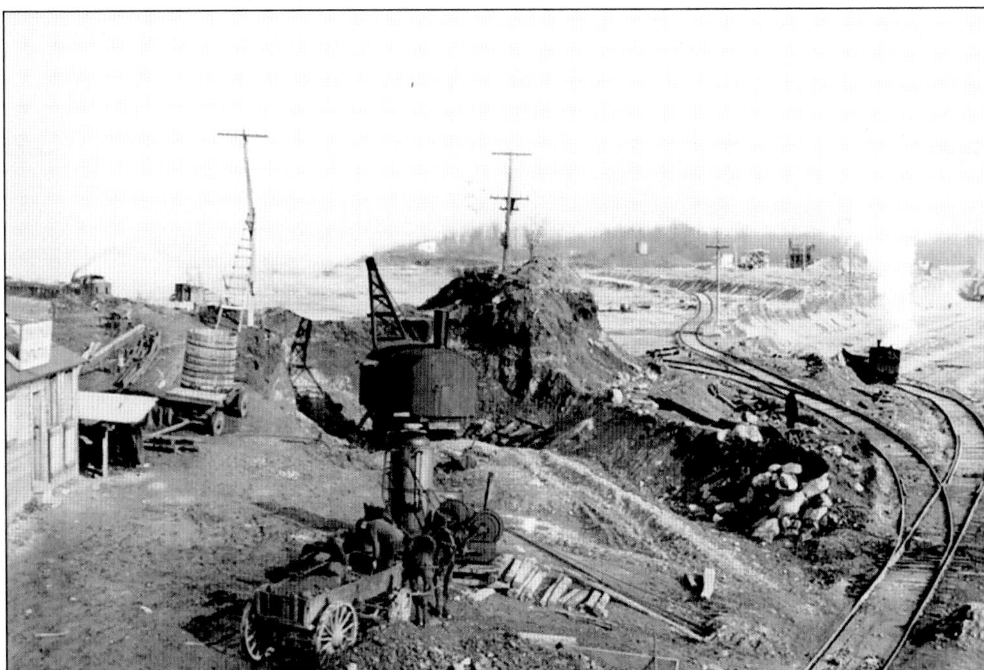

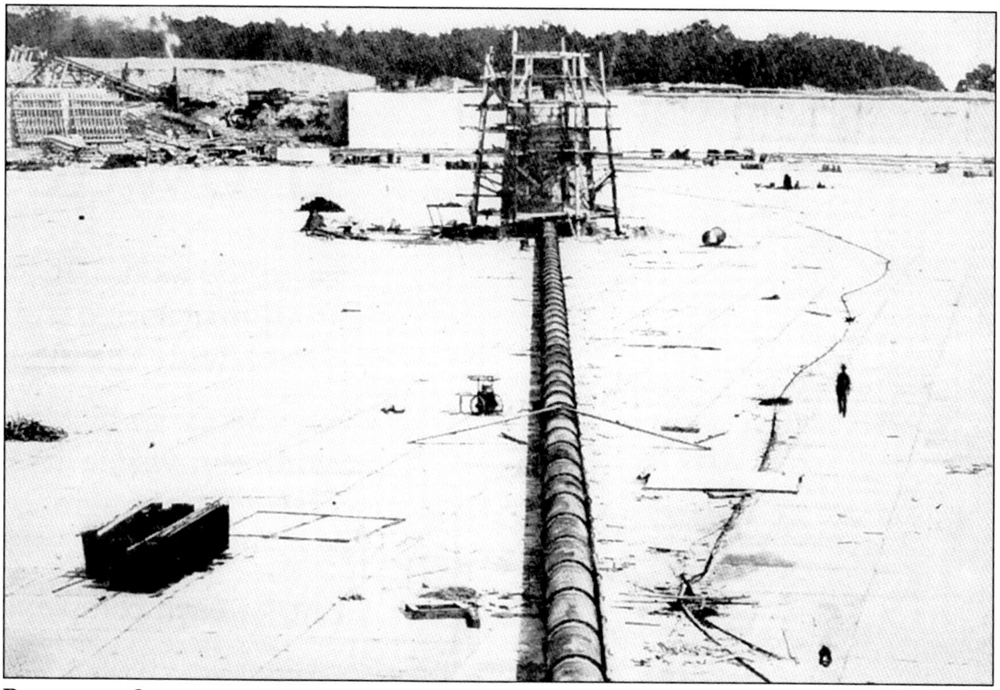

RESERVOIR CONSTRUCTION. Cobbs Hill Reservoir opened in 1908 to supplement the Mount Hope Reservoir at Highland Park dating from 1875. After a construction project that dug an average of 25 feet into the 400-foot-high hill, the new reservoir held 140 million gallons of water. The Cobbs Hill Pavilion, at the top of the hill by the reservoir and the gatehouse close to Monroe Avenue, was designed by notable local architect J. Foster Warner and built in 1908. (Courtesy City of Rochester Photo Lab.)

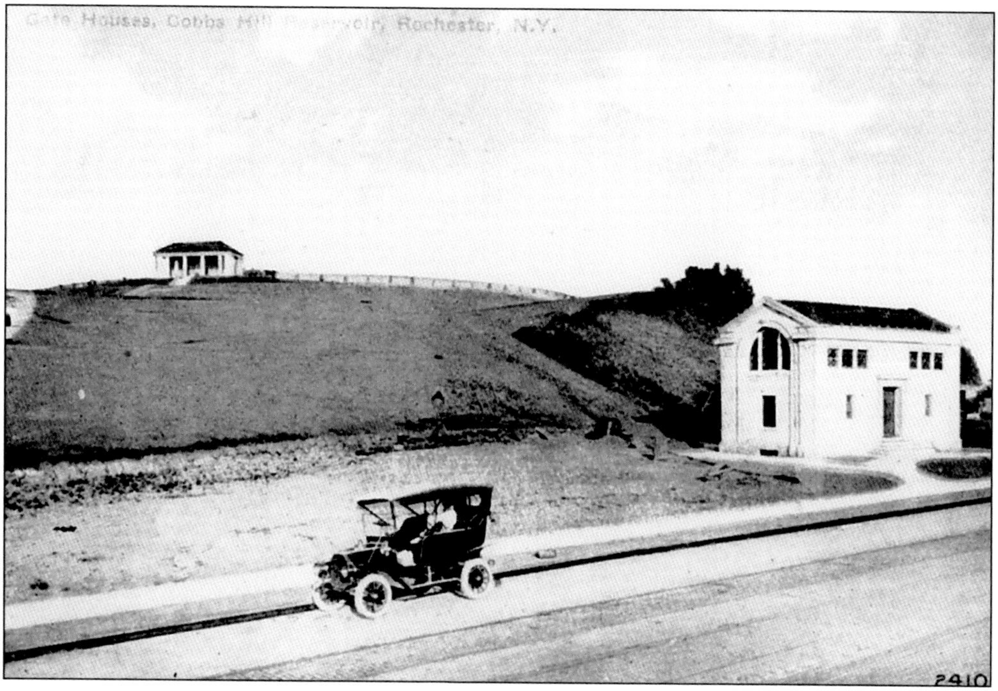

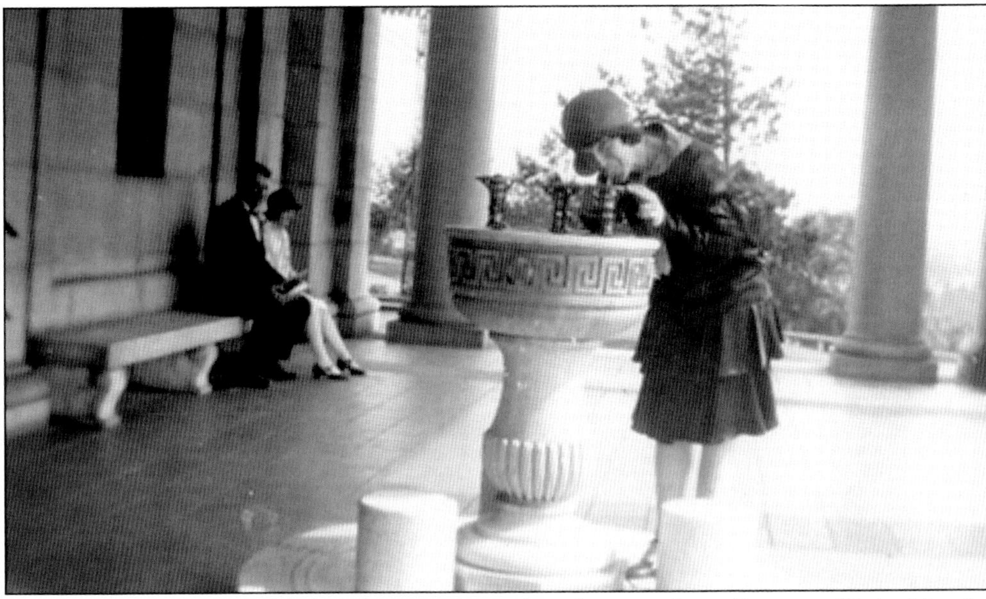

A COOL DRINK. This unlabeled photograph was found among the collection of Ruby Murphy, later of Averill Avenue. The ornate public water fountain was on the porch of the Cobbs Hill Pavilion in a Greek-style building by the reservoir that was designed by J. Foster Warner and built in 1908. (Courtesy Josh Canfield.)

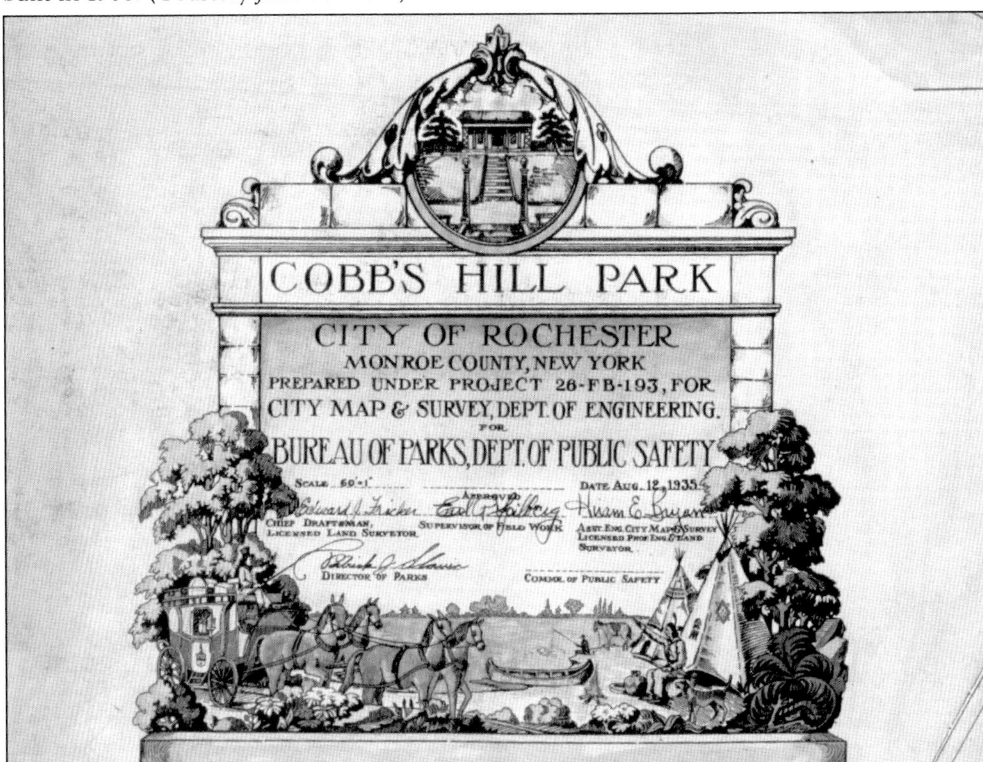

COBBS HILL PLAN. This attractive cover is from a 1935 Bureau of Parks, Department of Public Safety report on Cobbs Hill. (Courtesy City of Rochester Photo Lab.)

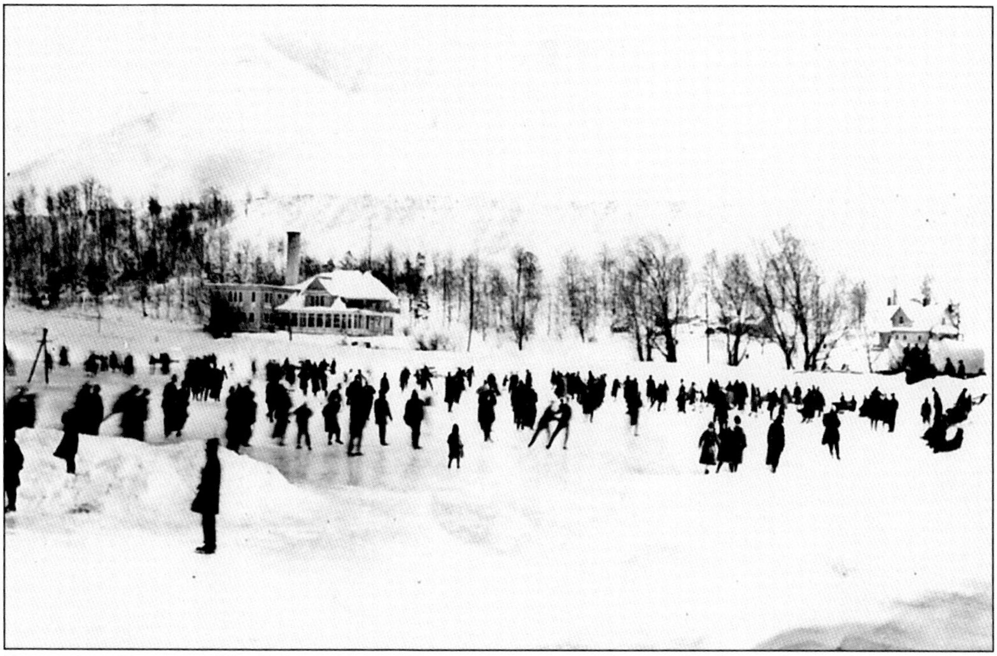

OPEN AIR SCHOOL. The Edward Mott Moore Open Air School, which was located in the former Rod and Gun Club building from 1913 to 1941, is in the background above. It began in 1909 as a day camp on the Municipal Hospital grounds for pre-tubercular children and after several moves, came to this site. The view of skaters on the frozen Eastern Widewaters was taken around 1915. The Eastern Widewaters first located south of the original Erie Canal, east of Culver Road, became known as Lake Riley in Cobb's Hill Park after the construction of the Barge Canal from 1905 to 1923. The lower picture is from 1935. (Courtesy Rochester Photo Images.)

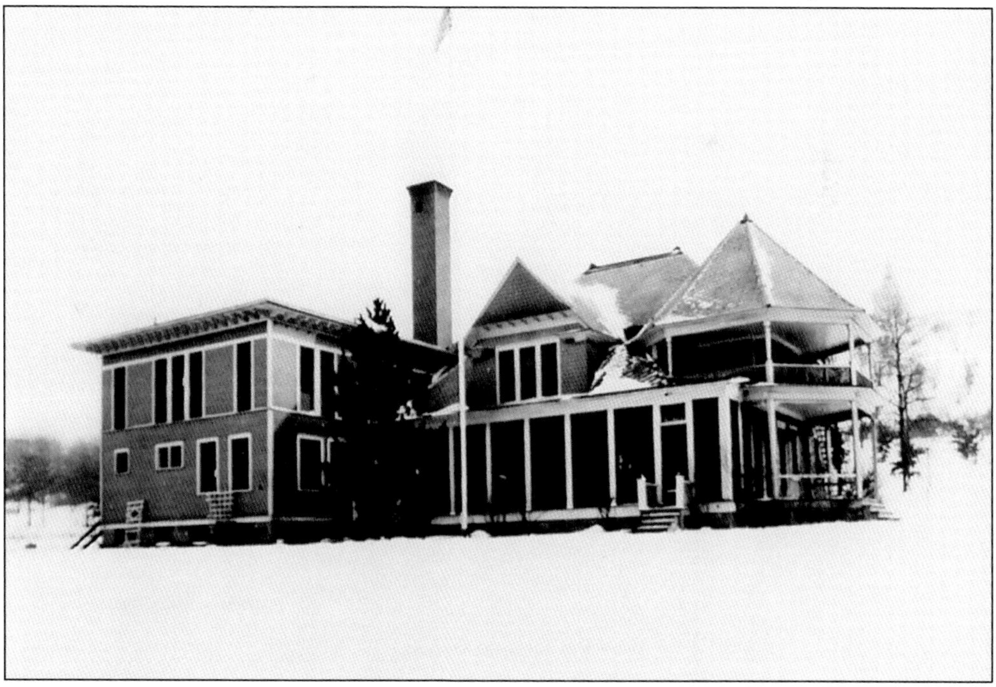

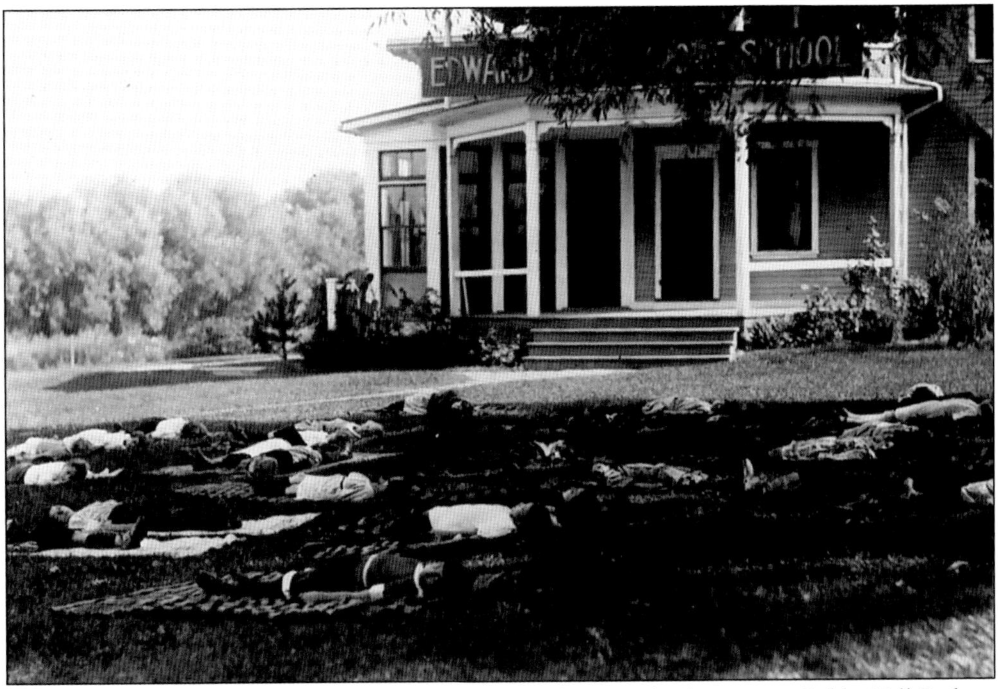

SUMMER AND WINTER CARE. Children rest on blankets on the lawn near Cobbs Hill Park in this *c.* 1913 photograph. The words "Edward" and "School" are partly visible behind branches overhanging the porch. The bottom photograph is titled *Winter Exercise at Open Air School No. 14*. Chester Dewey School No. 14 was built at Scio Street in 1916 to replace the old Riley School No. 14, which had been destroyed by fire the previous year. This is most likely near the old Riley School. (Above, courtesy Rochester Photo Images; below, courtesy City of Rochester Photo Lab.)

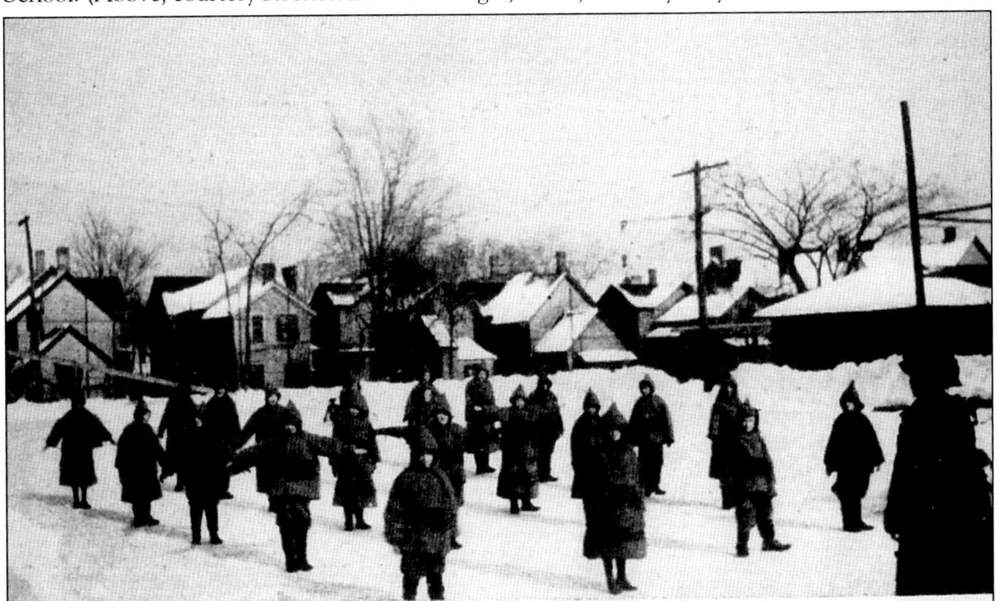

PLAYGROUND EXERCISES AT OPEN AIR SCHOOL, NO. 14

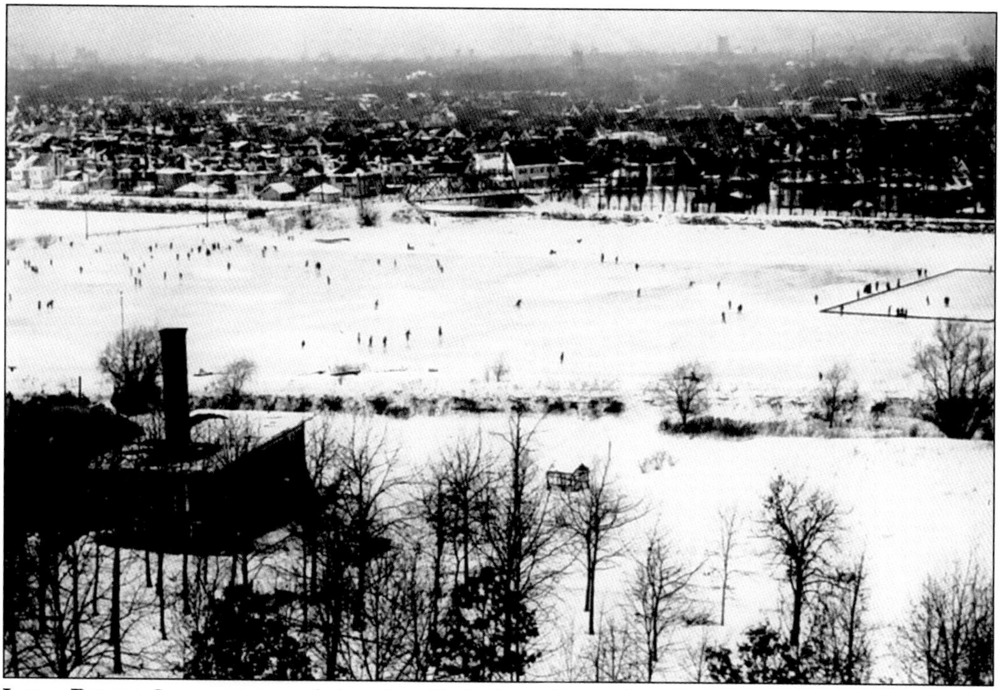

LAKE RILEY. Construction of the New York State Barge Canal south of the city cut off the Eastern Widewaters from the original Erie Canal. The large pond that remained was called Lake Riley. The building in the lower left of the top photograph from around 1915, seems to be the Edward Mott Moore Open Air School. The bottom view of Lake Riley on a sunny and cold winter day is from 1970. (Courtesy City of Rochester Photo Lab.)

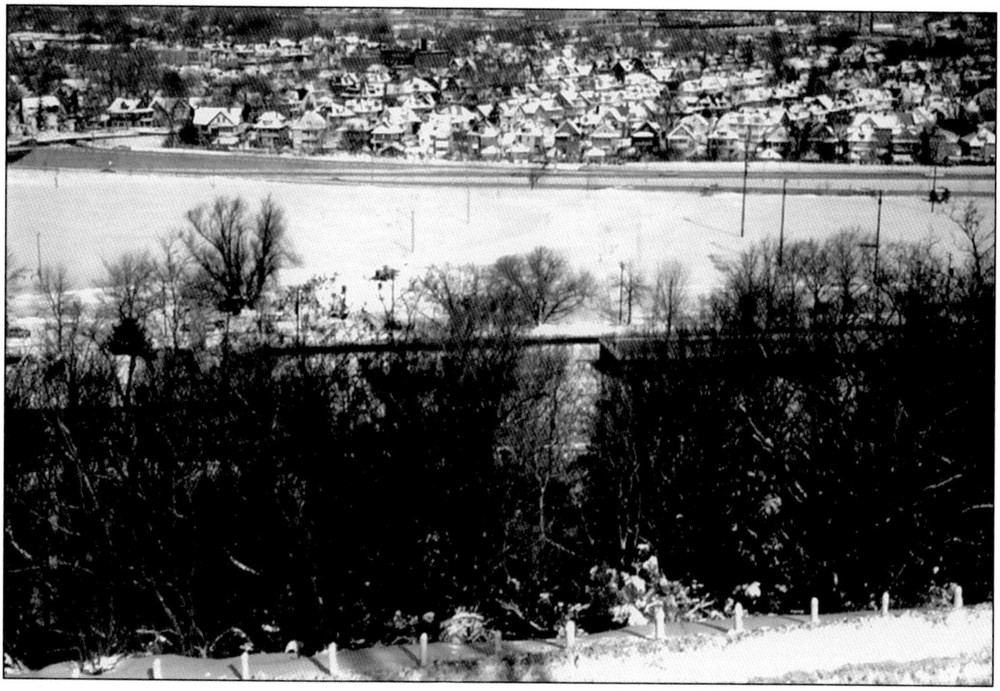

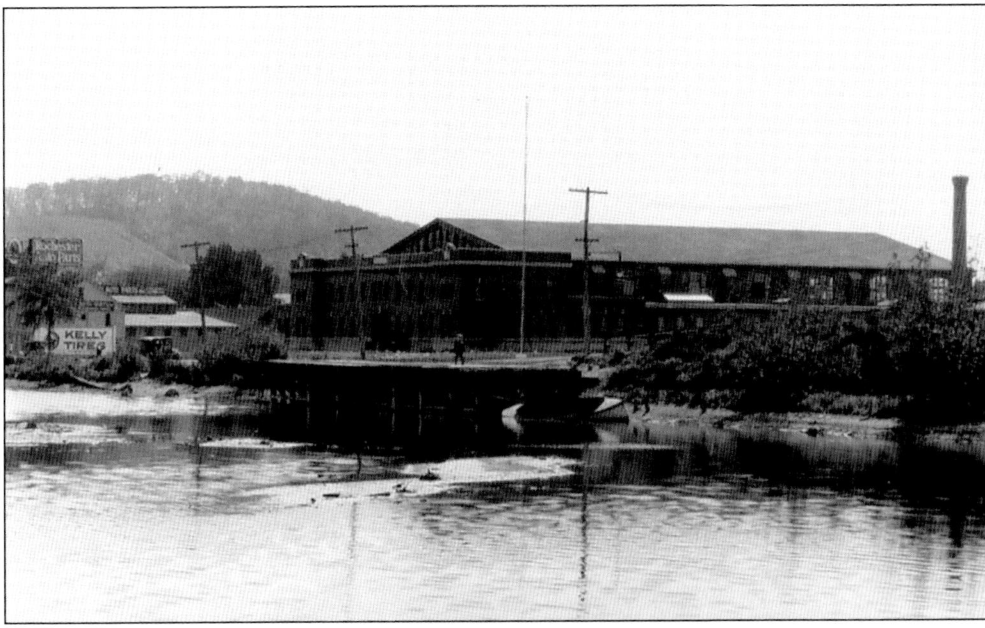

CAVALRY ARMORY. The New York National Guard Cavalry Armory was built in 1918 for Troop H, Rochester's first cavalry unit. This troop fought at the Mexican border in 1916 and in France during World War I. This view, looking southwest, was photographed around 1930 and shows the former Eastern Wide Waters on Culver Road; called Lake Riley since the early 1920s. (Courtesy Rochester Photo Images.)

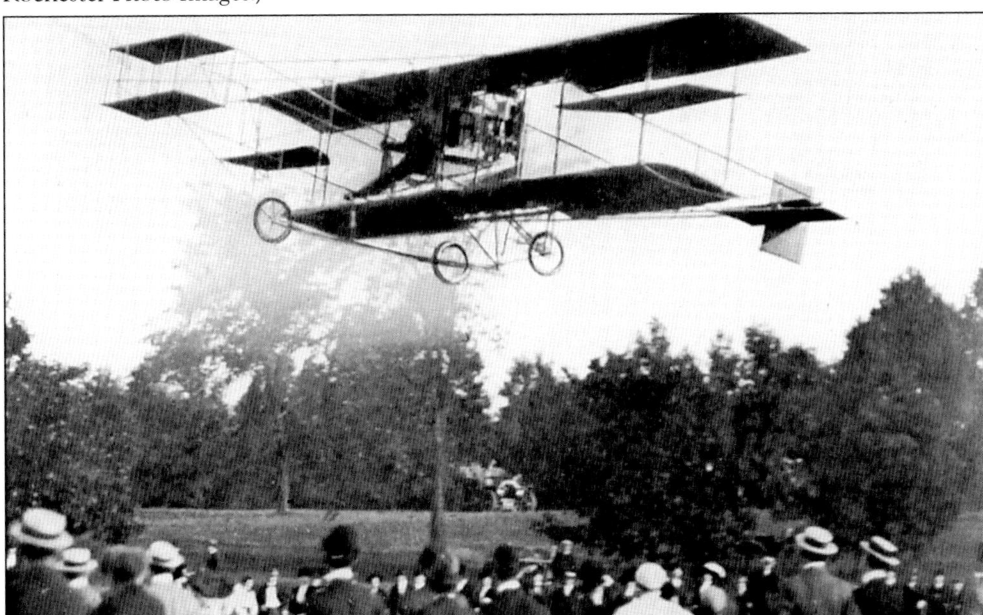

EARLY AIRPLANE. The crowd watches an early Curtiss biplane make its first flight over the city on July 7, 1911. The pilot, Rochester native John J. Frisbie, flew from Cobbs Hill, following the New York Central Railroad tracks at a height of 300 feet. In the following days, he demonstrated what planes could do in war by dropping flour bag "bombs" on Company H 3rd New York Infantry at the nearby armory. (Courtesy Rochester Photo Images.)

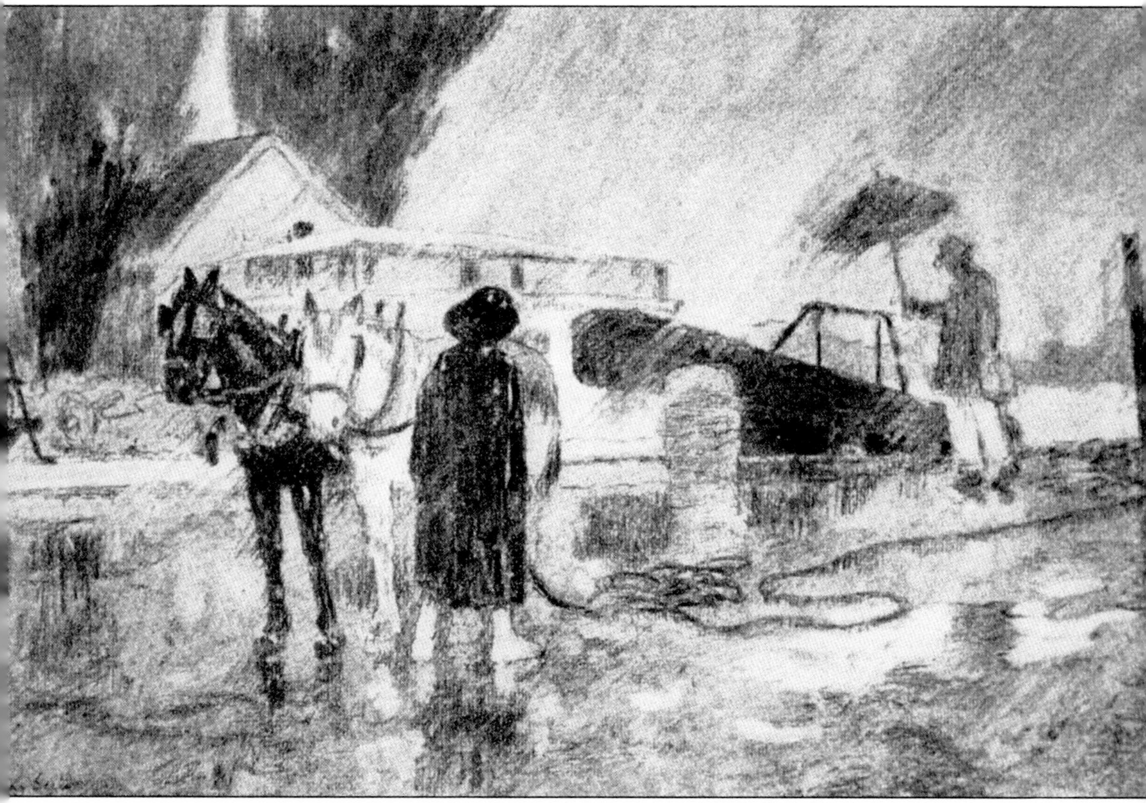

COMING DOWN IN BUCKETS. Harvey Ellis (1852–1904) was an architect who designed several commercial and industrial buildings downtown including the Court Exchange Building and what is now called the Ellis Building on Andrews Street. Unlike those two that still remain, the Nash Building at the corner of St. Paul and Mortimer Streets was torn down in 1967. Ellis also designed the Queen Anne–style house on East Avenue at Oxford Street of City Parks Commissioner Alexander Lamberton. This undated drawing is called *At the Eastern Wide Waters in a Rain Storm*. (Courtesy City of Rochester Photo Lab.)

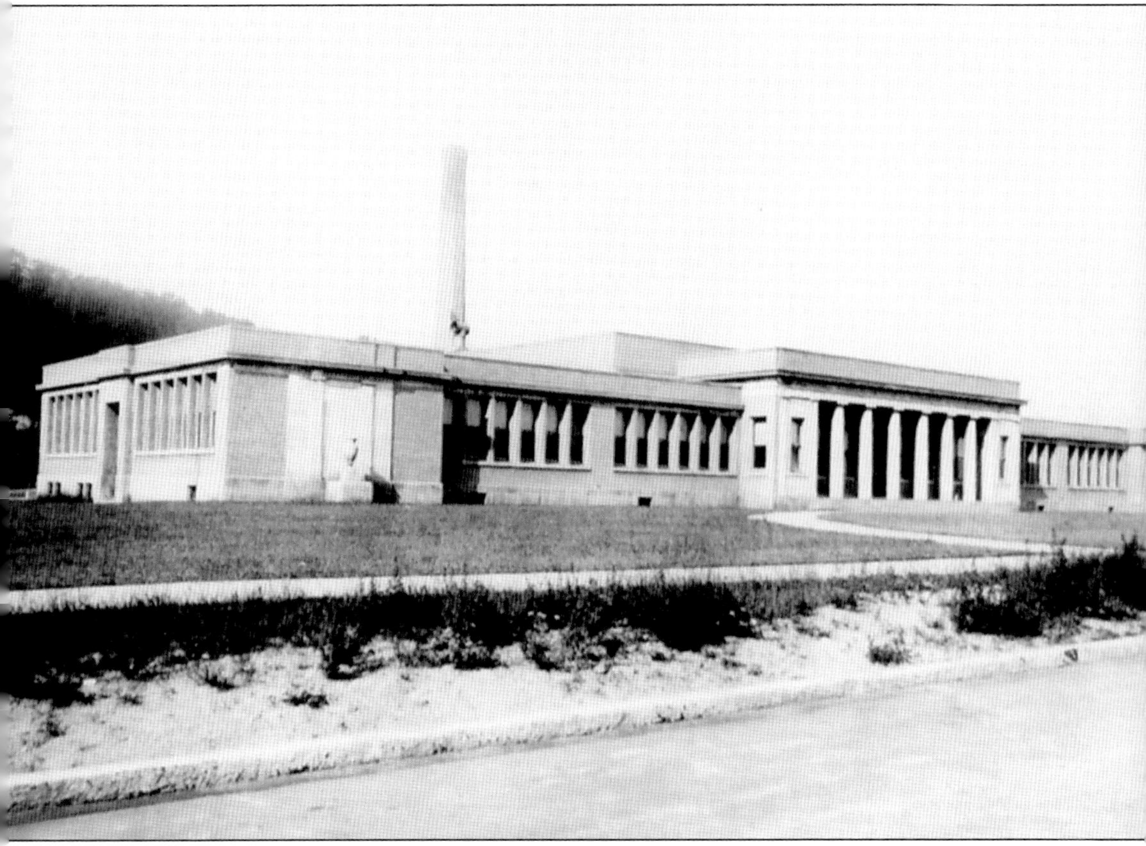

SCHOOL NO. 1. Martin Anderson School No. 1 was built in 1922 on Hillside Avenue to replace a building of the same name on Winton Road around East Avenue. This city school and Anderson Hall on Prince Street, built in 1861, were named for the first president of the University of Rochester. This photograph is from 1935. (Courtesy Rochester Photo Images.)